More praise for *The Practice of Preaching, Revis*

"Veteran preachers know that some of their v
they first preached when they were younger. Th ⎯ ⎯⎯ ⎯⎯⎯ ⎯⎯⎯⎯⎯ ⎯⎯⎯⎯⎯
that same sermon and pour into it the wisdom, the insights, and the
learning they have gained over the years. That's the way it is with the second, very much revised edition of Paul Scott Wilson's textbook, *The
Practice of Preaching*. The first edition was an excellent book; the second
edition is better. It is the mature work of one of the finest and most
respected teachers in the field of homiletics."
—Stephen Farris, Vancouver School of Theology

"In the revised edition of *The Practice of Preaching*, Paul Scott Wilson gets
to the theological heart of the preaching task. While engagingly teaching
the day-to-day techniques of crafting biblical sermons, he helps the
preaching student as well as the practiced preacher get to the point: the
gospel. Because there is no other point to preaching, this edition becomes
the essential tool for the teaching and the renewal of preaching."
—Clay Schmit, Fuller Theological Seminary

"A much-needed guide through the homiletical forest. Wilson not only
charts a path for students that clearly takes them through the step-by-step
process of sermon writing, but does so by pointing out the major land-
marks in homiletical theory, exegetical process, and pastoral considera-
tion along the way. A helpful, practical book that is also creative and full
of insight."
—Mary Hulst, Assistant Professor of Communication Arts and Sciences,
Calvin College

"I'll have to rewrite my course syllabus to use this book (and I mean that
as a compliment). The strength of Wilson's work has always been a practice informed, but not ruled, by theory, and he has kept himself busy
thinking his way through biblical preaching as it has and could be practiced. The second edition preserves his wise advice, now richly supple-
mented with new prompts to think theologically about the task and the
content of preaching. It asks students to begin at the beginning, engaging
the text with historical, literary, and theological questions so they can
finish by announcing the gospel."
—Paul E. Koptak, North Park Theological Seminary

"Wilson keeps the learner's needs clearly in view, bringing accessible insights into a sensible arrangement. The preaching task is compellingly taught in its theological depth and gospel aim. This book represents a wise, mature conversation with the diverse resources of the best of contemporary homiletical scholarship."
—James Nieman, Professor of Practical Theology, Hartford Seminary, Connecticut

"Paul Wilson has once again produced a masterful textbook on homiletics. This volume walks students through the homiletical landscape, equipping them to manage the complex maze of contemporary models and theories of preaching while at the same time giving them tools to theologically assess the terrain. Yet this is a practical book. In a clear and simple way, Wilson guides students through the weekly development of sermon preparation, taking a holistic approach to the task. Wilson's approach to sermon preparation is much more than technique. It involves the tasks of understanding the text, understanding the congregation, and most important understanding the power of the gospel. An appreciation and commitment to the gospel is one of the distinguishing features of this book. Those who teach preaching will find this volume to be an indispensable resource in preparing students to proclaim the gospel effectively and faithfully."
—Dave Bland, Harding University Graduate School of Religion

The PRACTICE of PREACHING

REVISED EDITION

PAUL SCOTT WILSON

Abingdon Press
Nashville

THE PRACTICE OF PREACHING, REVISED EDITION

This book is printed on acid-free paper.

Library of Congress Cataloging-in-Publication Data

Wilson, Paul Scott, 1949-
    The practice of preaching / Paul Scott Wilson.—Rev. ed., 2nd ed.
        p. cm.
    Includes bibliographical references (p.   ) and index.
    ISBN 978-0-687-64527-5 (binding: pbk. : alk. paper)
    1. Preaching.   I. Title.

    BV4211.2.W56 2007
    251—dc22

                                                                2007018822

07 08 09 10 11 12 13 14 15 16—10 9 8 7 6 5 4 3 2 1

MANUFACTURED IN THE UNITED STATES OF AMERICA

To Deanna, an exceptional minister, wonderful companion, and loving mother. She makes any place she is feel like home.

ACKNOWLEDGMENTS

Thanks are due to many people without whom this revised edition might not have appeared, at least in its present shape. My first thanks are as usual to my wife, Deanna, whose love, patience, and insight are a constant encouragement and blessing. Bob Ratcliff at Abingdon Press has been after me for several years to undertake this project, and his guidance and friendship I treasure greatly. Professor John Rottman of Calvin Seminary informs and sharpens my thinking through conversation and feedback; Casey Barton helped immensely with computer scanning of some lost chapters; and Professor Todd Townshend gave valuable advice from his own teaching at Huron College. I am grateful to Professor Laurence Stookey of Wesley Seminary and his colleagues for the invitation to present the inaugural Dunkle/Mackay Preaching Seminar at which I tested some of the new ideas here. Finally, thanks are due to my colleagues and students, at both the masters and doctoral levels, who continue to be my best teachers, to Principal Peter Wyatt of Emmanuel College, and to the President and Board of Regents of Victoria University in the University of Toronto for their support of this project.

A poem should be palpable and mute
As a globed fruit,

Dumb
As old medallions to the thumb,

Silent as the sleeve-worn stone
Of casement ledges where the moss has grown—

A poem should be wordless
As the flight of birds.

***

A poem should be motionless in time
As the moon climbs.

Leaving, as the moon releases
Twig by twig the night-entangled trees,

Leaving, as the moon behind the winter leaves,
Memory by memory the mind—

A poem should be motionless in time
As the moon climbs

***

A poem should be equal to:
Not true

For all the history of grief
An empty doorway and a maple leaf

For love
The leaning grasses and the two lights above the sea—

A poem should not mean
But be.

—Archibald Macleish, "Ars Poetica," 1926

CONTENTS

PREFACE TO THE REVISED EDITION

This introductory textbook is completely redesigned with clarity and ease of use in mind; what sets it apart from other approaches is its emphasis that gospel matters. Preaching the gospel is more than just preaching a text. I have provided a new yet simple and comprehensive overview in a step-by-step fashion of what that might mean for beginning preachers. At the same time, this approach encourages creativity and teaches a variety of approaches. Anyone who wants greater depth or complexity will find ample notation to the breadth and depth of what is most recent in the field.

When I undertook this second edition I was not prepared for all of the changes I would make. I did not expect I would rewrite so much of it and recast the entire project as I have now done. I knew that if possible I wanted to make this as simple and practical as possible, geared to the steps students might take in composing a sermon through the days of the week, one day at a time. I wanted to leave no phase of sermon development a complete mystery, at least insofar as the human tasks are concerned. It used to be common that second editions would be labeled "revised and expanded"; why did they always expand? The old saw about sermons—they should have a good beginning and a good end, and they should be as close together as possible—may apply to preaching textbooks as well. Much material is dropped or abbreviated, arguments are refined, and materials are updated in light of many exciting developments in homiletics over the last twelve years.

What I was not prepared for was how much my own homiletical thinking has evolved since 1995. Many of the things I thought then are the same, but other thoughts have shifted or matured in ways that may show evidence of a bigger, more comprehensive picture that offers greater coherence, depth, balance, and insight. That at least is the vision, but it may simply be the fond hope of any academic who is growing older.

I was also not prepared for the implications of some of these thoughts. The previous edition was designed to help any student to become a card-carrying member of the New Homiletic (or whatever term was being used then to classify the homiletical revolution since the 1950s). I still treasure those revolutionary learnings and I uphold them here, yet I have become aware also of their limitations. Sermons in the New Homiletic became more biblical, more in touch with the contemporary world, more imagistic. They taught in ways that did not just address the mind but allowed listeners to experience what was said; they had greater variety in form and allowed for diversity in the congregation. They were more artistic. But were they more faithful? Did the teachings of the New Homiletic enable better proclamation of the gospel?

I have returned to that question many times in the intervening years. I have explored it in written form in articles and books that include a four-page model and grammar of biblical preaching, an exploration of biblical interpretation for preaching in the first fifteen hundred years of the church, an annotated anthology of sermons of my own, and most recently an in-depth survey of contemporary homiletics. I bring many of the best fruits of those projects to this one.

Up to the time of probing the above question, I assumed that biblical sermons preached the gospel just as a matter of course. Now I am no longer confident. Some do, but many, perhaps most, do not. Challenging this widespread assumption has significant implications. While I remain enormously grateful for the New Homiletic, I am more and more convinced that homiletics needs fresh direction. It needs to reexamine its approach from the beginning of exegesis through the delivery in the pulpit, and this examination needs to be centered on the nature of the gospel.

It is to that task that I have dedicated this project. I was only part way along my own journey in the first edition. Now a clear and simple method is presented that engages students in biblical texts from the start. Along the way, readers learn not only traditional historical and literary criticism but also a newer form of theological criticism to balance it. They learn how to deconstruct texts and to make bridges between the Bible and today. The lessons of the New Homiletic and the old are laid out in a way that leads to appreciation of both in their times. Students are given many options of sermon form to choose from; at the same time, they are given guidance in theologically assessing those forms, something many textbooks omit. Student assignments are offered to help ensure that students engage the practice, not just the theory, by working through to a completed sermon of their own as they proceed through the book. Sidebars highlight material and numerous endnotes—more than are strictly required in an introduction—are provided both to give a fair representation of the discipline of homiletics and to encourage further reading. Other voices are included to offer alternative perspectives. Study guide questions appear at the end of each section to invite discussion and further thought. By the end of their actual course, students may have had a chance to preach once or twice using the exterior models here; they may also have some fluency in the deep structure or grammar needed to assist gospel and discover what it means to proclaim it.

I assume that a mere continuation of the New Homiletic will not suffice—in fact there may not be much new to harvest in its territory, though its lessons are still important and valuable. Something more is needed to equip students to meet the challenges of this new millennium. A key theme here is whether we preach the text or the gospel; the answer is both, but what is the difference? This current proposal goes in the face of many familiar and fond assumptions in the field—including my own—but I trust and pray that this departure will be for the strengthening of the church. In the way of thinking presented here, the gospel ought not to be conceived as a mere add-on to an old model of homiletics. New gospel headlights or taillights are not enough. An entire hermeneutic is required from beginning to end, a rethinking that gets at questions such as: What is a text? What does it mean to preach a text? What is gospel? Does the gospel have form as well as content? Is grace the same thing as gospel? What is the role of God in preaching? Are preaching and proclamation mere synonyms? These may be fresh questions for homiletics to ask, but in a way they are old because they address the commission of Christ to preach the gospel. Some of the answers are old, drawing on the best of our preaching forebears, yet adapted to postmodern times. I am hopeful that what is said here might stimulate fresh discussion and open new windows to creativity and faithful rendering of God's Word in the pulpit.

Emmanuel College
University of Toronto
April 2007

Preface to the Original Edition

Seminary students anxiously making their way down the hall to their first preaching class may ask questions like, "How long can I delay preaching before my peers?" or "Why not just submit written sermons?" or even "Why did I ever consider ministry?" There are good reasons for feeling anxious. Preaching is important. Our entire vocation may seem to come into focus, or question, once we sign up for our first preaching assignment. In spite of the fact that we know Christ, not the preacher, is the focus and that Christ speaks through us, these troubling thoughts start bubbling away. What if I cannot preach? Should I even be considering ministry? Am I wasting my time? Will I disappoint all of those who have encouraged me to be here? There are few other courses in seminary that evoke such questions about call to ministry.

On the other hand, as students, we may find some comfort in knowing that preaching classes are designed to provide the knowledge and skills we may be lacking, and seek to avoid competition. In the preaching class we are not like Cain and Abel, competing for the best offering to bring to God. We compete only with ourselves to be the best preacher we can be. Excellent preaching develops over many years in the pulpit, and only then with care, building on a solid foundation.

There can be other reasons for initial anxiety. Anyone who has been hiking through theological country in North America lately will know that it has been hit by the same forces that have hit society, culture, and politics in the last hundred years. We have changed the way we think about how institutions and structures function in their effective operation and management.

Power and authority are key issues. I suggest that two sources for our ideas of the nature of ministry have changed. No longer is the preacher automatically granted authority by virtue of the office. The church itself is no longer necessarily seen as a positive contributor to the social fabric, much less to the "good life" of the individual. There are now few "princes of the pulpit." They have been replaced by pastors with a variety of strengths in ministry. One popular model of ministry is the facilitator/enabler. In this model, (1) the minister, pastor, or priest resists claiming the authority of the pastoral office for himself or herself. (2) Ministry of the laity becomes the primary focus of vocational ministry. This affects the style and content of preaching. One important gift has been attention to the ways in which congregations actually contribute to the preacher's homiletical process.

Taken to its extreme, however, this tendency is at odds with preaching. Different voices arise: "No one person should have the authority to speak for everyone." "Everyone should share in the preaching." "Let us do away with preaching altogether." Relativism holds sway. How can the preacher speak authoritatively in that sort of relativistic climate? Moreover, if new role models are sought, there are few for women who, along with many men, may feel uncomfortable with some traditional models of preaching.

A prospective preacher therefore may feel torn in this cultural and ecclesial climate when it comes to learning to preach. Preaching presumes authority. Most congregations list preaching at the top, or near the top, of desired ministry skills. Ministry depends on it. Churches want it. We all need it. Christ mandated it. Yet who are we to place demands upon others? Still, our traditional claim nonetheless remains that preaching is one of the best means for us to exercise Christian instruction, pastoral care, and prophetic challenge. There is simply no substitute for it, and without it, the church would cease to exist. To be fine preachers we need a positive image and understanding of what we are doing, one that is suited to helping us meet the needs of churches in the twenty-first century.

There is a further reason for possible anxiety. Students also have heard that not since the Middle Ages or the Reformation have such mighty winds swept the homiletical highlands. If we ask some of the oldest preachers, we can be told how, in just one century, the average length of a sermon in many denominations has gone from nearly an hour, often to less than a quarter of that. Theorists now speak of propositional and narrative preaching; of deductive and inductive sermons; of different cultural understandings of preaching; of the role of parable in Jesus' teaching; of the pericope and various kinds of criticism (historical, redaction, form, sociological, literary, canonical, rhetorical, etc.); of the role of a reader's experience in interpreting texts; of greater ecumenical cooperation and sharing of scholarly resources; of the influence of the Roman, Lutheran, Episcopal, and Revised Common lectionaries; of changes in worship; of ways of thought being altered by mass media and computer technology; and of a host of other changes. What is at the heart of these changes? What are we leaving behind? What are we moving toward?

Given that the winds of change are still blowing, we undertake a tentative voyage of discovery here. It is tentative in part because the author is a middle-class, urban, white, North American, Protestant male, who brings many of the limitations of that perspective. In addition, changes are still happening. More changes will yet occur, the extent of which we can only guess. Why not wait until things are more settled?

On the other hand, when is there greater need to have a tour, something that can provide a fresh survey, new vision, and practical help, than when so much is in the process of change? Moreover, not everything is changing, and already there are strong indicators of what lies ahead. The changes in wind direction are symptomatic of a larger change, a change in climate. It is important to identify this climate now in order that we can make adequate preparations for the future.

If we go to the library and simply browse through the preaching books, we quickly get a sense of change. Many of the titles identify varieties of sermon form, from expository and doctrinal to sermons that adopt the form, function, or mode of expression of the biblical text. We also see changes in thematic concerns: for instance the number of preaching books devoted to feminist, liberation, cultural, and social justice preaching. Important as these formal and thematic matters are, they constitute but one part of a larger movement of long-term significance for the homiletical climate.

Fundamental to many of the changes we are seeing around us in theology as a whole is the increased importance being given to experience, in particular the experience of those who have been silent or oppressed or otherwise excluded from participation in decisions that affect individual and communal life. It was the experience of injustice by workers that led to the social gospel movement; of poverty in Latin America that led to liberation theology; of white, male, middle-class bias in traditional theology that led to feminist theology; of racial, cultural, and economic bias that led to black and womanist theology; and, within the limited sphere of worship in some denominations, the experience of exclusion of laity that led to theology of liturgical revision.

Many, though not all, of the changes in homiletics today are also related to various claims of experience, even beyond these theological movements. David James Randolph made four claims for the renewal of preaching in 1969 that now seem prophetic concerning the current emphasis upon experience in contemporary forms of preaching:

1) The sermon ... proceeds from the Bible as God's Word to us and connects with the situation of the hearers; it does not arise from religion in general and address the universe.

2) The sermon moves fundamentally to *confirmation* from affirmation, rather than to evidence from axiom.

3) The sermon seeks *concretion* by bringing the meaning of the text to expression in the situation of the hearers, rather than abstraction by merely exhibiting the text against its own background.

4) The sermon seeks forms of *construction* and *communication* which are consistent with the message it intends to convey, not necessarily those which are most traditional, most readily available, or most "successful."[1]

Of course the call for preaching to relate to the experience or situation of the hearers is at one level simply a call for relevance, and this is a cry of every age. However, in recent decades it has also become a call for new sermon forms that reflect human experience and demonstrate integration of form and content.

This book is intended as a textbook that introduces students to the breadth and depth of the homiletical field, much in the manner that we might expect of an introductory textbook in any other field, for instance New Testament. As in other fields, use of the term *introduction* need not imply anything about its readers (that is, whether they are undergraduate or graduate theological students or experienced preachers). It is addressed directly to students engaged in theological education and tries to speak to the concerns and questions they have as they begin studying homiletics. It is written to challenge students in helpful ways, without the expectation that they necessarily will have finished with their learnings when their preaching course is done. Excellent preaching is, after all, a lifelong goal for all of us. Attention is given to all stages in the development of a sermon, to major developments in homiletics, as well as to the relationship of preaching to other key courses in the theological curriculum.

At the same time, this book is written to enable preachers already serving churches to overhear what is being said in the classrooms; Fred Craddock has helped us to understand the importance of overhearing in the preaching and learning process (*Overhearing the Gospel*). Assistance is provided here for ministers, pastors, and priests to apply learnings in their own situations. I have chosen simply to use the word *sermon* rather than a dual reference to sermon/homily, hoping that readers who prefer *homily* will forgive this attempt at being less clumsy.

Several assumptions were at work in the formation of this introduction. A textbook in preaching should: (1) foster a love of preaching and a love of language; (2) draw on the history of preaching; (3) fairly represent a variety of approaches; (4) present preaching as a theological task; (5) be practical; (6) be challenging; (7) present a coherent vision of future homiletical directions; (8) contribute new insights; (9) assist readers and instructors with examples, exercises, and guidelines along with theoretical understanding; and (10) meet the needs of students in helping them actually to prepare a sermon.

The primary purpose here, however, is not to identify major traditions informing preaching or even to identify changes affecting the contemporary homiletics or to point to new or emergent directions. It is rather to assist preaching today and to encourage us all to think how we may better assist God, who meets us all, especially in proclamation of the Word.

Section I

Monday: Getting Started

Early in the week, the preacher needs to start thinking about the upcoming sermon. With any sermon, it helps to have an idea in one's mind about what it means to preach the gospel. What is the effect of the proclaimed Word? A marvelous statement about this is made in a painting by Jean-Paul Lemieux, a Quebec artist, in 1941 during World War II, titled *Lazare* or Lazarus (see the cover of this book). In the top left corner is a terrible scene: barely visible against the clouds, six bombers are flying and two soldiers, who drop in parachute from the sky, are shooting at families walking to church. A child appears dead, and a man is falling while another returns fire. In the bottom right corner is a traditional Quebec funeral; the hearse leads the way to the graveyard, followed by the men in formal attire, and had the artist extended the picture, one presumably would see the women and children walking behind. That axis, top left to bottom right, is the death axis of the painting, yet it is not dominant.

Of greater focus and dominance in the picture is the life axis. In the bottom left and covering much of the canvas is a cut-away church with the worship service in progress; the roof mostly has been omitted so the viewer can see inside. The worshipers are wonderfully normal; many listen to the preacher attentively; one may be dozing; another is craning his neck to look back; a boy hangs his arms over the balcony rail; the woman playing the organ is partly turned from the keyboard, perhaps half listening. As one gazes on the scene one becomes aware that most of the lines of the church point to one place, like in grade-school art when one is taught to draw train tracks by having a vanishing point where the lines converge. In this case, the lines of the tile floor, the ends of the pews, the tops of the walls, the various portions of the roof—they all point to the top right and specifically to the man in a suit with a halo over his head, that is, to Jesus. Jesus, for his part, stands by a grave with Martha dressed in black, the color of mourning, and Mary in blue, the color of faith;

Lazarus is rising from the dead. Someone else is present as a witness, perhaps the gospel writer John, but more likely the artist himself.

The painting as a whole says that in the midst of war and death, something else goes on connected with it, the church gathers for worship, the gospel is preached, and faith continues to bear fruit. However strong the axis of death may be, the axis of life is stronger. The two axes form the cross. Everything in the picture points to Jesus—even the preacher points to Jesus—and if you look closely Jesus points straight up to God. In other words, preaching is effective and has some connection with death being overcome, the dead being raised. Through the Word the old order is put to death and a new world is begun. Lemieux makes a powerful statement about the effectiveness of preaching.

Christians are, of course, a people of the Book. The Bible is at the center of worship in a manner that mirrors its significance for life in general; Christians center their lives on God in Jesus Christ as revealed by the Holy Spirit through Scripture. One may claim, "I know that the One I have met is Christ because of Scripture. And I believe Scripture because it leads to Christ."

Being people of the Book immediately poses challenges. Written texts require interpretation. Who has authority to interpret for the community? What is a correct interpretation or can such a term even be used in a postmodern world? What are the roles of contemporary experience and the Holy Spirit? Not every biblical text is plain in meaning and not every interpretation is an expression of what the church believes, so the early church developed the idea of the rule of faith, reserving for the church the right to determine. Origen commented that Christ reads Scripture to us, meaning something similar to Luther, who looked for the meaning of Scripture in relationship to Christ; Calvin affirmed "objective" study of Scripture of the sort modeled by Erasmus and the humanists yet also affirmed that the Holy Spirit gives the right reading. Given that Scripture has both human and divine elements, how does one discern what to preach?

Many preaching textbooks start by talking at length about theology of the Word. In fact, the first edition of this book started in that way. Whatever advantage that approach has in laying a foundation, it has the effect of delaying students in introductory preaching class from engaging the biblical text upon which they will preach. Since typically students benefit from dealing with the biblical text as early as possible in an introductory course, it is good to start, for instance, in the first week. Other matters can be discussed in the midst of the process, as issues arise, when students can see and experience their practical implications. Thus, we turn immediately to doing exegesis.

Since in these pages we will go step-by-step through sermon preparation to the final product, I will do what I have done in other places and break down the preacher's week into days, assigning tasks for each day. Whether one does this in one's own regular preaching is up to the individual preacher—I often cannot because of time pressures, but I always start early in the week and try to finish by Friday, with some revision and rehearsal on Saturday. Preachers do need a day off, and some put this day at the beginning of the week, some at the end, some in the middle. Let this layout of the week at least be a gentle encouragement to spread out work over several days and spend some time on each of them on the sermon. Be as disciplined as possible and guard sermon time because preaching is central to the church's life. In the sermon one has the potential to reach more people at a deeper level than in any other normal activity in ministry. One's creativity, spiritual insight, and critical perspective will be greatly increased if one allows maximum time to process materials at both conscious and subconscious levels. The mind can process much even over several nights of sleep.

CHAPTER 1

BIBLICAL EXEGESIS

I f you recall your best experience of preaching, what stands out? What happened? What did that sermon do? What did it achieve? In the best sermons, Christians not only learn something but also feel renewed hope, stronger faith, and recommitment to mission or Christian living. Simply stated, they experience God. Thus one may claim that preaching is an event in which the congregation hears God's Word, meets their Savior, and is transformed through the power of the Holy Spirit to be the kind of community God intends. Preaching is an event, an action; something happens in the lives of the hearers by way of a divine encounter. Christ commissioned preaching. Since this encounter is a salvation event, it effects an end to the old ways, reconciliation with God, and empowerment for ministries. All of this is part of the purpose of preaching.

This dynamic perspective represents a departure from more common ways of thinking about sermons. These old ways fall somewhat short of meeting God in an

> Preaching is an event of encounter with God that leaves the congregation with stronger faith and deeper commitment to doing God's work.

event; my hope, in these pages, is that, by keeping God as a focus, one may find better ways to communicate God's love. What can we as humans do to make preaching more of an event of divine encounter? Many things, and they all start with the Bible.

The immediate purpose here is to take the student through the exegetical process step-by-step, from the beginning to the end. Thus, here we turn immediately to the Bible and choosing a text.

Choosing a Text

A preacher needs a biblical text upon which to base the sermon since the sermon gains much of its authority because it renders God's Word. Christ commissioned the church to preach the gospel. With prayer, scholarship, and discernment given of the Spirit, preachers seek what God wants to say.

Nothing is more important for the quality of the finished sermon than the time allotted to it over the greatest number of days. Some of a preacher's best thoughts initially form at a subconscious level when doing other things. Sixteen hours of rushed preparation on Saturday are not worth eight or ten quality hours spread throughout the week (and this still might be minimal preparation!).

A text may be chosen in any number of ways, and each has its strengths and dangers. One can choose favorite texts that ensure one has something to say, although favorites run out, or choose texts out of the congregation's study program. Some preachers choose texts from their general reading and studies; here a danger can be that one spends too long settling on a text and not enough time developing it for the sermon. Preachers who choose their own lessons belong to a free church or free pulpit tradition that allows preachers to proclaim the Word of God wherever it is found. Other preachers belong to traditions in which a bishop or other denominational leader stipulates what texts are to be read, normally from a lectionary, as a means of encouraging unity.

Many free-church preachers today use a lectionary in text selection. Even if one's own denomination does not follow one, preachers need at least to know that a lectionary is a collection of Bible readings or lections. Scholars suggest that Jesus may have followed a lectionary when he was asked to read the Scripture in the synagogue of his hometown of Nazareth (Luke 4). Lectionaries are designed for particular occasions: Sundays, weddings, funerals, daily services, as well as personal lectionaries that a preacher might individually compose in advance of a year's preaching schedule.

The most frequently used lectionary today is the ecumenical lectionary (published as *The Revised Common Lectionary*, 1992). Derived from the Roman Catholic lectionary produced out of Vatican II (1962–65), this ecumenical lectionary was complied by a group of scholars with representatives from many denominations. It observes the church year, which follows Jesus' life and gives an annual review of it and his ministry: the four Sundays of Advent lead to Christmas and anticipate Christ's coming in three ways: at the end of time, in history in the incarnation, and in the renewal of individual faith. They are followed by the season of Epiphany in which the manifestation of God in Christ was made known to various people. Ash Wednesday is the beginning of the fifty days of Lent, a time of penance that culminates in Holy Week, including Palm/Passion Sunday, Good Friday, and Easter. The Sundays after Easter lead to Jesus' Ascension to heaven, Pentecost, and Trinity Sunday. The Sundays of ordinary time then focus on the life of the church and end at the Reign of Christ (or Christ the King) Sunday, affirming his rule over all, just prior to Advent starting once again.

The ecumenical lectionary offers three readings for each Sunday—Old Testament, epistle, and gospel—plus a psalm. The psalm is considered to be a sung response to the first reading, though it is a preaching text in itself. The lectionary brings before congregations a wide selection of scriptural readings in a systematic way by rotating through a three-year cycle: Year A focuses on the Gospel of Matthew, Year B on Mark, Year C on Luke, and John is dealt with each year mainly in Lent and Sundays after Easter.

A lectionary ensures that preachers do not stick with their own favorites and that congregations hear a wide selection of texts. A wide range of resources is available to preachers who follow the lectionary, such as ministerial study groups and published aids including hymn and art selections, suggestions for speaking with children, and so forth. Dangers also exist: large portions of scripture are never read (the same thing can be said of any method of text selection except for *lectio continua,* continuous reading/preaching through the Bible). With four readings prescribed per Sunday, if all are read, pressure is put on the sermon to be shorter. Preachers might not think of using a text not prescribed even though it has obvious application on a day. Also, some preachers try to preach all three readings instead of one and end up dealing with none adequately. On the whole, however, preachers who use the lectionary find an advantage in spending their time on actual sermon preparation rather than hunting for a text or searching for a topic.

Harry Emerson Fosdick, who held the congregation's needs in high regard, once criticized use of historical criticism in the pulpit, saying that a congregation rarely came to church "desperately anxious to discover what happened to the Jebusites."[1] The same thing can be said concerning the biblical texts that are read on Sunday: the congregation rarely comes to church with a desperate need to know how the psalm relates to the epistle. They want to know what God has to say to their lives, to the teenager who is experimenting with drugs, to the man who has cancer, to the woman who is unemployed, to violence in the world.

On special days like anniversaries, high holy days, or civic holidays, both the biblical text and the meaning of the day may need to be expounded in relation to the congregational needs, thus preachers are under even tighter constraint to concentrate on only one primary biblical text.

Generally choose only one text to preach—in the sermon one normally only has time to deal with one in depth—the norm in the church being the gospel lesson, yet with a good mixture of Old Testament and epistle sermons. Normally make reference to any other biblical text (not just the other texts read in the service) if helpful, using obvious images, ideas or story lines, not probing deeply. A general rule can be that if one of these other texts needs more than a few words of explanation, it may not clarify or reinforce what is said, but detract from it.

However you choose a text, select one for which you have some passion, that either initially excites or annoys. Initial positive or negative response to a text is energy that can be channeled constructively through study and composition during the week. A text that provokes no personal response in the preacher may produce an uninspired sermon.[2]

Novelist Doris Lessing once advised that one should never read a book if it carries no interest because at any moment there will be hundreds of books that will have appeal. The same might be said for preaching: do not preach a text that has no initial effect on you.

What Preachers Do with the Text: Exegesis

Exegesis means "to draw meaning out" of a biblical text as opposed to eisegesis, "to read something into" a text making it say what one wants it to say. Exegesis has become synonymous with historical criticism, a method of determining what a text actually says, the steps of which are well established. Exegesis is a process of bringing the text's meaning forward to today across linguistic, cultural and other barriers and of bringing worldly reality to bear fully on the text. Even as late as the 1960s this process was thought to be an objective science. Nowadays, scholars tell us that discovery of what a text says and means is never objective, it is inescapably influenced by the biases and experiences a reader brings.

Some current ways of reading texts, like reader-response criticism, would have been dismissed in previous eras as eisegesis, and while the latter term perhaps has lost some of its sharp edge, it can be still useful to help distinguish good and bad interpretative practices. Good practices nourish the faith and life of the Christian community, and the church has always used the rule of faith to assist its own ways of reading texts. The historical-critical exegetical process still stands as the best means available to ensure a fair hearing of the text in its time and context.

The purpose of this first stage of encounter with the biblical text is simply to understand what it says. What it says often is not self-evident. One needs to ensure that one has an accurate version or translation of the text. Even then, the careful reader will keep on reading until things previously unnoticed in a text begin to appear. Thomas Troeger described this process of being "attentive to what is" as imagination.[3] In other words, imagination is not culling something from nothing but rather is discovering what is given. With a text one knows well, one seeks to penetrate the barrier of familiarity so that it may be experienced afresh.

The first step is prayer. This can be anything from a simple prayer all the way up to praying the text, a practice known as *lectio divina* in Ignatian spirituality in which one holds up each word, phase, or image as a means of envisioning it, experiencing it, and discovering its meaning. Michael J. Quicke outlines four stages of this in dealing with the parable of the lost sheep: *lectio* (slow reading) turns to *meditatio* (meditation, experiencing the drama); for instance, "I listen as Jesus tells the parable to me in the crowd.... I sense both the love and hostility around Jesus. Jesus' identification jumps out at me: 'Suppose one of you has a hundred sheep.'" *Oratio* (praying) is the next step, "focusing on what God is saying to sinners, mutterers, shepherds, lost sheep, found sheep, and friends of the shepherd." The final step is *contemplatio* (contemplation, waiting to receive God's grace), often in silence. Quicke shows the importance of encountering a biblical text on one's own before seeking what others say about it.[4]

Linda Clader follows a simpler practice of prayer: "I often read the texts with prayer beforehand. I ask God to open my ears and heart to receive the Word, and I ask for guidance from the Holy Spirit so that I can proclaim what God's people need to hear. I do it about as simply as I just wrote it, and then I read the texts."[5] For her, prayer continues throughout the week, "I pray for my congregation and ask God to give them a gift from the text for that day. I also ask God to give me a gift, to open my imagination to reorganize how the Word nourishes and heals me. I pray for faith and I pray for inspiration."[6] The process takes place within a relationship with God. Learning to do good exegesis can be fun because it involves newness and depth, a sense of being led.

Some people might still question whether exegesis is necessary. Why not just get a text and run with it? A colleague in student days wanted to avoid exegesis and rely simply upon the Holy Spirit in the pulpit. Our preaching professor reminded us that the devil took Jesus to the highest pinnacle of the temple and commanded him to throw himself down, and the angels would bear him up: Jesus resisted that temptation (Luke 4:9-12) and so should we. The Holy Spirit works in many ways, not least through scholarship.

Still, holding out for the importance of scholarly exegesis in guiding the preacher to deeper understandings is like an episode of *The Simpsons* that Casey Barton, a graduate student in homiletics, reported:

> I was watching *The Simpsons* the other night, and Ned Flanders was making movies out of biblical scenes, which were all quite bloody, and everybody loved. The films were shown at church, and there was this exchange between Lenny and Rev. Lovejoy:
>
> Lenny: Reverend Lovejoy, I think that people might be more interested in your sermons if you added in a little "razzle dazzle," like Ned.
>
> Rev. Lovejoy: Well, I do have "razzle dazzle" in my sermons. If by "razzle" you mean a healthy dose of piety. And by "dazzle" you mean accurate scriptural interpretation.
>
> Lenny (whispering to Carl): What a tool.[7]

As preachers, we are all in danger of taking our tasks too seriously.

Perhaps the best way to introduce the important task of exegesis is to give a brief overview of the development of its method for the pulpit in three stages. We will consider: (1) traditional historical criticism, which began with the Enlightenment and matured by the 1900s, (2) literary criticism that arose as a distinct way of treating literary texts in the 1900s when literature departments began in universities, (3) theological criticism, a step still resisted in most biblical departments because it engages the text from the perspective of faith, not simply history. A theological stage of exegesis is essential for preaching, yet it is frequently ignored. Finally, we will blend and unify the whole process with a demonstration exegesis that students may imitate. First, the overview.

Historical Criticism

Translation and interpretation for most of history were thought to be linear exercises, like substituting one word for another, the way one might substitute one brick for another in a wall. Words were substituted according to rules of grammar and syntax in order to support, clarify, and secure the text's meaning.[8] In fact, for much of history it was possible to hold the doctrine that the content of Scripture is univocal and clear. Thus the Reformers claimed that their doctrines were essentially the content of the New Testament in a different form. Most preachers, prior to the general acceptance of higher criticism, identified a doctrine in their scriptural verse and moved, in the body of the sermon, to discuss that doctrine (not their biblical text) anywhere it was found in Scripture.

J. G. Eichorn (1752–1827) is one of the founders of historical criticism. His three-volume introduction to the Old Testament swept away doctrinal presuppositions that stood in the way of scholarly investigations of the texts. Scholars using humanist methods began asking troubling questions like, what views of the ancient world did the biblical writers have? What did they think? How did their language and culture affect how they thought? How did these various factors affect what they wrote? Critics recognized that there was a distance (1) between the biblical text and the events it described and (2) between the biblical text and the contemporary scholar or preacher. Interpretation came to be visualized not in linear ways but as a circular exercise (hence the "hermeneutical circle"), or more accurately a spiral of ongoing dialogue between the text, its background, and contemporary language and times. One looks for an equivalent word or phrase, takes it back to the text, comes back to today for another more precise word or phrase, goes back to the text, then moves on to take in more of the text, and gradually moves to comprehension of the whole.

The Contribution of Higher Criticism

With higher criticism two things happened. First, the understanding of text, in effect, expanded: new bodies of material were seen as relevant to the text that had not been acknowledged before.[9] That is, to translate a biblical text meant going beyond the Bible itself; some of the text's meaning lay elsewhere. Other texts and fields of study like world history and archeology had to be considered because these gave access to ancient cultures and worldviews. Thus modern historical-critical approaches to the Bible arose.

Second, two stages in interpretation were conceived. The first stage became referred to as "understanding" a text (*verstehen*),[10] or what we may call, "what the text says." Alongside it there appeared an interrelated, second stage. This second stage is "explaining" a text (erklaren) and offers "what the text means." Sometimes what a text says does not clarify its meaning, thus this second step became necessary. It concerns what the text means when adjustments are made for time and culture.

In the 1960s, Otto Kaiser and Werner G. Kummel wrote a slim volume entitled *Exegetical Method: a Student's Handbook*. They basically summarized what was standard by then. They spoke of exegesis as a "scientific" process concerned with the text's original form and purpose and its "objective meaning."[11] Their approach was quickly dated. Today scholars generally agree that texts have many meanings, depending on one's perspective. The original form of a text in history is important in helping to know what the text originally meant, but the form that it currently has in the biblical canon is also important; this is the form the church affirmed in receiving it as the book to guide its faith and life. In spite of weaknesses, the basic historical-critical method still stands. Its essential steps are as follows:

- Determine how much of a biblical text to consider. Read what comes before and after it. Does it have unity and coherence on its own or do you need to consider a larger section? For example, The Revised Common Lectionary provides only

Genesis 9:8-17 of the Noah story; there is no judgment on humanity, no building of the ark, no gathering of the animals, no storm. As Eugene Lowry notes, "What we have is the rainbow (in a redundant passage)."[12] An assigned reading may be extended or shortened if the preacher deems it appropriate. By the same token, an entire story need not be read in church in order for that story in its fullness to be preached. Nonetheless, the passage ideally represents a complete unit of thought. Identify its form or genre: is it song, letter, law, epic, parable, sayings, something else?

- Identify key words and phrases that provide clues to the theme of the passage and check in a concordance or lexicon for meanings of important words.

- Make a provisional translation of the text if you have the original language; read various translations and, using a scholarly edition of the Bible, check the critical apparatus (that is, the footnotes) to see if there are textual problems or variant readings.

- Outline the plot or sequence of thoughts; sketch their movement if possible in order to understand the text's structure.

- Consult various scholarly resources like Bible commentaries, dictionaries, and atlases to determine as much as possible the historical life situation of the text, or its *Sitz im Leben*, and its history of transmission. Answer basic historical questions about the text from evidence you find within it: Who wrote it? What can you say about the human author? To whom was it written? On what occasion; to what situation? For what purpose? Determine from research if your text has been edited and what purposes the editing served. Discover what biblical scholars have said about the passage.

- Determine the theme of the entire book. What is the theme of this particular passage? What connection is there between the two?

- Check to see if the text has parallels elsewhere in the Bible or cites other texts that might give clues about the source or meaning. What was going on in Israel's (or the church's or the world's) history at this time? What has just happened or is about to happen? Do the events of this passage or book cause anything to happen?

13

- Seek the meaning of a text in a sentence if possible. Offer an interpretation only after all of the evidence has been carefully analyzed and synthesized.
- Venture an interpretation of the text.

Historical criticism generally does not yield a meaning of the biblical text that will preach. This is all the more the case since biblical studies in general moved toward history and provable data and away from theology and questions of faith. Historical criticism often clarifies what the text does not say, even as it continues to give access to essential background and meaning of texts.

Literary Criticism

Historical criticism examines a text through history (diachronically = through time) and literary criticism exams it mainly in this moment (synchronically = at the same time) for what is says on its own, apart from history. Literary criticism as a discipline is new within the last century, and it overlaps with historical criticism. Northrop Frye, the great literary critic, was an ordained minister who taught the Bible as literature. In his classes, students with no biblical background would read the stories in remarkable and fresh ways. They did not necessarily favor the people God favored. Some could not overlook the fact that the land given to Israel was stolen from the Canaanites. Many felt Jesus was foolish to die as he did and that he in fact committed suicide by entering Jerusalem. Their interpretations were among a variety of legitimate possibilities, if one were reading the Bible only as literature. They were honest, human responses to the text of the sort that many in our congregation might share at some level. Preachers should seek this kind of response as a starting place with any biblical text, putting aside for the moment the fact that the church has established a range of normative readings.

Literary analysis brings a measure of playfulness and imagination. One impact has been to encourage preachers to get to know the biblical text on their own before going to any other sources for help. Read and reread it; read it out loud. Summarize it. What details stand out in your mind? What happens in the text? Look for something you never noticed before. Using your senses (and your imagination), what does the text allow you to see, hear, feel, smell, or taste? Who does what? What is the result?

Three basic principles of literary criticism are helpful. The first is that *each literary text can stand on its own as a source of interpretative data.* Literary critics say that a poem's meaning does not rely on any meanings it does not itself suggest and does not even depend on what its author might say was her intent. A naive first reading of a biblical text offers some initial understandings. Subsequent rereadings will support or correct them.

A second principle of literary criticism is this: *there are many possible correct understandings of any work of literature, and some contradict each other.* One may have seen this among friends when discussing a poem, movie, or biblical text, and individuals understand it differently. Each interpretation may offer new insight, yet some seem stronger than others.

A third principle is that *valid interpretations require three separate pieces of information pointing to the same truth.* "Why three?" we may ask, "Is this not arbitrary?" In some ways it is. For instance, one does not always have three and must go with what one has. Nonetheless, the strongest case is still made with three because literary criticism looks for repeating patterns. Someone's behavior may strike one as strange and raise questions; two similar incidents suggest a possible pattern; but three incidents suggest a theory in which one may have some confidence, perhaps enabling one to anticipate future behavior or to identify a personality trait.

To take another approach, in a sermon one can discuss the psychological motives Ruth had for staying with Naomi only if the text itself states it plainly, or gives three solid clues pointing to the same motive. If these are not provided, motive is not a focus of the text and one has no textual basis for discussing it. (One can venture why we might do it, but that is different from finding it in the text.) One ends up psychologizing the text, attributing motive that the text actually does not support.

Concerning Ruth, the biblical text does offer at least three pieces of information that allow one to draw some conclusions about love as her motive: she did not choose to return to her own mother; she wanted to stay with Naomi past death (Ruth 1:17); she is loyal (3:10). These pieces of information need to be communicated to the congregation in order to allow them to be partners in concluding with you that Ruth loved Naomi.

One of the earliest forms of literary criticism was formal criticism. It took the piece of literature and read it to discover within its form its own principles of coherence and unity; questions of history or authorial intent were irrelevant. There are many types of literary criticism today (feminist, reader-response, postcolonial, and so on), each with its own questions to address a text. Literary criticism asks:

What is the form of the text (is it an epic, a letter, a hymn, a benediction, a lament, an argument, a story)? In what style is it written (for example, poetic, formal, familiar)? What are its parts? How does each part relate to the whole? Why was it written? How does its form relate to its function? What is the text trying to accomplish rhetorically (that is, what effect is it meant to have)? What difference would be made to the book if this passage were left out? Who are the main characters in the text? What is the conflict? What do they do (that is, what is the plot)? What is the resolution? How does the thought or action in the text connect with the passages that went before and go after? Who is in power? Who are the primary characters, the minor ones, and what might this suggest? With whom do you identify in the text? Who is excluded from power? Is there a difference in the way rich and poor are treated? or men and women? Are their words given equal weight? What repeated patterns in action, thought, or expression emerge? What links does this text suggest with other Bible passages? What does not fit or is a puzzle?

By listening in this manner preachers are led by the biblical text to an understanding of it. The process is never as linear as this. One converses with the text, listening to it in a humble and receptive fashion, yet listening also to oneself as a real participant in the relationship. As interpreters, we come with preconceived ideas or preunderstandings. We try to identify them and minimize their effect. Throughout the exegetical process we make guesses about the overall meaning and application but nonetheless withhold final judgment until exegesis is complete.

Theological Criticism

Theological exegesis is in some ways the new kid on the exegetical block, and in some ways it is the old one. Historical criticism sometimes engages theological questions, if the text raises them from within. Theological criticism has been developed in homiletics to recover what seems to have been lost, mainly in the last century, from how the Reformers viewed Scripture. In many ways they still teach us how to read Scripture because they helped shape an era in which there was more balance. They combined close study of the original texts with critical theological readings that opened the Scriptures for the church. John Calvin, for instance, understood that scientific tools were needed for reading Scripture, but he also understood that the Holy Spirit needed to inform and inspire any reading. Modern approaches to the Bible have led to historical and literary readings that mainly focus on humans and leave out God.

Theological criticism engages something that the previous two stages ignore, namely, the text as revelation, and it addresses what the text says about God and humanity in relationship to God. The Protestant Reformers were in agreement that Scripture could be interpreted by the authority of Scripture alone (*sola Scriptura*) and not by unwritten oral traditions. They protested interpretations and principles for interpretation that had no basis in Scripture and reason. Scripture interprets Scripture. They agreed with Augustine in giving primacy to the literal interpretation, in reading obscure passages in the light of clear ones, and in rendering the interpretation that fosters love with figurative passages where the meaning is in doubt.[13] Like many scholars in the medieval church before them, they in fact had a double literal sense: one was historical (or grammatical) and the other was theological, and it was the latter that offered the higher and authentic true meaning of the text. This was the literal meaning that allowed Luther to speak of Christ, and for Calvin it was the reading the Holy Spirit inspired.[14] One might say that theological criticism tries to recover something of this second literal sense while avoiding some of the errors of previous ages, and in so doing tries to recover the Bible as the church's book, not just the academy's.

Some traditions have been less vulnerable than others to the loss of a divine focus. Cleophus J. Larue says three features are common to contemporary African American preaching. The preacher (1) "attempts to name God's presence in the text and in the sermon," (2) "pairs the biblical text to the life experiences of the hearers," and (3) considers "the end to which God's power is used ... to liberate, deliver, provide, protect, empower, or transform."[15] As William H. Stewart Sr. has said, "'In the beginning God ...' and so it is in any act of preaching and biblical interpretation."[16]

Here are some basic theological questions that help preachers move to what will preach. These questions, unlike most of those of the historical critic or literary student, are not anthropocentric, putting human activity at the center. Rather, they are theocentric, putting God at the center. Michael J. Quicke says, "responsible exegetes must investigate what God is saying and doing in a text."[17] Theological reading is of course larger than this. David Bartlett encourages preachers to read biblical texts listening for other voices: Latin American, feminist, African American, third world.[18]

Some questions overlap and not every text is able to answer each one: What is God (in one of the persons of the Trinity) doing in this biblical text? Or, what is God doing behind this biblical text, in the larger story? What group or person represents God in this text? What does this text say about who God is? What does this text say about who we are as human beings? What does this text say about how humanity has fallen short of God's purposes? What sin does this text reveal? What divine judgment upon that sin does this text reveal? What human brokenness or vulnerability does this text reveal? What divine judgment rests upon those in this text who inflict brokenness or who take advantage of the vulnerable? What change must the people make in the text? Why does God choose to act? What hope does this text imply or offer? What action of God communicates that hope? What does this text say about God's will for human beings? What does this text say about how God will restore humanity to God's purpose? What does this text say about God's love? What does God do in this text to provide or accomplish what is needed? What does God do behind this text in the larger story to accomplish what is needed? What is God enabling the people in the text to accomplish? What does this text say or imply about God's future promises? What verb best captures God's help (that is, what God does) in this passage? What sentence with God as the subject best establishes the text's theme? What action of the people in this text makes it necessary for God to act in this way? What other central biblical texts display similar actions of God? What teaching or doctrine of the church most closely corresponds to the theme? What aspect of that doctrine applies? What does this text say, imply, anticipate, or echo about Jesus Christ? How might it connect to the cross, resurrection, ascension, and/or pentecost? What does the resurrection say to this text?[19]

Unifying the Process: a Practical Example

Now is the time for the reader to choose a biblical text and to engage it by working through the exegetical process. I have chosen my own text, in this case, the call of Isaiah (Isaiah 6:1-13) that I will work through with the student. In the process, we will unify historical, literary, and theological criticism into one exciting exegetical model. Students might take the example below and use it as a model for working on their own text. The answers that one gives need not be longer than those provided here. The purpose is not to exhaust either the meaning of the text or the student, but to awaken the student to rich gifts. The questions are numerous yet the process is not overly difficult; it is at least not more difficult than it needs to be. If you get stuck on any question, move along and return to it later, or leave it blank. The entire exercise initially need not take more than a few hours.

Students should have a few basic resources on hand: a dictionary and atlas of the Bible to explain such things as key terms, places, and social practices; a concordance of the Bible to help one locate related texts; at least one good scholarly commentary devoted to the particular book of the Bible (in other words, not a one-volume commentary devoted to the entire Bible although the latter can be excellent in providing a quick overview of an entire biblical book); several translations of the Bible (these are available online); a Greek or Hebrew lexicon for those who can use the biblical languages; and theological books and dictionaries that explain key doctrines. In Reformed understanding, study of the biblical text is the preacher's spiritual discipline.

Again, students need not answer every one of the following questions in relationship to their own preaching text. If a particular text does not yield an answer to a particular question, move to the next. Also, some questions may overlap, and these questions may open new doors with some texts and not with others. Ignore questions that will result in mere duplication of previous answers. The purpose of the exercise is to help the reader see what is in the text from various angles.

> 1. *Read and reread the text on your own. Close your eyes and picture its events or the events surrounding the author or receivers, relying on clues that the text actually offers. You might even pray the text, thinking about each detail. Look in the text for things you may not have noticed before.* Isaiah pictures God not in some celestial heaven but in a celestial version of the earthly temple. This is in contrast to the book of Revelation in which there is no temple or church. The six-winged seraphs are unlike any angels I imagine.

> 2. *Determine the boundaries of your text by reading what comes before and after it. Does it have unity and coherence*

on its own or do you need to consider a larger section? Identify its form or genre. This text in the lectionary ends at verse 8. On this occasion I want to treat it as a whole, including verses 9-13, because they remove any romantic notions of Isaiah's call: he is not being called to a big church and fancy robes with a hood from Harvard but to an unpopular ministry. The unit is an autobiographical call story or oracle in a series of oracles. It functions as a unit with two parts: the call itself when Isaiah was still a young man (vv. 1-6) and the details of his assignment (9-13).

3. *What function is this text designed to serve?* This text is an oracle that functions in at least two ways: to establish the divine authority of Isaiah and to indicate divine purpose behind the destruction of Judah. By placement of his call in chapter 6 instead of chapter 1 (as in Jeremiah's call), the author or editor wants first to establish the wickedness of Judah and Jerusalem in order that Isaiah's call may be seen as God's response to that wickedness.

4. *Make an initial statement: what is God doing in or behind this text?* (I like to ask this question early in the exegetical process because it awakens the preacher to a key purpose of the entire exercise and directly helps identify a theological theme. Keep it simple. We will return to this question later in the exercise.) God calls Isaiah. God's purpose in calling him is to correct the people of Judah and Jerusalem and bring them back to faithfulness.

5. *Identify key words and phrases that provide clues to the theme of the passage and check in a concordance or lexicon for meanings of important words. Make a provisional translation of the text if you have the original language; read various translations and, using a scholarly edition of the Bible, check the critical apparatus to see if there are textual problems or variant readings.* The theme concerns God's action in calling Isaiah. Key words I find include: I am

lost; unclean lips; your guilt has departed; send me; make the minds of this people dull; and the holy seed is in its stump.

6. *Who are the main characters?* King Uzziah is dead. Isaiah is afraid to be in the presence of God and considers himself and his people unworthy. The flying seraphs have powerful voices. The Lord is not pleased with the people of Judah.

7. *What happens; what is the plot or movement of thought?* In a vision of a heavenly temple, Isaiah sees God sitting on high. Thinking he will die for looking on God, he finds instead that his lips are purified by a coal. God chooses him to condemn the people of Judah to exile.

8. *What happens before and after this text (that is, what is the context)?* The vision is preceded by oracles of destruction, in particular of a foreign power destroying Israel at God's command. Following the vision is a confrontation with King Ahaz who is slow to hear. Ultimately, the people will experience exile and eventual return.

9. *What is the conflict in the text?* The main conflict is between God and Judah for its sin. There is conflict within Isaiah, for he is unclean and looks on God, and he must deliver a harsh message to his people.

10. *What resolution of the conflict does the text offer?* A messenger must be sent to pronounce God's judgment and to prevent Judah from turning to be healed. They must be exiled and their land destroyed leaving only a burned "stump." The stump will be the hope.

11. *What is known about the author, narrator, or editor?* Isaiah gives an account of his call and, hence, of his own authority to prophesy, which suggests he is facing opposition. He does not want to give the harsh message ("How long, O Lord?"). Scholars disagree about whether or not there is a first, second, and third Isaiah.

12. *Who is the intended audience?* This is written for the people of Judah, for the king of Judah, and it is preserved for a future time when Israel has been restored.

13. *With whom do you as reader identify?* I personally identify with Isaiah, since he is the main human being and perhaps because he is portrayed as being good. However, I suspect I am more like the unclean people of Judah.

14. *What would the structure of the text look like if you sketched it?* The first part of the text focuses on Isaiah in the heavenly court, at first unworthy and then purified; in other words it moves from low to high. The second part is dominated by the Lord's speech and the harsh nature of Isaiah's assignment, a movement that suggests high to low. At the center is Isaiah's "Here am I; send me!" My sketch would be an "inverted V" with "send me" at the apex.

15. *What are the power relationships in this text?* Judah has presumed to act as though it is God. God is all-powerful, free to destroy Isaiah and Judah. Both have freedom to decide what to do. Isaiah models what Judah should do: confess, repent, and dedicate oneself to God's purpose.

16. *What patterns do you find in the text?* There is also threefold bringing low: A high earthly King Uzziah is brought low by death. A vision of the high heavenly King brings Isaiah low in confession. The Lord purifies and raises Isaiah to pronounce that Judah will be brought low. There are other threefold references: Holy, Holy, Holy; seraphs with three sets of wings; the destruction of cities, houses, and land.

17. *What parallels exist between this text and others?* (Parallels are most obvious with the Gospels, but they are important with all texts.) Other call stories have similar structure: Moses, David, Jeremiah, and the disci-

ples of Jesus. There is a parallel with 1 Kings 22:19-23 where Micaiah in a vision sees the Lord on a throne, and a lying spirit is called to entice King Ahab to destruction.

18. *What is puzzling in this text? What questions does it raise?* Why does the Lord want Isaiah to prevent the people of Judah from turning and being healed? How does what will happen to Judah relate to Israel? Is this written before or after the exile it predicts?

19. *Name how you feel about this text—what emotions does it raise?* I like the cleansing of Isaiah in the heavenly court. I do not like the harshness of the judgment upon Judah because I am afraid I might be the recipient of God's wrath. I love the implication that if Judah would turn, it would be healed.

20. *What hopeful action is God performing in the text?* God calls Isaiah to preach the Word. God brings forth righteousness. The hope that there will be a "holy seed" in the "stump" that remains is not for this generation but for those to come. Nonetheless, God is the only source of hope, and the implication is that God could not help healing the people if they would turn. This hope in verse 10 at first seems as small as the seed in verse 13.

> We must decide for ourselves how much of a particular biblical text to preach upon or how many of the details to cover, often largely on the basis of the projected unity of the imagined sermon.

21. *What hopeful action is God performing behind the text, in the larger events?* With this text, this is already considered. See 20, above.

22. *What is God's judgment (that is, name the law, condemnation, or human failing)?* The people have ceased to distinguish good and evil, and God will banish them and destroy their lands.

23. *What change is demanded of humanity?* The people are to return to God, but it seems almost too late for change here, for the Lord will harden their hearts.

24. *What empowerment or change does the text suggest that God enables?* God sends Isaiah in order that the people may at least understand what is happening.

25. *What empowerment or change does God enable in the larger story to which this text belongs?* God does restore God's people and Jerusalem in Isaiah 40–66.

26. *What does this tell us about who we are? who God is?* We are a people liable to a self-deception of the sort God will not tolerate.

27. *What does this text say about God's love?* God's love for Israel is unending.

28. *What are we asked to believe or trust?* God will take action even against God's loved ones to achieve God's purposes. God's love is unending.

29. *What are we asked to do?* It depends on who we are. If we are those who are wronged by the unfaithful people (5:7-8), we are to trust that God is righteous and will end their evil ways. If we are God's unrighteous people, we are to repent of our evil and turn to God's purposes.

30. *What verbs best capture God's action in this text?* Calls. Forgives. Judges. Purifies. Promises restoration.

31. *What sentence with God as the subject best establishes the text's theme in your estimation?* God calls Isaiah to ministry.

32. *What teaching or doctrine of the church most closely corresponds to the theme? What aspect of that doctrine applies?* Several doctrines apply: call, salvation, God's righteousness, the sovereignty of God. I would focus primarily on call and on God's ability to raise up a leader in any time or season; I would not focus in this sermon for instance on election, which is also part of call, or on something we affirm in ecclesiology, the need for the community of faith to confirm the call of an individual.

33. *What does this text say, imply, anticipate, or echo about other major biblical stories?* The live coal that does not burn Isaiah's lips is akin to Moses' burning bush that is not consumed. The small hope for the present generation (Isaiah 6:10) and the small seed of hope (6:13) are reminiscent of Jesus' words about the mustard seed.

34. *How might it connect to the cross, resurrection, ascension, and/or Pentecost (that is, the heart of the gospel)?* The words that the seraph says to Isaiah are the same words that Jesus says to us from the cross, "your guilt has departed and your sin is blotted out" (6:7).

35. *How does the fact of the resurrection affect or alter the import of this text?* In Christ we have an advocate who has taken upon himself our hardened hearts. The "holy seed" has come to fruition, and we may partake of the righteousness Christ offers.

Student Assignment 1: Do an exegesis of the text for your first sermon for the class following the model above.

CHAPTER 2

PURPOSES OF PREACHING

Seeing a biblical text open like a flower and bloom before one's eyes is an exciting adventure. Ideally, this has happened by the end of the exegetical process and results in one appreciating a text in new ways. Even more important, because of the theological criticism embedded in the process, a preacher has a good number of things to say about God that were not evident before. In fact, through exegesis, a preacher ideally discovers strengthened faith and a renewed sense of being led by God to deeper understanding and witness. As any experienced preacher knows, the sermon must first speak to the one who composes it.

The blessing of having many things to say about a text comes with its own problems, however. Before proper exegesis, one may feel one does not have enough to say in a sermon, and afterward there is too much to say. Preachers at this stage typically have mixed feelings: they are excited by everything they have found, and they are eager to communicate it. They also feel overwhelmed; there is information overload. If the sermon were to be composed immediately, it might head off in six different directions at once.

Isn't there a happy medium, a way of doing exegesis so that one just gets the information that one needs, no less and no more? Cleophus LaRue says that, in his tradition, there is something known as "preaching out of the overflow"—having more to say than one can possibly say.[1] This begins early on. One needs more information than one can use in order to select what is best.

Exegesis expands the text, and the next step of determining the theme of the sermon will narrow it. The sermon needs focus, some way to ensure

27

that it will not be all over the map. I think it is important not to decide the direction of the sermon on the basis of exegesis alone but to take into account the purposes of preaching and the people to whom one is preaching (see chapter 6). Whatever purposes are most central to the preaching task will help determine the selection of a sermon theme and the best path to follow. Four theological purposes will be explored here, namely, preaching as: teaching, a relationship with God, an event of God's encounter, and proclamation of the gospel.

Preaching as Teaching

If preaching does nothing else, it must provide sound teaching about the Bible: who God is, what it means to be human, salvation, the meaning of life, and God's intentions for creation. The New Testament uses separate words for teaching (*didache*) and preaching (*kerygma*), though they overlap. *Didache* is teaching about the consequences of Christ's coming. *Kerygma* is witnessing or proclaiming the coming of God's realm in Jesus Christ. Early church preaching took a variety of shapes and included martyrdom.[2]

Even in the Middle Ages, preaching remained broadly understood, when Alan of Lille (1128–1202) identified it as what is spoken, what is written in a letter, and what is done by deed.[3] By then the church regularized four ways of reading biblical texts called the four senses or meanings of Scripture. Essentially, these were four things that Scripture teaches: a text literally describes a historical event and, hence, has a literal sense; a text says something about theology of the church and, hence, has an allegorical sense; a text calls for a change in how life is lived and, hence, has a moral sense; and a text implies something about the next life and, hence, has a prophetic or soul sense (they sometimes called this *anagogy*, to go up, that is, a higher sense).

What an inventive idea for preachers, that they could approach any text and mine at least four different meanings for their sermon! Early and medieval preachers used these four senses like four different sets of eyeglasses and thereby discovered four different kinds of things to say. So reliable were these glasses that, until the Reformation, they provided the basis for biblical interpretation and preaching. Though the church has since then affirmed that texts have one sense—the literal one—it nonetheless still often practices the others without naming them.[4]

Teaching remains an essential part of preaching. Ideally some balance is sought between teaching history, theology, and ethics, for all three of these areas inform preaching. When balance is lost, the sermon can fail. For example, some preachers today preach historical criticism, perhaps influenced by the Jesus Seminar, and everything may seem called into question. Other preachers are so much into teaching about God and theology that congregations have a hard time connecting the sermon with their lives; faith seems to be a matter of right doctrines. Still other preachers turn every text into a moral lesson, something the people must do. One former student humorously identified that particular denominations have their own slant for every text, "Southern Baptists tend to find a message of personal salvation in texts; Mennonites tend to find peacemaking; Roman Catholics tend to find a message for moral living; Episcopalians tend to find the Eucharist; and Methodists tend to find social justice."[5] When preachers turn every text into what we humans must do, they communicate that faith is what we do and that everything is up to us.

Every sermon teaches, intending to or not, something central to the faith or otherwise. When preaching is reduced to teaching, lecturing, or instructing, it becomes too narrow. It ceases to be God's event, establishing a relationship with God.

Preaching as a Relationship with God

Homiletical literature commonly speaks of three sets of stories that come together in the sermon: the stories of God, the congregation, and the preacher.[6] Teaching helps to establish a relationship between the congregation and the preacher, and preaching (that inescapably includes teaching) goes one step further, establishing a relationship with God. The sermon is largely what God does: God comes in the Holy Spirit, corrects and calls to repentance, and makes atonement for sin, once more to bring us face-to-face with the One who died for us. Charles Bartow has a good phrase for this; he claims of the Word of God that it is "*actio divina*, God's self-performance."[7] The Word is something God performs even now.

Language for this relationship is never fully adequate. Though God's identity is revealed in Scripture, what is essentially mysterious does not lose its mystery in being revealed. Human knowledge is imperfect. Preaching cannot give all the answers, for instance, to questions such as, why does evil exist? Paul says, "Now we see through a glass, darkly" (1 Corinthians 13:12). Yet, preaching does give answers and more than that, together with the sacraments and the other parts of the worship service, it fosters a relationship with the living triune God. It does this because Christ commissioned the church to preach the gospel, and he promised to be present where two or three are gathered in his name.

People long to experience God as a reality in their lives. As Karl Barth said:

> they want to find out and thoroughly understand the answer to this one question, *Is it true?*—and not some other answer which beats about the bush.... [They have] a passionate longing to lay hold of *that* which, or rather of *him* who, overcomes the world because he is its Creator and Redeemer.[8]

What one may rightly expect of this relationship is witnessed through the ages: God is unconditionally for us, desiring our fullness of life with a love that is without end. God corrects, sustains, and empowers us for ministry each day according to our needs. God uses our words to reconciling purposes in the shaping of community. And God bestows identity in Christ through the proclamation and sacraments of the church.

> The sermon at one level is God's doing from beginning to end. It is God's action through the preacher, during the week and in the pulpit, and through the listeners, in the pews and throughout the week. The sermon is a manifestation of God.

What one may not expect of this relationship is also clear: we are not in control; God's ways are not our ways nor are they determined by our ways; and God will play no favorites, for all people are loved, as the rain falls equally on the just and unjust. God is against much that we do.

Relationship as an Event of God's Encounter

It is common to conceive of the sermon as something less than an event of encounter with God. In pastoral life, preachers may conceive of the sermon to be like a college assignment; it is an essay to write or a task to be done; it is a paper that is due or a theological, biblical, or ethical presentation. These are all relevant activities in themselves, but they are not normally events of divine encounter. Jana Childers says the words of "some Greeks" to Philip in John 12:20-21 are the words of the congregation: "We wish to see Jesus." If we agree, preaching Christ is an incarnational act, the word becomes flesh.[9] Through preaching, the church is renewed as the body of Christ that exists to be a servant to the world. Moreover, preaching reveals Christ in Scripture, in the preaching and sacraments of the church, and in people around us. Through the Spirit, preaching introduces people to Jesus.

> Preachers tend to think of the sermon as an object or a thing, like an essay or lecture, rather than a vehicle God uses to establish a relationship with God's people. Salvation is communicated and authentic life bestowed. God's advent in part is through preaching.

How one thinks of a task affects how one does it. Phillips Brooks (1835–93), the great Episcopalian preacher of Trinity Church in Boston, spoke of one difference between lecturing and preaching as he thought it should be:

> Much of our preaching is like delivering lectures upon medicine to sick people. The lecture is true. The lecture is interesting. Nay, the truth of the lecture is important, and if the sick man could learn the truth of the lecture he would be a better patient, he would take his medicine more

responsibly and regulate his diet more intelligently. But still the fact remains that the lecture is not medicine, and that to give the medicine, not to deliver the lecture, is the preacher's duty.[10]

Something should happen. The sermon is an intimate and personal event in a communal context with community-shaping power. Understood this way, it is God's salvation breaking into the world. Jesus said, "Whoever listens to you listens to me" (Luke 10:16).

Consequently, language may need to shift in order to begin and maintain a relationship with God, not just ideas. God is forming the church in Christ's image. Listeners do not so much hear witness about Christ, they experience Christ's love. They do not so much receive a summons to authentic life, as they experience anointing.

Other claims could follow: Good preaching is less instruction about community than community happening. Preaching can be less a discussion of the things wrong than it is Christ beginning a new creation. The sermon can be less a talk than it is a relationship renewed.

This idea of God reaching out through preaching is not original or innovative, nor should it be, though it has languished much in recent years, arguably at great cost to the church. If one holds that the sermon is God's event, that God is the one doing the acting, that God has called the preacher and the community of the church, that the Spirit gives words and empowers the preacher to preach, that the Spirit inspires the listeners to hear and do, that through the sermon God saves and knits community, that the sermon itself is a manifestation of God, then preaching will not be received as just another task done in the course of a busy week. While the preacher obviously preaches and the listener actively listens, even these roles can be said to be products of God's work: no one can testify to Christ, nor comprehend such testimony, separate from God.[11]

Other Voices

This idea of event is at the heart of biblical understandings of the Word.[12] Paul Scherer, former teacher of preaching at Union Seminary in New York, put the matter succinctly in 1965:

[The voice of God] is forever associated with the act by which God confronts us, in Bible or in church, in worship or history or person. He is not intent on sharing conceptual truth. That must come later. It is not some saving measure of information he wants to impart; it is himself he wants to bestow: that not having seen him one may meet him and know and trust him and live our life in him, freely and for love's sake.[13]

David James Randolph in 1969, seeking to bring fruits of the school of interpretation then called the New Hermeneutic into what became the New Homiletic, spoke of preaching as event: "The key to this approach is that its emphasis falls on what the sermon *does*, rather than what it is." He identified what it does by quoting John Wesley: "To invite. To convince. To offer Christ. To build up; and do this in some measure in every sermon."[14]

The idea of event has grown in acceptance and implication in recent decades, as a quick sampling may indicate.[15] Eugene Lowry notes that, "While philosophers may be centering on the question of truth, the preacher's goals focus on experienced truth."[16] Sallie McFague said of Jesus' parables, "They are not primarily concerned with knowing but with doing."[17] Fred B. Craddock says the sermon needs "realization not information," and adds: "Preaching both proclaims an event and participates in that event, both reports on revelation and participates in that revelation ... here and now."[18] Don M. Wardlaw says, "the Word of God happens; it becomes a proclamation event in the lives of the people experiencing the sermon."[19] Eduard Riegert notes, "We receive too much information as it is. People are hungry for an encounter with God; they do not merely want to know about God, they want to know God."[20] Finally, David J. Schlafer notes:

> In catholic tradition, the sacraments of the church, through word and gesture, achieve what they symbolically announce.... All of these perfectly natural elements, touched by grace, are transformed and do transform. Similarly, the words of preaching are merely, fully, human words. Yet, engraced by the Word, they actually accomplish the salvation they announce.[21]

The idea of divine encounter in preaching is as old as the church and derives from understandings of the sermon as a breaking open of God's Word. Justin Martyr wrote (ca. 150) concerning the hearing of Scripture:

> When you hear the words of the prophets spoken as in a particular character, do not think them as spoken by the inspired men themselves, but by the divine Word that moved them. For sometimes he speaks as in the character of God the Master and Father of all, sometimes in the

character of Christ, sometimes in the character of the people answering the Lord or his Father.[22]

One does not make Christ present by preaching. Christ is already present in the church, and surely it is only through this presence of Christ that preaching is made possible.[23] However, Christ's historic presence in the church is active, and one cannot take it for granted, as though Christ is at our disposal. Ongoing self-giving through Word and Sacrament is essential for the life of the church, not least because by this the sinful church becomes the true church.[24] Our task, then, is not to bring Christ to the church but to find him there and to bring our people before God's throne of judgment and grace.

Preaching as the Gospel

In order for preaching to establish a relationship with the triune God and for it to an event of God's encounter it needs to proclaim the gospel. This is an area in which much preaching falls short. Christ commissioned the church to preach the gospel, and God's promise to meet us in the sermon can be said to be dependent upon that. One might ask, how is it possible that the gospel is not preached? We will explore this in greater detail later, but for now we can cite a few possible reasons. Some folks have not stopped to question what the gospel is and may assume that it is enough to preach a text. We have tended to assume that when one preaches the Word of God, one preaches the gospel, but much that is God's Word is not gospel; the Word may instruct, correct, edify, lament, condemn, and tear down without necessarily clarifying the good news. The New Homiletic adopted historical criticism as its norm, without making God a deliberate focus. Some people maintain that the gospel does not need to be preached in the presence of the hymns, prayers, and sacraments. Others assume that it is enough over the long haul for the church to preach the gospel, this does not need to be done each week. Finally, some people may find what Paul calls "the offense of the cross" (Galatians 5:11) to be inappropriate for a technologically advanced and informed society such as ours and are content to equate gospel with the world's understanding of good news.

What is the gospel? This seemingly obvious question now needs deliberate focus because we live in a postmodern era, and all assumptions benefit from examination. Such questioning provides a healthy and fresh opportunity for preachers to be clear about what they do.

The gospel is literally good news. It centers on God in Jesus Christ through the Holy Spirit, an announcement or proclaiming of the saving acts that God has done, is doing, and will do. The gospel is contained in the Bible, and the ancient creeds of the church are an attempt to state it, as are many prayers, hymns, and songs. The gospel can be summarized, but one needs the entire Bible to communicate it adequately. It is not narrowly confined to the New Testament; the good news is found wherever God acts with saving power. There is one God in both Testaments, yet the character of that saving power is fully disclosed in Christ. (We will say more on preaching the Old Testament below.) The gospel is not identical to the Bible; God's Word needs to be sought in Scripture (some readings are not the church's). As Luther said, the Bible is the manger in which Christ is laid; if one seeks the gospel in Scripture one may avoid making an idol of the Bible.

The gospel is centered in Jesus Christ, yet not narrowly so to the exclusion of the other persons of the Trinity, as can seem to be the case in some worship settings where he alone is mentioned, where prayers are addressed to Jesus rather than to God in the name of Christ and through the Holy Spirit. Where Christomonism reigns, Jesus may become a kind of idol.

Some people are tempted to identify the gospel with what Jesus preached, that is, the kingdom or realm of God. A student asked if it was necessary to preach the resurrection if one preached Jesus' words. In fact, Jesus did preach his death and resurrection, for instance, when he said, "Thus it is written, that the Messiah is to suffer and to rise from the dead on the third day, and that repentance and forgiveness of sins is to be proclaimed in his name to all nations, beginning from Jerusalem" (Luke 24:45-47). However, one could argue that the full content of his message is only appreciated in light of the cross and resurrection. They are focal points of his identity as the One who is willing to be servant of all, even unto death and the One whom God raised from the dead that all might know God's love. Christ's identity makes clear the character of the realm of God that breaks into the present. In Mark, Jesus keeps telling his disciples to say nothing, the reason being that they cannot understand the implications of what he says until his words are understood in light of his death and resurrection. If preachers avoid the cross and resurrection, people may find no reason to believe Jesus, for he is then just another person.

The Gospel as Scandal

It is perhaps natural to avoid the scandal or stumbling block of the resurrection. Paul identifies the problem when he says, "but we proclaim Christ crucified, a stumbling block [*skandalon*] to Jews and foolishness to Gentiles" (1 Corinthians 1:23). It is an embarrassment to the postmodern mind that we need a Savior, that this Savior happened to come as a male, that he ate with sinners, that he refused to defend himself, that he died the death of a common criminal, that he died for us, that he rose from the dead, that he sits at the right hand of God, that he will come again at the end of time, and that we drink his blood and eat his body to our salvation. In a casual conversation recently about the future of the church, someone suggested that it needs to put less emphasis on Jesus and more on other things, such as the Bhagavad Gita, in order to attract youth. The church could try any number of innovative practices, yet Paul said, "but we proclaim Christ crucified" (1 Corinthians 1:23), and "If Christ has not been raised ... we are of all people most to be pitied" (1 Corinthians 15:17-19). We can only preach the God we know.

Rather than conceive of the cross as a problematic barrier to faith, one may think of it as the doorway to faith. Many people get stuck on questions like, is it possible for the Red Sea to part, or for a virgin to give birth, or for a blind person to see again? But, these are in some ways secondary questions of faith. There may be no better place for people to stand or stumble in their faith journeys than at the empty tomb asking, is the One put to death on a cross as testified in Scripture the same One whom I have met today? Are his traits the same; does he show the same love; do the words that he spoke match the words he speaks today? Is Jesus of Nazareth dead or alive or not? If he is dead he remains the Jesus of history, but if he is alive he becomes the Christ of faith. If the answer is yes, a God who works other seemingly lesser miracles should be no real stumbling block. If the answer is no, the matter rests between the individual and God, and love, of course, remains.

The Gospel as Announcement of a New Age

Something happened on the cross. The world is different. What died with Jesus on the cross was the power of the old ways of violence and degradation, abuse and humiliation, injustice and greed. They rule no more. We are yet at what James F. Kay calls the "turn of the age"[25] and while even our preaching still has one foot in that old age, the other foot is firmly planted in the new creation of Christ ("See, I am making all things new," Revelation 21:5). Proclamation of the gospel is like midnight on New Year's Eve at Times Square every Sunday. Preaching not only heralds the death of the old age, in preaching the cross it ushers in the new. That makes the power of the cross not just a past event but a now event in preaching.

Kay, drawing on Paul, puts the matter well: "If the turn of the ages has taken place in the cross and continues to take place in the work of the cross, then what is required of preachers are not simply illustrations from history and nature, but illustrations that place history and nature, indeed all of life, into the crisis of the cross." By "crisis of the cross" he means see things new: "What assumptions of the old world are called into question by the new?"[26] Thus every image, story, and experience in the sermon needs to be viewed from this two-world perspective.

David Buttrick said something similar when he said "we have lost sight of the image of a coming realm of God" and "a sense of the presence of God-with-us seems to have vanished."[27] Preaching the gospel means to preach God's future, to picture in sermons the new age with vivid images of a world reconciled in God's love. Buttrick makes an important point about the need for eschatology not just to inform preaching but to assist preachers in preaching boldly about social injustice in the present. As he says, "Let us paint images of the new creation on an age that seems tumbling down. Although the age may well tumble, our images are painted on the eternal mystery of God and, therefore, sure."[28]

The Gospel and Sermon Variety

The nature of God's identity is not separable from the gospel and what is revealed in Jesus Christ. Richard Lischer puts it this way:

> Death and resurrection—this fugal theme is at the center of Christian worship. The drama of the church year unfolds it; the Sunday service, which originated as a little Easter, reenacts it, and the Holy Communion represents it. Baptism as burial and rising in Christ, sacramentally recapitulates it, and the Holy Communion represents it. The first and only feast of the church was the Pasch, the two-day vigil that commemorated the death and resurrection of Jesus in a single, fused experience, beginning with baptisms on Holy Saturday and culminating in the Eucharist at Easter dawn.... The church ... orchestrate[s] its

preaching, spiritual discipline, and liturgical and sacramental life according to the rhythm of death and resurrection.[29]

Because of the centrality of the resurrection for the good news, does this mean that every sermon will bring the same news, like endless deliveries of yesterday's newspaper? Yes and no, though we will have to wait for later chapters to see how this is possible. Yes in that Christian preaching is Christ-centered and the cross has saving power. No in that how the gospel is proclaimed in relationship to specific occasions will vary widely from week to week. Listeners vary in their needs and this adds variety; Joseph R. Jeter Jr. and Ronald J. Allen speak of "one gospel, many ears."[30] In fact one could say that until the gospel has been proclaimed in a manner such that the listeners can understand it in terms of their own lives, it is not the gospel, it is just abstract or remote truth.

Christine Smith develops a fine image of the sermon as weaving that helps to emphasize sermon variety.[31] Celtic tartans had their own colors and weavings to distinguish the clans; First Nations people in North America wove patterns into their fabrics to designate their own tribes and regions. By the same token, each sermon is woven such that the distinctive Christian markings of the gospel may be found, yet with seemingly endless variety.

CHAPTER 3

THE GOSPEL AND THE THEME SENTENCE

It is now time to take the rich harvest of exegesis and determine a direction for the sermon. We have completed our exegetical study of the biblical text; to traditional historical-critical and literary exegesis we have added theological exegesis. We have also considered the purposes of preaching. Now we need to narrow the range of rich possibilities and choose a theme sentence in light of who our listeners will be.

The Relevance of a Theme Sentence

Recently in homiletics this notion of even having a theme sentence has proved to be more controversial than one might expect. The discussion is helpful because it highlights a shift that has taken place in preaching over the last fifty years, from propositional preaching to the New Homiletic. Some homileticians claim that no theme sentence is needed—sermons ought not to be conceived in the old propositional ways, and sermons ought not to be designed to appeal to reason alone. Fred Craddock has argued that sermons ought not to proceed deductively, stating a point and then building a case to prove it; rather, they ought to move inductively, using narrative and gradually narrowing experiences to a particular understanding: for example, not this, not this, not this, but this.[1] He said that this inductive development mirrors the preacher's own experience of the biblical text during the week and could be an effective model, therefore, for listeners as well. He was still arguing for a theme sentence, but it came at the end.

Let us continue for another moment to listen to the discussion because it tells us much about the movement away from sermons being idea-dominated. David Buttrick went further, "Preachers do not explicate teachings; they explore symbols. Faith does have content, but not a content that can be spelled out in propositional statements for instruction."[2] The purpose of a sermon "cannot be stated in some clear single sentence"; rather, preachers discover in the text "an intending *of*," a field of meaning that, like film in a camera, will eventually allow us to "see what we are seeing."[3] He encourages preachers to think of a structure of meanings that they want to bring forth through the subject matter, thus they would sketch a series of "moves" and work through them. Richard L. Eslinger thinks sermons should present patterns, images, and symbols with "narrative modesty" such that the character of God becomes known through them.[4] For Lucy Rose and others, the sermon is multifocused, tentative, and open-ended like a conversation.[5]

These suggestions have merit. There is general agreement today that the sermon's appeal ought not to be just intellectual because people are not solely governed by reason, they learn in different ways that have emotional and spiritual dimensions. Biblical texts are not just wheelbarrows of ideas that one dumps into some waiting sermon form.

Nonetheless, the sermon still needs to start with some idea that takes shape in the preacher's own consciousness that will open a gate to meaning for the listener. Thoughts need words and images, and words and images need sentences and paragraphs to enable listeners to receive them. Preachers need to be clear about their own intentions. In other words, one can argue that in seeking to escape static "points" in a sermon or sermons that only try to communicate ideas, preachers do not escape the need for clarity about a theme.

Parishioners have the right to ask what that sermon was about, and if they cannot identify some sort of coherent claim, the sermon arguably has fallen short. The sermon needs to appeal to the head, heart, mind, and body, and a theme sentence simply ensures clear communication.[6] It is the sermon in microcosm. When people know clearly what the preacher means they can more easily determine what the sermon means for them.

The Grand Canyon of Biblical Preaching

The theme sentence states the heart of the text's message and the heart of the sermon. To determine it we need to draw it from the text, yet how this is done is a matter of considerable controversy. What lens do we use? Do we use the historical, the literary, the theological, or some other lens? Some say the historical and literary, and others say the theological. Another way of approaching this subject is to ask, is the goal of preaching to preach the text or to preach the gospel?

Here one comes to the Grand Canyon of biblical preaching. Anyone who has been to the Grand Canyon in Arizona knows that one comes upon it suddenly; the ground just drops away and, after some considerable distance across, continues on again. The terrain on both sides of the divide is similar but the divide is real and has large implications for the sermon, starting with the theme sentence. On one side of the great divide are biblical preachers who say we preach the text, but let us not rush to a decision—this entire book is devoted to this issue. On the other side of the divide are those who say we preach the gospel.

Preachers will answer both ways, and good arguments support both sides. To say that we preach the text is natural because most of our teachers in biblical studies assume this stance. The unit of scripture or pericope is the source of the sermon and largely determines its direction. What the text communicates at its literal or plain level to its own people is what the sermon tries to communicate to listeners today. One seeks the Word of God in the intention of the original writer against the historical and cultural background of the time. The Bible says, "All scripture is inspired by God and is useful for teaching, for reproof, for correction, and for training in righteousness" (2 Timothy 3:16). Having found the message in a biblical text through exegesis, one is ready to preach. The operating assumption here is that the word one finds in the text is the gospel. Nearly every preacher, if asked, says, "I preach the gospel." However, in the practical reality of today's sermons, one cannot be confident that this is in fact what is preached.

The terrain on the preach-the-gospel side of the divide is much the same. Those who represent that position agree with their preach-the-text colleagues on most points and procedures, especially on starting with the text. They would agree that the bald way the above question is framed— Do we preach the text or the gospel?—implies "either/or" when the right answer is "both/and"; we preach the text and the gospel. However, those who argue preach-the-gospel tend to disagree that the message one finds in a text is necessarily the gospel. It may be, but it may not be. Not every text immediately yields the gospel, and as Calvin noted, one needs the Holy Spirit to read it rightly. Every approach is a lens, a perspective, and the same is true for the gospel.

Scholars in both camps believe it is false that there is a single objective meaning of a text. Even the gospel meaning of a text is an interpretation. Still, the preach-the-gospel argument contends that when the text does not directly yield the gospel, it needs to be treated as an essential lens to it, a portal if you like, that offers a way to read the larger Christian story so that the gospel comes into focus through it. Seen another way, biblical texts are treasured windows through which the light of the gospel is projected upon and into the lives of the hearers.

> "Do we preach the text or the gospel?" implies "either/or" when the right answer is "both/and"; we preach the text and the gospel. However, those who argue preach-the-text tend to assume the presence of the gospel and those who argue preach-the-gospel argue that the message one finds in a text is not necessarily the gospel.

Both positions are steeped in historical-critical and literary thought, yet preach-the-text is resistant to making God a deliberate focus where God may not be directly mentioned in a text. A theological purpose of the text is often sought, yet no safeguards ensure it. The great Scottish preacher of the 1900s, James S. Stewart, had a theological test of a sermon for a congregation: "Did they, or did they not, meet God today?"[7] What does one preach when a text like the good Samaritan does not mention God, as is true of many texts? Is Christ only to be mentioned when a text mentions Christ? Many experienced preach-the-text preachers, in fact, instinctively arrive at God, but there is nothing in their explicit exegetical or homiletical methods or sermon forms to ensure that they do. If a homiletical method does not offer substantial discussion of how to make God a primary focus, chances are that sermons following that method will not get to God. The preach-the-text methodology does not instruct the student of preaching how to do this. Advocates of preach-the-gospel developed the kind of detailed theological exegetical method recommended earlier as a means to compensate for what is missing.

Edward Farley is one scholar who encourages preachers not to think narrowly about preaching a text or unit of Scripture, but to concentrate on the theological task of preaching the gospel and to allow it to set the themes of the sermon.[8] James F. Kay and David Buttrick agree and have written papers that are among the best recent theological treatments of preaching.[9]

The point here is plain: Christ commissioned the church to preach the gospel. Preachers must preach individual texts, and often they do not contain the gospel; yet all texts in their own particularities can serve as windows to and from it. The texts are essential and vital starting points for biblical preaching; they are the means whereby preachers arrive at the gospel. Not all sermons based on the Bible are biblical, and many biblical sermons are not the gospel. Preaching is no better than the instruments one uses to guide its formation. If preachers do not look for God in texts, they may not find God. If they do not find God, how can they know they have found God's Word? If they do not in some way seek the gospel, it may not be discerned.

Hermeneutical Method

The Grand Canyon in biblical preaching represents a cutting edge of current homiletical thought. Traditional biblical exegesis is essential; its limitations however are apparent in sermons that do not arrive at the gospel. Of course, God can still use sermons on biblical history, ideas, characters, events, and images, yet they are likely to have only modest success in fanning the glowing embers of congregational faith if that is all they focus upon.

A basic requirement for a hermeneutical method is that it account for how the Word of God in a previous age is the Word of God today. Historical criticism, for all its excellence, can be argued never to have met this requirement. It tempts preachers to preach the text as history, without the gospel, yet in doing so, preachers ironically ignore a histori-cal truth: the texts are Scripture because they are not only texts of history but also texts of faith. In the 1950s at Union Seminary, Paul Scherer stated the matter in brilliant simplicity:

> Do you realize that the Bible does not primarily invite us to any knowl-edge about God?... We are invited to meet God.
>
> That's what the Gospel is about. Nothing else.... If you want to try an experiment, take any page and strip it of God, as we strip our lives, down to the bone, with that infinite mind away somewhere, and that eternal heart just a grand perhaps. And all of a sudden you'll be right back in the world that you know all too well, where a sower sowing his seed is just a sower sowing his seed, nothing more than that, where laborers stand idle in the market place, and where nothing is a parable because God hasn't anything to do with any of it, and the whole place is stale, flat and unprofitable, and makes you sick.
>
> The difference between us and these more stalwart souls of the Bible was simply this: that when they looked at the world they saw Him, when they listened to the Babel of the world's voices they heard his voice. Everywhere in their days there was something God wanted them to do.[10]

In other words, until preachers read their texts theologically, looking for God and viewing individuals in the Bible as people of faith and doubt for whom salvation is a possibility, the texts are not being read as they were historically intended to be read, which is the goal of historical-critical readings.

Still, awareness of this great divide in homiletics is not great, if one is to judge from the academic literature. There may be good reasons for this seeming silence. First, awareness of the problem is relatively recent; homiletics has been shifting from propositional preaching to the New Homiletic, and attention has been focused on all of the implications of this. The focus has been on how communication is made, however, not on the theological nature of the message. Second, historical-critical method is still the best means of getting deep into a biblical text in its his-torical setting to discover what it says, even if something more is often needed by way of getting to what also matters. Third, students learn the historical-critical method not so much from their homiletics professors but from biblical scholars. Teaching students to look first at the meaning of a text in its original context is always a difficult task. Teachers of preaching are therefore reluctant to undermine their colleagues' work by pointing out the problems with historical-critical method.

Finally, teachers of historical criticism seem not to comment on its weaknesses as a hermeneutical approach. Perhaps they are not aware of it or matters of the Word of God are deemed beyond the boundaries of their discipline. They may have a different understanding of gospel than the one presented here. Or they may equate God's Word from a text with the gospel, perhaps because many texts have an obvious gospel component. With those other biblical texts that may be in the majority, preachers may have learned at some intuitive or other unstated level either to compensate or to accept the status quo as normal, thus they may see no need to correct the basic approach. Truth be told, no homiletical method is fail-safe, and something important can be learned from most approaches.

Both preach-the-text and preach-the-gospel are presented here because, in fact, one needs to preach the text to preach the gospel. Students will be better preachers for knowing the strong arguments on both sides. Here we make the case for preaching the gospel as the much-needed next stage of homiletical development beyond the New Homiletic. It involves one's entire approach to preaching.

The Theme Sentence

The difference between the two biblical stances can be quickly demonstrated as we finally return to our task of selecting a theme sentence for the sermon. Most writers today think of the theme sentence in double-barreled ways, in which two related statements take the place of the former notion of a theme sentence.[11] Tom Long and Fred Craddock are in the preach-the-text school and advocate that sermon direction comes from the preacher answering two questions: "What is the text saying?" and "What is the text doing?" As Craddock says:

> This question [What is the text doing?] is not only identifying the nature and function of the text but is also providing an early guideline for the sermon to come. After all, the preacher will want to be clear not only about what is being said in the sermon but also about what is being done in the sermon. And just as one's message is informed by what the text is saying, the sermon's function is informed by what the text is doing. If, for example, one were to state as *what the text is saying*, "Every Christian is a charismatic," and as *what the text is doing*, "Encouraging

those believers who felt second-class," then content and tone and purpose of the sermon have come into focus.[12]

Long argues that this double variation of the traditional theme sentence makes the sermon eventful and avoids the propositional dominance of an idea-centered approach. Texts not only have a message, they have a rhetorical intention; they make a claim and seek an effect.[13] This is in line with the New Homiletic that, as a whole, shifts the emphasis in preaching from what the sermon says to what it does. A bridge connects the historical text and the sermon, and the preacher is to carry over from the text what it says and does.[14]

The strength of this approach is obvious. The event captured in this approach is the event of the text: "the eventfulness of the text is expressed in the claim of the text, which then guides the eventfulness of the sermon."[15] "Something happens between text and people; a claim is made, a voice is heard, a textual will is exerted, and the sermon will be a bearing witness to this event."[16] This approach gives to the text rhetorical freedom to determine the direction of the sermon. Contemporary textbooks using this approach offer few if any guidelines in speaking about gospel from the text.[17]

By comparison, those who stress preach-the-gospel treat the sermon first and foremost as God's event, not the text's. This approach also uses a double-barreled adaptation of a theme sentence. It asks, what is God doing in or behind the text? (that is, in the larger story if God is not directly mentioned) and, what is God doing today? The answer to the first is designated the major concern of the text (MCT) because the preacher will treat it as though it is the main route to the heart of the text's original meaning (in fact, there are other possibilities). The answer to the second is designated as the major concern of the sermon (MCS) because the preacher uses that as the main bridge across which to transport the significance of the text today.

This approach ensures that the sermon will deal with the text in responsible ways and will also teach about God and God's relationship to humanity and creation. God will be the center. Jana Childers says that some years ago she freed herself of the enormous burden to come up with something original in every sermon. She discovered:

> *It is more important to say something timely than something original. . . .* God was not expecting a fresh, new insight every time I preached. . . . [The congregation] didn't need me to invent new spiritual gadgets for them;

they needed to hear the connection made between their worlds and God's....The purpose of a theme sentence is to help you keep your focus, not to advertise the erudition of your sermon.[18]

Haddon Robinson recently recommended four questions to ask of every text in relationship to God: "First, what is the vision of God in this particular text?...Second, where precisely do I find that in the passage?...Third, what is the function of this vision of God?...Fourth, what is the significance of that picture of God for me and for others."[19] Focusing on God ensures that the sermon can foster a relationship with the triune God. It ensures the eventfulness of the sermon by focusing on an action of God. Without this, it is easy to imply that God is remote and abstract, indifferent, impersonal, passive, or apparently irrelevant; propositions can become dominant. In cases in which God does not seem to be the subject of the text, this approach helps the preacher still to find God. The text remains one's primary authority for preaching, yet Christ's mandate to preach the gospel determines the sermon direction. In broad terms, this approach understands the gospel to be the rhetorical purpose of the text.

What is God doing in or behind the text? This is an important question. Texts have many meanings or senses, and each lens that a preacher uses yields other meanings; this one we may call the God sense of the text. A problem faces preachers however: a God focus is ensured, but does this in itself ensure that the gospel will be proclaimed? No, it does not.

> A God focus does not in itself ensure that the gospel will be proclaimed. One can say many things about God—indeed one can teach many things about the gospel—without ever getting to proclaiming or performing the gospel in the sermon.

One can say many things about God without ever getting to the gospel. Indeed, one can teach many things about even the gospel and still stop short of performing the gospel. We are getting ahead of ourselves—we will have to wait to see how all of this plays out. For now it is enough to ensure that the God focus of the theme sentence will be a good news focus: the sermon needs to be conceived as an event of hope.

The Gospel as Hope

When one speaks of a theme sentence, one speaks of far more than a sentence, for the shape and theological thrust of the entire sermon is at stake. The theme sentence is the sermon in microcosm, thus if it is not focused on the gospel, the preacher will have to hike through backcountry in the sermon to get there and may get lost along the way. One might ask, how can one sentence (even a double-barreled sentence) focus on the gospel? The simple answer is that while it cannot contain the gospel, it can at least point in the right direction. It points to liberation, deliverance, healing, empowerment, a new beginning, salvation—whatever God provides.

A theme sentence that has one of the persons of the Trinity as the subject is a good start, but gospel means good news, and the theme needs to sound like good news. Good news comes from God, it points to God's help, and it is what God does. The theme sentence must be hopeful.

Preaching hope is but one theological possibility among many legitimate alternatives. For instance, John Calvin, seeking to enable regeneration through preaching, drew on 2 Timothy 3:16-17 when he emphasized edification, reproof, correction, and instruction. One may similarly preach condemnation, fear of God, repentance, spiritual discipline, moral rectitude, endurance, acceptance, obedience, submission, self-denial, forgiveness, justice, peace, reconciliation, and a long list of other possibilities. There are many biblical texts that have just this kind of thrust, and one can be faithful to the biblical text in preaching this kind of message, but in and of themselves they are not the gospel. If one were strict with preach-the-text, one might preach the gospel only when a text explicitly deals with it.

The good news of Christ has dire consequences if people do not change their ways. Many preachers apparently think that sermons need to stress what is required of us, precisely because of the gospel promise. To tell people they must change is hopeful by its nature, since it brings them closer to God. Hellfire-and-brimstone preaching may sound hopeful to some people by some process of inversion because they count themselves among the saved. In this way of thinking, one might decide that the theme of hope is just one of a number of possibilities to use in rotation, over the course of many weeks.

Some preachers dismiss having a gospel focus for every sermon because they claim it reduces the Bible to a single doctrine. However, hope is not the theme per se of every sermon any more than the sun is the theme of every daytime conversation. Rather, hope is the nature and tenor of the gospel, thus hope is the ultimate nature and tenor of each sermon. If preaching is to be the gospel, something has to change in the pulpit, in the way the Bible is taught in seminary, and in the way homiletics often is taught.

The problem of hopeless sermons is not the Bible; it is the familiar ways of reading it, the tools one brings to it, not seeing what is there. Reading the Bible without looking for gospel is a product of relatively recent biblical scholarship and does not represent what the Reformers intended when they pioneered responsible theological criticism for us, nor is it what they meant when they claimed the literal sense of scripture as normative, nor may it even represent the original goal of historical criticism. Yet the problem is not new. Karl Barth faced many of the same issues when he wrote his groundbreaking and controversial commentary, *The Epistle to the Romans*, in 1921. History was not enough; theology was also needed.

If great preaching is hard to find, those of us who teach homiletics may be part of the problem. We may not have been rigorous in analyzing and assessing the preaching of the church, in naming its goals and weaknesses, and in helping to change the way preachers are taught. Excellent preachers of the gospel can be found, but most do what they do by instinct rather than by principles they were taught or teach.

Many preachers in history and today do preach hope. As Gardner Taylor, the dean of African American preaching, once said, "God is out to get back" whatever has gone astray.[20] The heart of the Christian faith is Easter. Jesus Christ is risen. A new age has begun. The power of death has been broken. This is both a promise of the future and the character of hope that already breaks into our present. God meets us not least in the sermon, confronting the reality of human sin and negating the future that we deserve as sin's consequence. Christ is making all things new. Of course we cease to follow Christ's way if we abandon hope and thereby look away from God; we put our trust elsewhere, for instance, in possibilities of human accomplishment or human measurements of success. Cast on our own resources, there is no hope; as Jesus said, "apart from me you can do nothing" (John 15:5). However, by trusting in God's grace, all things are possible.

Such clear truths have obvious implications for preaching. The sermon should ultimately sound like good news, not bad. Its overall character should be hopeful as numerous biblical passages suggest. Isaiah says:

> For I am about to create new heavens
>   and a new earth;
> the former things shall not be remembered.
> . . . .
> But be glad and rejoice forever in what I am
>   creating. (65:17-18)

And Paul speaks of the "God of hope" (Romans 15:13). It is this hopeful word of the gospel that redirects, restores, and equips listeners for their ministries of outreach in service to the world. It unites them as communities of love and faith.

The Importance of an Active Verb

Even focusing on God one can speak of God in ways that portray a passive or ineffective God. Luther thought the problem was avoided just by the act of preaching. His "God not preached" was precisely of this nature: abstract, hidden, remote, passive, majestic, refusing to become known, reluctant to act, unwilling to save, against sinful humanity. By contrast, "God preached" reveals God's true nature as the one who makes atonement for our sins.[21]

The language one commonly uses in preaching may inadvertently portray God in the manner Luther sought to avoid. Consider common phrases that are often used: God knows what we suffer; God understands our pain; God hears our cries. On closer examination one finds that these verbs are passive, and through them, God is unintentionally portrayed as an observer who is content to understand, know, or hear, without doing anything to help. If we are suffering pain or loss, it is good to know that God is actively doing something. The God we preach intercedes in history and does not avoid getting caught up in our lives, even to the point of death on a cross. By portraying God's action, and eventually depicting

50

what this might look like in the midst of particular local and global situations, one facilitates the event of God in our midst.[22]

The Gospel and the Theme Sentence

In light of the above remarks, we are now able to choose a theme sentence for the sermon in line with its gospel purpose. We have already recommended that the theme sentence be derived by asking, what is God doing in or behind this text? and what is God doing in our world? Several helpful guidelines may be offered:

• *In order to ensure that the sermon gets to the gospel, choose an action of God's that is hopeful, that helps the people meet whatever demands are placed on them.* For example, Cleophus LaRue determines from the text whether "God's power is used to liberate, deliver, provide, protect, empower, or transform."[23] Ronald J. Allen speaks of the "sermon-in-a-sentence": "(a) The subject is normally God. (b) The verb is usually an activity of God. (c) The predicate is normally a benefit or other outflow of God's love and justice.... (d) The sermon-in-a-sentence is usually positive and offers the community hope and encouragement."[24] Henry H. Mitchell advocates a "controlling idea" from a "succinct, positive, biblical verse."[25]

• *Make a simple sentence, not compound.* By keeping the sentence simple, it will be memorable. You will repeat it many times in your actual sermon as a way of indicating to listeners its centrality, and thus you will help them to understand and follow what is said. What you might say by way of a compound sentence can be put into the sermon.

• *Make God the subject of the sentence.*

• *Choose a verb that is as active as possible* (for example, saves, heals, cleanses, unites, forgives) because active verbs are easier for listeners to visualize and help guard against unnecessary abstraction.

• *Make a claim, do not ask a question.*

Sample Theme Sentences That Focus on Gospel

Here are some possible major concerns. These have God as the subject and focus on actions of grace. Identify a few potential major concerns from your own biblical text.

Biblical Text	Possible Major Concerns
Genesis 9—Noah and the rainbow	God initiates the covenant.
Exodus 20—Ten Commandments	God gives the way to life.
Ruth 4—Ruth and Boaz	God restores the outcast.
Isaiah 6—Isaiah's call	God gives a new identity.
Luke 11:33-36—Letting light shine	Christ lights our lives.
John 4—The woman at the well	Christ bestows true identity.
Acts 13—The Holy Spirit and Paul	The Spirit guides the Church.
Philippians 2—Christ's self-emptying	God exalts the lowly.
Revelation 21—God wipes away tears	God in Christ comforts the suffering.

If the sentence around which one develops the sermon focuses on an action of God, one is more likely to avoid the problem of sermons that marginalize God or leave God out. By regularly focusing on God, the preacher helps maintain an active faith life and is less likely to burn out.

To review: here are the main options concerning a sermon theme. What you identify as your theme sentence will depend on your purpose: (1) if you write a sermon from one of a variety of possible purposes, for instance preaching the text or teaching some doctrine, any strong theological idea or topic may stand as your theme. Keep the idea short so that you can repeat it and listeners can remember it, exactly as you said it. (2) If you want to do more than this and have your people meet God through the preaching, then focus on an action of God (or an action of one of the persons of the Trinity) for the sentence around which to develop the sermon. (3) However, if you want to do even more than this and preach hope, the idea you choose should focus on God's action of grace and empowerment and move toward the gospel.

> Student Assignment 2: Using the exegesis exercise that
> you have done, list a few potential major concerns of
> the text. Now select one as your theme sentence.

For Further Reflection and Study Concerning Monday

1. Is it realistic in the busy life of a preacher to spread sermon preparation throughout the week? How do you plan to budget your sermon preparation time to get your best results?

2. Theological criticism of the sort developed here is traditionally not part of traditional exegesis because it introduces bias and prevents the reader from encountering the text as a historical document. Might this be true?

3. What do you understand by the word *gospel*? If one preaches the gospel every week, do you feel preaching would become tedious? or too dominated by Christ?

4. Preach-the-text assumes that when one finds the Word of God in a text one has found the gospel and preach-the-gospel assumes one may need something else in addition. What do you think one needs to do to preach the gospel? Is a focus on grace sufficient in itself?

Section II

Tuesday: Connecting the Bible and Today

If Monday of the preacher's week is devoted to exegesis and what the text says, Tuesday can be devoted to what the text means, or explaining the text. Hermeneutics is a fancy name given to the study of the process of interpretation. The term is derived in part from what may seem like a strange source for Christian interpretation: the name of the Greek messenger god, Hermes, hence hermeneutics is the study of how messages are communicated. This exciting field of study traditionally has two phases: what the text says and what the text means.

What a text says is determined by accurate versions of the original text—good translations—in fact by much of the activity that makes historical criticism important. What a text says does not always clarify what it means, however. Jesus' disciples in Matthew hear what he says, but almost as though they are dense, they repeatedly ask what he means. Understanding a text, says Paul Ricoeur, is to follow its movement "from what it says to what it talks about."[1] Explanation or clarification is the key here, and exegesis has begun the process. We have even chosen a theme sentence as a means to focus thoughts, yet a whole range of materials has been opened up for our use. How can they be employed? That is the issue at hand in the next two chapters, which bridge then and now.

CHAPTER 4

BRIDGING FROM THE TEXT

Origen handled the problem of a broad potential field of meanings in Scripture by throwing the door wide open: he assumed that since Scripture was dictated by God, every jot and tittle was pregnant with meaning for those who were spiritually enlightened. As a result, some of his interpretations were wild and allegorical without textual support. Augustine took a more sensible route that history followed. He favored the literal, particularly on passages of faith and morals; in cases of dispute, Scripture meant what the church said it meant, the rule of faith. For us in our own time, we discern what Scripture means in part through scholarship.

The Role of Scholarship

Preachers can scarcely conceive of preaching without using scholars to explain what a text means. Preachers today know immensely more than their ancestors about how Scripture was written, the historical background of the writers, their biases, the role of editors in reshaping material, and the like. This helps preachers to address many issues that stain the fabric of Christian history (for example, anti-Semitism, racism, sexism) and other situations of injustice in communities.

Still, some today express caution. Recovery of early forms of the biblical texts (for example, the Jesus Seminar in which scholars voted on the likelihood of the historical Jesus having said his various words) does not result in texts that are more foundational for preaching. Historical methods are limited and even if one were able to get closer to the Jesus of history, one would not necessarily be any closer to the Christ of faith. Preachers do not preach the version of the parable of the wedding guests found in the Gospel of Thomas even though some think it may be closer to the original version Jesus told. It is not Scripture, the church's book, what the church receives as revelation.

> Recovery of early forms of the biblical texts does not result in texts that are more foundational for preaching.

Also, preachers should not give higher faith value to words that Jesus is voted most likely to have said. Gerald T. Sheppard noted about Isaiah, "One should not confuse the recovery of a more 'reliable' historical portrait of the eighth-century B.C. prophet with the discovery of a more reliable 'Scripture,' since ancient traditions do not become Scripture through their fidelity to principles of modern historiography."[1] Said another way, the church has a canon that was settled on through study, discussion, prayer, and the guidance of the Spirit. If one affirms that the Holy Spirit speaks through Scripture, one might even say for purposes of the faith that there are no words of Jesus that Christ does not speak, and no teachings that are more preachable than others.

Perhaps the most acerbic critic of modern directions is Thomas G. Oden, who is critical of "the bone-dry valley into which [Bultmann's] form criticism has lately shepherded preaching."[2] He calls historical biblical criticism a "broken promise": "Have the texts been made more understandable? Have the texts been made more accessible? Has critical method elicited or inhibited moral decision?"[3] He cites Walter Wink, with whom he agrees, "The outcome of biblical studies in the academy is a trained incapacity to deal with the real problems of actual living persons in their daily lives."[4]

These barbed criticisms are as much about preaching as they are about biblical studies. They can serve as a caution to preachers, first, that essays and lectures in biblical courses have their own value and rhetorical purposes, but they do not themselves preach or constitute preaching.

Second, exegesis yields far more information about biblical texts than is helpfully communicated in a sermon. Particularly when theological criticism is added to traditional exegesis, preachers will not have a shortage of meaningful things to say. The theme sentence ideally keeps the focus on God, not humanity. Historical-critical study yields information only on what the science and art of history can tell us, namely, what humans in another time have thought, said, and done. Because God is outside the scope of what history can claim to confirm, historical-critical exegesis *alone* will not give us a sermon.

Practical Implications of God's Encounter

Preaching can be an event of God's encounter, resulting in a renewed relationship of faith and action. This can mean four things for the preacher:

1. Approach the biblical text in part as a document of faith. In other words do not give priority to the text merely as a lesson in history—it is about people struggling with faith issues. Martin Luther said:

> This [Bible] lesson is just like the sun: in a placid pond it can be seen clearly and warms the water powerfully, but in a rushing current it cannot be seen as well nor can it warm up the water as much. So if you wish to be illumined and warmed ... then go to where you may be still and impress the picture deep into your hearts.[5]

When I was a student, a colleague preached a raging sermon that disguised any contemplative dimension, and the instructor wittily responded, "Trying to get a drink from your sermon was like trying to get a drink from an open fire hydrant." When the text is treated in large part as a document of faith, one looks for issues of faith in the text. Ask, how is this text a metaphor of the faith of this community?

2. Continue to ask of every biblical text, What is God doing in or behind the events of this passage? Warren H. Stewart is only one of several preachers who note how important it is that the starting place of biblical interpretation for preachers is with God: "Hermeneutics in preaching does not begin with the text but with the *Author* of the text."[6] Even when contemporary needs are brought into focus, God still needs to remain the subject of much that the sermon says. As Cleophus J. LaRue notes, people on Sunday need "to be assured and reassured that God has acted and will act for them and for their salvation."[7]

3. Identify the implications of the text for your own life. If the text is to come alive in one's people, it must first have happened in the preacher's life. What did God say through it? One should be able to identify the difference this has made or could make.

4. Name the idea(s) from the biblical text to develop. This is the beginning point of composition, the naming and selection of biblical ideas to develop in the sermon. It is to this specific practice that we turn.

Starting to Make Bridges

One task of hermenutics is to have the text "then" speak with clarity "now" such that the gap between them is closed; one then experiences what Hans Georg Gadamer identified as the "fusion of two horizons."[8] He thought this fusion happened in the scholar's study, rendering an interpretation of the text. One could argue that it truly happens only in the sermon, when the people begin living out the text in their lives. A bridge has been made.

Many scholars remain uncertain what to suggest as a way of moving from the text into our world. Some are even unsure if the move is valid. The issue is, how are bridges built? Bridges go from one place to another place. A basic norm for biblical preaching is that one starts in the Bible and moves to now (though as in the hermeneutical circle the movement is never quite so simple or one-way). Here we will speak of what is needed in the text to build a strong foundation for a bridge to today.

It is helpful to think of every text as having many concerns. We have already spoken of the theme sentence as the major concern of the text. It is major only because: (1) it is a clear statement of what the preacher discerns is the heart of the text, and (2) the preacher will give it major emphasis in the sermon. However, what I might choose might differ from what you would choose, therefore many possible themes can arise out of one text. A change of one key word in a major concern of the text will result in a different sermon. Every text yields a host of concerns, and they vary in strength.

Concerns of the Text

Concerns of the text normally emerge in doing exegesis and may be discovered in three places: the biblical text itself, biblical commentaries, and background knowledge or reference books relevant to the culture and times. Only by breaking the text down can one discern how much is in it. In theory at least, each concern of the text represents a single complete thought that may be the subject of an entire paragraph (or sermon). In fact, every paragraph can be stated in a simple sentence: that is what makes a paragraph what it is.

The clearest communicators know how small a thought is. One good short sentence can be unpacked for an hour if one learns how to explain or expand it. There may be no more important practice for the preacher to learn than to slow down the pace of thoughts, images, and feelings for oral delivery in the sermon. Ideas need a chance to form in listener's minds, and they must grow, not race, do cartwheels, or leap tall buildings. However, nearly all seminary training is geared for the page, not the ear and eye, and what makes a good essay makes tedious pew-sitting.

Any idea, image or emotion expressed by a biblical text is a concern of the text. The goal is to break down a text into as many small ideas as possible and state them as simple sentences. Each one states only one complete thought. By identifying them one is able to do several things: (1) see things in the text that one has not previously seen, (2) break down complex thought to simple expression, (3) determine which concerns have most sermon potential, and (4) decide which ones to use and how.

For purposes of a teaching example, even a nursery rhyme can yield concerns of the text, for example, "Mary had a little lamb, its fleece was white as snow; and everywhere that Mary went, the lamb was sure to go." It suggests the following:

> Mary was a girl.
>
> She was a shepherd. (Or, she had a pet.)
>
> The lamb belonged to her.
>
> The lamb had wool.
>
> The wool was white.
>
> Mary kept the lamb clean.
>
> The lamb followed Mary.
>
> The lamb was loyal.
>
> Mary was kind. (Or, Mary was needy; or, the lamb was needy.)
>
> Mary and the lamb were inseparable.

Mary went nowhere without the lamb.

Mary did not go many places.

> **Concerns of the text** are ideas, images, and emotions that a biblical text expresses. They are stated in short sentences and may be discovered in the biblical text itself, biblical commentaries, and background knowledge or reference books relevant to the culture and times.

In the exegetical exercise done earlier, many of the answers to the assigned questions could be simplified and stated as concerns of the text. The text now becomes useable. In the sermon itself the preacher will need to reconstruct the biblical text in order for the congregation to truly hear it. One may think that an idea for preaching just "happens" in one's mind, and often this is true. However, when it does, it is only because the mind, at some subconscious level, has broken the text to find some unit of meaning. Some form of deconstruction of the text has occurred. If preachers do not name concerns of the text, they may struggle to find enough things to preach in a text, or their thoughts will be too complicated, or they will not readily discover fresh insight to a passage.

Concerns of the Text in Isaiah 6:1-13

Here are a few of the concerns of the text from Isaiah 6:1-13, Isaiah's Call:

> King Uzziah died. The country was in mourning. Isaiah had a vision.

> The Lord appeared to Isaiah. Six-winged seraphs praised the Lord.

All earth is full of the Lord's glory. Isaiah fears for his life. He is unclean. He has seen God. The angel brings an altar coal. The coal touches Isaiah's lips. The coal does not burn his lips. His sin is blotted out. God needs a messenger. Isaiah offers to go.

God calls Isaiah forth. God gives Isaiah what he will need. Isaiah's word will dull the people's minds. God prevents some from understanding God's Word. They will not be healed. They will be made desolate. The Lord will send them away. Not one-tenth will remain. A remnant will survive. The remnant will be a holy seed.

Uzziah died around 735 B.C. Judah is threatened with war from the north. Isaiah 1–39 anticipates the Babylonian exodus (Isaiah 40–55). Isaiah sees heaven's holy courts. The holy realm is dangerous to the profane world. God creates a new identity for Isaiah. God will not tolerate disobedience. Isaiah pleads for God's people ("How long?"). The desolation is like the destruction of the vineyard (Isaiah 5).

The seed will sprout a light for all nations (Isaiah 9:2). God's purpose is larger than any one group of people. God's purpose is salvation. God will not be thwarted. Ability to understand God's Word is a gift of God. Failure to understand has perils.

Note that none of these is phrased as a question. Similarly these sentences are not statements about things in general that merely announce a topic but tell nothing about it (for example, "This is the meaning of call"); they give a complete thought.

> Student Assignment 3: Using your exegesis assignment, make a list of the concerns of the text.

Discerning Theological Potential

The exercise becomes all the more important when concerns of the text are evaluated for basic theological potential. Here one asks, what ideas seem to emphasize hope and will serve in developing the gospel? Here it does not matter whether one leans primarily in the direction of preach-the-text or preach-the-gospel because all preachers benefit from being able to make the following assessments.

Hope for Christians is not generic, it springs from the events of the cross and resurrection. It has to do with the heart of the gospel message that on our own we are lost, but with God's help through faith, all things are possible. Something of the relationship between the two must be preserved, both the sin and the grace, the lostness and the foundness, the old world and the new creation.

The traditional theological language for this is the classical language of law and gospel or judgment and grace. The terms I sometimes prefer are trouble and grace; they help get away from old understandings that falsely connect law with Old Testament and gospel with New. Also, trouble seems broader and less freighted than judgment. In any case, both trouble and grace are needed. Trouble has three possible expressions: (1) God judging, that is, commandments from God to correct our ways; (2) the human condition after the fall, that is, descriptions of the world in the old order that indicate things are not as God wills; (3) God suffering, that is, ways in which Christ's crucifixion is ongoing in places where unrighteousness, injustice, and violence are perpetrated.

Students sometimes ask, why not just call trouble sin? Somehow sin is not large enough. It does not get at God's law, which is a gift—though in any moment it may not be experienced as such—or at what Gardner Taylor called "God as the Troublemaker"[9]; sin is not a satisfactory way of speaking about the suffering of many through no cause of their own. In all theological trouble, the burden to do something falls on humanity; repentance is needed—and a change in behavior.

Clearly, however, hope cannot be found in judgment alone (though in being a correction, it is a gift). Trouble leads to the crucifixion. Hope is most clearly defined by the resurrection, though hope cannot narrowly be confined only to the resurrection. Hope is incorrectly equated with grace on its own because grace always appears in relation to sin and judgment.[10] Grace without cost is a fiction; it is what Bonhoeffer called cheap grace. Thus to have the correct equation we must write: hope = trouble + grace, where grace is greater than trouble. True hope takes account of our troubles and sets them in the context of abounding grace.

At the simplest level, trouble places the burden on people. To decide if a concern of the text is trouble, ask, does it feel like trouble? Is it something that we

$$hope \neq being\ nice$$
$$hope \neq grace$$
$$hope = trouble +$$
$$grace,\ where$$
$$grace > trouble$$

as humans must do? As Paul said, "For I do not do the good I want, but the evil I do not want is what I do" (Romans 7:19). Thus, trouble is what we get into on our own, apart from God. If the future is up to us, we are toast.

At the simplest level, grace is God's acceptance of the human burden to act. Grace may also be defined in three ways: (1) God forgiving, that is, Jesus Christ taking on the burden of judgment in atonement; (2) God overturning the powers and principalities of the world, intervening in history, that is, the norms marking the old age are put to death in Christ; and (3) God acting through people in ways that demonstrate the new creation. In each of these the cross is central.

To determine if a concern of the text is grace, ask, is God doing something here that seems hopeful? Does it feel like hope? Does God give what is needed to do God's will? Grace is what God does, not what we do. In preaching, if something feels like trouble or if it feels like good news, it often is.

Trouble puts the burden on humans. Grace puts the burden on God in Christ.

Some concerns of the text function as neither trouble nor grace; they have no theological value, thus we brand them as neutral. Let us now return to our previous exercise to see how this works.

Trouble and Grace in Concerns of the Text

t = trouble
g = grace
n = neutral
Text: Isaiah 6:1-13, Isaiah's Call

> King Uzziah died. (t)
>
> The country was in mourning. (t)
>
> Isaiah had a vision. (g)
>
> The Lord appeared to Isaiah. (g)
>
> Six-winged seraphs praised the Lord. (g)
>
> All earth is full of the Lord's glory. (g)
>
> Isaiah fears for his life. (t)
>
> He is unclean. (t)
>
> He has seen God. (t)
>
> The angel brings an altar coal. (g)
>
> The coal touches Isaiah's lips. (g)
>
> The coal does not burn his lips. (g)
>
> His sin is blotted out. (g)
>
> God needs a messenger. (g)
>
> Isaiah offers to go. (n)
>
> God calls Isaiah forth. (g)
>
> God gives Isaiah what he will need. (g)
>
> Isaiah's word will dull the people's minds. (t)
>
> God prevents some from understanding God's Word. (t)
>
> They will not be healed. (t)
>
> They will be made desolate. (t)
>
> The Lord will send them away. (t)

Not one-tenth will remain. (t)

A remnant will survive. (g)

The remnant will be a holy seed. (g)

Uzziah died around 735 B.C. (n)

Judah is threatened with war from the north. (t)

Isaiah sees heaven's holy courts. (g)

The holy realm is dangerous to the profane world. (t)

God creates a new identity for Isaiah. (g)

God will not tolerate disobedience. (t)

Isaiah pleads for God's people ("How long?"). (g)

The desolation is like the destruction of the vineyard (Isaiah 5). (t)

The seed will sprout a light for all nations (Isaiah 9:2). (g)

God's purpose is larger than any one group of people. (g)

God's purpose is salvation. (g)

God will not be thwarted. (g)

Isaiah 1–39 anticipates the Babylonian exodus (Isaiah 40–55). (n)

Ability to understand God's Word is a gift of God. (g)

Failure to understand has perils. (t)

Student Assignment 4: Indicate on your own list of concerns which texts are trouble and which are grace.

Encouragement for the Journey

Even at this early stage of sermon preparation, students may need some reassurance that these exercises are not merely technical. Trouble and grace will have a rich payoff in sermon composition that can easily be demonstrated in the poetry of Kilian McDonnell, a Benedictine monk and theologian who, for the past ten years, has devoted himself to writing poetry. His poems are beautiful and may be considered a form of preaching in another key; all preachers might do well to read them. They are based on biblical texts on which he has done his exegetical homework. More than this, his poems have simplicity and depth, an honest response to the texts, the kind of engagement one hopes for in students of preaching. He sees life in the texts, not just ideas but experience, doubt, and faith, as in the following:

Joseph, I'm Pregnant by the Holy Ghost

Her husband Joseph, being a righteous man . . .
Planned to dismiss her quietly. Matthew 1:19

Life was simple before that angel
pushed open the kitchen door,
announced light and trouble, as though
a foe had roiled the bottom of the well
and now the pail brings up only

murky water. I'm chosen for some
terrible grace beyond the well.
After short light long dark,
left to stumble through the Sinai

Desert. No manna to gather, no quail
to catch. Nothing. When I tell Joseph
I'm pregnant by the Holy Ghost,
he stares, ox-dumb in hurt. I've asked

him to believe that I, God's
Moses-girl, part seas, give
Torah. He turns, leaves
without a word. Why should my dearest

love believe? Yahweh's not fair.
Where's the voice of light? Where
the pillar of fire? My man drops
me cold, as though I were a concubine

dismissed without a drachma for cheating
on her master's blanket with that
swarthy Roman soldier from the barracks.
Joseph doesn't expose me; I will not

be stoned. My heart eats Yahweh's
cinders; I drink the last date wine
gone sour at the dregs.
God does nothing. But I carry life.[11]

McDonnell has an obvious gift for words. He somewhat humorously describes Mary's experience of God as "short light long dark"; he speaks of Joseph dropping her "cold, as though I were a concubine" and of her heart eating "Yahweh's cinders," leading to her plaintive yet profound cry: "God does nothing. But I carry life."

There is rich paradox in his poems, as in even the title of one of his poems (and books), "Swift, Lord, You Are Not," a poem that concludes with instruction to God:

Think less of galaxies.
Think small.
Then, without the heavy equipment,
stoop and hasten to help me.[12]

The paradox is of the serious and the humorous, tragedy and comedy, doubt and faith, and what we are calling trouble and grace, and faith and grace prevail. As he says of his own writing, "My basic paradigm in writing religious poetry is Jacob wrestling with God, confronting God.... I wrestle with God 'flesh to flesh, sweat to mystery' and I limp away.... I am not teaching but sharing an experience; truth tags along."[13] Author Debra Farrington once wrote similar words, "Engaging with God is hard work, as Jacob and Job can attest. It is more often like a wrestling match than a civilized conversation. If we're being truthful, we'd have to admit that we want a simpler prescription—a pill to take. We don't want to be vulnerable with God."[14]

Preachers can learn not least from the way McDonnell's poems are like many psalms that balance vulnerable human engagement of the Bible with the "nonetheless" of faith. It is hard not to feel some degree of identity with someone who says more beautifully than you can say what you yourself may feel at times. Too often students will either ignore or smooth over natural human reactions to situations and people in the Bible or life and rush to assert the truth of some doctrine, or worse, leave faith out entirely.

Roberta Bondi does an exercise with students in writing prayer that is very similar to what we see practiced in McDonnell's poetry. It could be a good exercise for preaching students as well. She writes:

> I ask everybody to include three elements in their prayer. One is some portion of scripture every day. I explain to them the Liturgy of the Hours, and how the backbone of monastic prayer was the psalms. The other part of their prayer is conversation with God in which they really speak their minds. We talk about the things that make it difficult to speak our minds to God, especially about being afraid of God. The third part of their prayer is silence: just sitting in God's presence without saying anything or having any expectations of God or of themselves. I call it kitchen table prayer. Just spending time with God as we spend time with a friend without talking.[15]

In our own exegetical exercises both above and in what will follow, trouble and grace provide an early foundation for preaching that can have some of the richness one finds in McDonnell's poems that is, after all, the richness of life itself.

Student Assignment 5: Write your own poem/prayer based on your biblical text. Conclude with some powerful dimension of grace in the manner of McDonnell.

Chapter Five

Bridging to Today

Preachers naturally seek to apply texts. Until a connection to today is made, the text may seem like remote history. In the previous chapter we discussed how to find a foundation in the text for the bridge. Now we discuss completing the bridge to today. The preacher always interprets using what David Buttrick calls a double hermeneutic that both scans the field of meaning in the text and the field of meaning to which the text relates in congregational experience.[1] The text points to events today. The process can be demystified and spoken about in plain terms.

The following exercise transposes concerns of the text into concerns of the sermon. Preachers may use it to preview the strength of proposed thoughts for a sermon and thereby save many hours of wasted work in writing. On one level, it is difficult, and students initially struggle with it. On another level, when one is able to do it, it seems deceptively simple, yet still it retains intrigue and surprise. In my own teaching, no exercise is more valuable to help students discover connections between the Bible and now, to correct and strengthen them, and to show the range of rich possibilities. One can isolate sources of potential problems and find stronger alternatives. Students who do this exercise (and if necessary repeat it) can gain the experience equivalent to writing many sermons in terms of identifying pitfalls and good connections to today. Equally important, the exercise done regularly strengthens one's ability to do theology in the pulpit.

Concerns of the Sermon

Concerns of the text (= T) are simply paired with equivalent statements for our day, called concerns of the sermon (= S). These are natural links and provide the sermon with natural bridges of thought between the biblical text and contemporary experience. Every sermon uses them even if a preacher has never had terminology for them. We defined "concern of the text" as any idea with which the biblical text is concerned. It is true to the text and is a short sentence. It can arise from the text itself, from the commentaries, or from our background scholarly knowledge. In the sermon, a concern of the text might be developed into at least a substantial paragraph.

> A concern of the sermon is a transposed version of the concern of the text that makes a true statement about now.

A concern of the sermon normally arises from the concern of the text. It is a transposed version that makes a true statement about now. One affirms its truth by testing it not as a true statement of the text per se but as a true statement of experience, either how the world is experienced or how it is understood theologically.

Transposing

Rather than try to explain transposition, which I have done elsewhere,[2] let me simply provide numerous examples, for it is more readily observed than explained and more readily imitated than analyzed. A helpful clue can be given: keep at least one term constant in transposing from then to now. We start with our Isaiah text and later move to other examples to demonstrate some typical problems. Trouble and grace are again identified according to how I imagine I would develop the idea (you might see something different). In the following list, I have discarded ideas of neutral theological significance.

Text: Isaiah 6:1-13, Isaiah's Call

T = *Concerns of the text*
S = *Concerns of the Sermon*
(t) = *trouble*
(g) = *grace*

Samples from the biblical text itself:

T: King Uzziah died. (t)
S: Many die today. Or: Rulers die; or: Earthly powers pass away. (t)

T: The country was in mourning. (t)
S: Many are in mourning. Or: Our nations mourn; or: The world lacks direction. (t)

T: Isaiah had a vision. (g) Or: Isaiah had a vision (t)
S: Christ is our vision. (g) Or: We have no visions. (t) Or: God seems absent to us. (t)

T: The Lord appeared to Isaiah. (g)
S: God appears to us. (g)

T: Six-winged seraphs praised the Lord. (g)
S: We praise God. Or: God praises us.

T: All earth is full of the Lord's glory. (g)
S: God's glory cannot be contained. (g)

T: Isaiah fears for his life. (t)
S: Many live in fear. (t) Or: Life can be lost. (t)

T: He is unclean. (t)
S: We are unclean. (t) Or: Our ways are unclean. (t)

T: He has seen God. (t)
S: God has seen us. (t)

T: The angel brings an altar coal. (g)
S: We have been made clean. (g)

T: The coal touches Isaiah's lips. (g)
S: Salvation does not stay remote from us. (g)

T: The coal does not burn his lips. (g)
S: Destruction of our sin does not injure us. (g)

T: His sin is blotted out. (g)
S: Our sin is blotted out. (g)

T: God needs a messenger. (t) Or: God needs a messenger. (g)
S: We need a messenger. (t) Or: God sent a messenger. (g)

T: God calls Isaiah forth. (g)
S: God calls us forth. (g) Or: God calls many forth. (g)

T: God gives Isaiah what he will need. (g)
S: God gives us what we need. (g)

T: Isaiah's word will dull the people's minds. (t)
S: Our minds are dull. (t) Or: We don't know salvation when we hear it. (t)

T: God prevents some from understanding God's Word. (t)
S: We prevent others from understanding God's Word. (t)

T: They will not be healed. (t)
S: Many will not be healed. (t)

T: They will be made desolate. (t)
S: Much has been laid waste. (t) Or: We have made much desolate. (t)

T: The Lord will send them away. (t)
S: God seems to have sent us away. (t)

T: Not one-tenth will remain. (t)
S: Things will get worse. (t) Or: There is little hope. (t)

T: A remnant will survive. (g)
S: A remnant has survived. (g) Or: Hope is alive. (g)

T: The remnant will be a holy seed. (g)
S: The seed has sprouted. (g) Or: A new realm is breaking in. (g)

T: Judah is threatened with war from the north. (t)
S: War faces people on all sides. (t)

T: Isaiah sees heaven's holy courts. (g)
S: We glimpse God's heavenly realm. (g)

T: The holy realm is dangerous to the profane world. (t)
S: God's ways are not our ways. (t)

T: God creates a new identity for Isaiah. (g)
S: God gives us a new identity in Christ. (g)

T: God will not tolerate disobedience. (t)

T: God will not tolerate us. (t) Or: We tolerate disobedience. (t)

T: Isaiah pleads for God's people ("How long?"). (g)
S: Christ pleads our case. (g)

T: The desolation is like the destruction of the vineyard (Isaiah 5). (t)

T: God will not stand lack of fruit.

T: The seed will sprout a light for all nations (Isaiah 9:2). (g)
S: We are a light for all nations. (g) Or: Christ is a light for all people. (g)

T: God's purpose is larger than any one group of people. (t/g)
S: God's purpose cannot be stopped. (g)

T: God's purpose is salvation. (g)
S: God is determined to accomplish our salvation. (g)

T: God will not be thwarted. (g)
S: God wins. (g)

T: Understanding God's Word is a gift. (t/g)
S: God illumines God's Word. (g)

From a list such as this, a number of preaching possibilities begins to emerge not all of which can be used in one sermon. Even though a preacher will use only a few of these to structure the overall sermon, the rest are not wasted. They can still be used to help one re-create or represent the text in the sermon or to help in the development of thoughts about today. They provide something to say. Readers seeking to go beyond these suggestions to full sermons on Isaiah 6 may find three quite different examples in two readily available sources: Paul Tillich's *The Shaking of the Foundations*[3] and James W. Cox's *The Twentieth Century Pulpit*.[4]

Student Examples

Here are some typical examples that I imagine might appear, for instance, in a class working with different biblical texts. They highlight typical slipping places that could have appeared in a sermon if the exercise had not caught them. I add comments to suggest stronger alternatives:

Text: Matthew 5:13:

T: Salt cannot restore its saltiness. (t)
S: Some people lack saltiness. (t) (Do they? Better: For many, life seems without salt.)

T: Useless salt is no good for anything. (t)
S: Choose life or death. (t) (Stay closer to the above: Without God, we are no good for anything.)

T: You, the disciples, are the salt of the world. (g) (Better: The disciples are ...)
S: The Christian community is valued as salt. (g) (For grace it is better to focus on an action of God: God in Christ gives us our saltiness.)

Text: Matthew 21:23-32

T: Jesus questioned the religious authorities. (t)
S: We question the religious authorities. (t) (Better: We question God.)

T: The religious authorities argue among themselves about the right answer. (t)
S: Why would they do this? Do they know what they are afraid of? (t)

(Avoid questions at this stage and make a statement that links from the text: The religious authorities are confounded by Jesus.)

T: The religious authorities failed to recognize God's action. (t)

S: We should consider our shortcomings. (t) (Better: We fail to recognize God. [We can still talk about our shortcomings in developing this in the sermon].)

T: Jesus' response was ambiguous. (t)
S: We rarely get clear answers from God. (t) (Another possibility: At times God seems devious.)

T: Tax collectors and prostitutes will enter God's realm first. (g)
S: Red-light hookers are eligible for salvation. (g) (This would be better at this stage if it were more general. In the sermon we can make it more specific, but now is a time to open possibilities. It would be stronger as a statement of grace if the action was shifted to God: God welcomes the sinners and despised.)

T: The religious authorities are not denied entry to God's realm. (g)

(This could be stated positively: Even the religious authorities will be given entry.)

S: God reaches to all with salvation. (g)

Text: Matthew 21:33-46

T: The landowner rented the vineyard to tenants. (t)
S: We borrow and lend. (t) (Better: Our life at times seems on borrowed time.)

T: The landowner left the tenants to manage on their own. (t)
S: God gives us free will. (g) (Better: Sometimes God seems to have left us. Transpositions from judgment to grace or from grace to judgment are harder for listeners to grasp and are best used as devices preachers use to find judgment or grace when they seem absent.)

T: The landowner sent servants for the rent. (t)
S: God sent the prophets to warn us. (t) (Better: God's messengers come to us. This idea could be developed with the concern of the text in the sermon itself. Concerns of the sermon are about us and our time.)

T: The tenants kill the son. (t)
S: We hurt Jesus by our hardness of heart. (t) (Better:
We continue to crucify Christ today.)

T: The landowner sent many messengers. (g)
S: God sent Jesus to us. (g) (Better: God keeps reaching
out to us.)

T: The landowner sent his son. (g)
S: God sent Jesus. (g) (Better if held to our time: God
sends Jesus to us. [that is, even our worst actions will
not have the final say].)

Each of these paired sets affords a bridge: a paragraph or two on a concern of the text moves to a paragraph or two on its matching concern of the sermon. The first is developed using the text, commentaries, and theology; the second is developed using theology, contemporary experience, and resources such as television and newspapers. Even the major concern of the text (MT) has its own major concern of the sermon (MS).

Every preacher at some deep or intuitive level makes these comparisons. Laying them out gives a preacher control of the process; they offer the sermon in microcosm before it is written, and thus enable the best bridge(s) to be selected.

Student Assignment 6: Transpose your list of concerns
of the text into concerns of the sermon. Transpose trouble into trouble and grace into grace.

Other Voices

One of the most detailed (and difficult) studies in homiletics is David Buttrick's *Homiletic: Moves and Structures*. A strength of his project was to make preachers attentive to how ideas become conscious in the minds of listeners. He indicates how often a new idea may be ventured (for example, every three to four minutes), how many diverse thoughts may be entertained at once, for instance in a paragraph (he says a maximum of three), and what is needed before a new subject is ventured (that is, the current idea or topic must be repeated, as a way of closure, followed by a pause).

He calls a unit of thought centered about a single meaning in consciousness a "move" (essentially a paragraph or two). Each "move" initially arises from the biblical text and then shifts to our contemporary situation.[5] Hearers are thus led through individual "moves" to discover the "field of meaning" the biblical text discloses. Buttrick recommends "moves" located in sequenced "structures." He suggests a maximum of five to six in a sermon of twenty minutes. I suggest only a few generally longer "moves" of three to eight minutes to prevent the sermon from feeling choppy.

Nancy Lamers Gross gives an alternative metaphor to a bridge. She visualizes a swing in which the preacher is like a gymnast on a high bar, swinging between engagement of the text and engagement of various dialogue partners.[6]

Stephen Farris made a valuable contribution to the subject of bridging—his book cover actually has a picture of a bridge. Bridges are analogies. He recommends that preachers determine the persons or groups in a biblical text or behind it—for example, the people to whom Jesus addresses his parables—and the historical faith communities of the gospel writers. To make a bridge, compare the biblical person or group with a person or group today. Thus Israel in the Bible may be compared with the church; Babylon with unjust power structures; the priest, Levite, and Samaritan with listeners.[7] Jesus in any text is a possible analogy for us.[8] Analogies may be made on the basis of differences; various kinds of analogy are important to keep in mind as one develops bridges in the sermon.

> A Move = a unit or paragraph of thought centered about a single meaning initially arising from a biblical text and then shifting to our situation

Implications

There are several implications of concerns of the sermon. The first is practical. Generally, preachers make only a couple of points of contact using a couple of bridges between the biblical text and our day, and one of them is with the theme sentence. One or two other various concerns may become paragraphs, even as the rest may be ideas mentioned in passing. Second, concerns of the sermon ensure that the sermon connects the text with the listeners. A third implication is theological; concerns of the sermon fall into six theological categories in relation to the world: three trouble and three grace. They are easier to remember if one notes that trouble and grace mirror each other, that is, that the one list is an inversion of the other. If you remember either set of three, you can invert them to remember the others:

TROUBLE

1. God judging/commanding us

2. The human condition after the fall / the old order

3. God suffering (that is, Christ's ongoing crucifixion in the world)

GRACE

1. God forgiving/atonement

2. God overturning the powers, principalities, and old norms

3. God acting through people / the new creation

In other words, each concern of the sermon (dealing with our times) points to one of these theological perspectives from which to interpret our world. They are categories with which we may view events around us. This is very important for people who have countless files of stories for future sermons and cannot find them when they are needed: here, only two (or at the most six) files are required.

A final implication of concerns of the sermon is pastoral and prophetic. Most students wonder how to find stories for the sermon. Any story for instance about human need and suffering, can be used to develop a concern of the sermon pointing to human need and suffering. Or any story about Christ acting by the Spirit through people can be used to develop a concern of the sermon pointing to Christ. We will speak more about developing stories according to trouble and grace in a later chapter.

The next step will be to select just a few of these bridges or paired statements to structure the sermon. Only one set of these will function as the theme sentence (that is, the major concern of the text and the major concern of the sermon). A few other pairs will function as theme statements of individual paragraphs (the one leads into the text, the other leads into our situation). It is important to use their exact wording (usually in the first sentence of the appropriate section) in order to preserve these important bridges as bridges for our hearers. A few of these paired statements can sketch a possible outline for the sermon. I suggest at least two pairs (one trouble and one grace) and no more than one pair for every five minutes of sermon.

For example, on the call of Isaiah, one might structure the sermon using the following two pairings:

Concern of the text: Isaiah was not good enough.

Concern of the sermon: Our world is not good enough.

Major concern of the text: God gives Isaiah a new identity.

Major concern of the sermon: God gives us a new identity (that is, in Christ).

These can serve as an essential outline of my sermon on this text. In order that the first half of the sermon fit with the last half, it is often wise to choose first one's major concern and then work backward to locate a concern that represents in some ways its opposite, thus the one will flow into the other. Further examples and discussion of using these paired concerns to structure sermons can be found in chapter 9. Examples of other ways to organize sermons can be found in chapter 8. For now, it is important at least to understand how one makes bridges between the biblical text and today.

> Student Assignment 7: Choose from among your list of
> concerns of the text and concerns of the sermon two
> pairs, one to serve as trouble and one to serve as grace.
> Consider these as a possible outline of your sermon.

We conclude our discussion of Tuesday in the preacher's week with a brief review:

For Further Reflection and Study Concerning Tuesday

1. Analogy is a key way of moving the Word of God "then" to the Word of God "now." Might there be other ways? For example, texts such as many of the psalms or sections of the epistles tell us little of their original communities. Can they speak directly to our own?

2. Trouble and grace are two ways of ensuring theological discussion. They also echo the predominant movement of the faith. Do you agree? Does the gospel have a movement, a form? Are there other forms you might suggest of the gospel that are not from trouble to grace or law to gospel or crucifixion to resurrection?

Section III

Wednesday: Drawing on Experience

T he day is Wednesday and it is time to start composing the sermon and connecting the text to real experience. We have spoken of (1) what the text says, and (2) what the text means, and now in turning to (3) what experience says—one applies the text to specific situations today. Later we will more fully turn to (4) what the preacher says.

The hermeneutical circle is a way to picture translation from another language: it is a repeating cycle, back and forth between a text and now, gradually getting the sense of what is meant. The same circle applies for a preacher coming to an understanding of a Bible passage. It can also be adopted for the overall repeating process of preparing a sermon each week. The four stages just named represent four quadrants of the hermeneutical circle for preachers:[1]

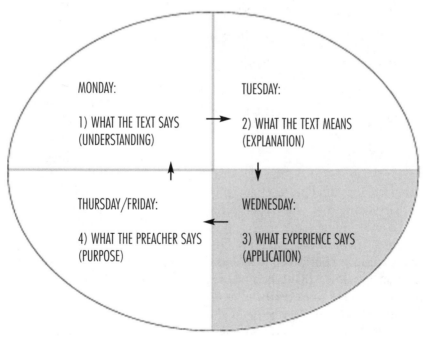

MONDAY:

1) WHAT THE TEXT SAYS
(UNDERSTANDING)

TUESDAY:

2) WHAT THE TEXT MEANS
(EXPLANATION)

THURSDAY/FRIDAY:

4) WHAT THE PREACHER SAYS
(PURPOSE)

WEDNESDAY:

3) WHAT EXPERIENCE SAYS
(APPLICATION)

The Role of Experience

In the last two centuries nothing has affected preaching more than the role of experience. It represents key hermeneutical issues of our time. Everyone reads texts from a different perspective, and each perspective yields different understandings. While the canon of the Bible is closed and preaching texts remain fixed, sermons are always different because preachers read biblical texts with the lenses of new experiences. Many of the "new theologies" in recent decades have arisen out of the experience of particular groups and subcultures. Part of what characterizes our own time as postmodern is the appreciation of differences.

It became apparent to interpreters in the last century that experience affected the interpretative process from the beginning. Bultmann's idea of preunderstanding has found general scholarly acceptance: "no exegesis is without presuppositions."[2] He meant that one approaches a text with preconceived ideas of what it means. By identifying these, the reader gains some control over their influence. The reader's experience also plays a key role in the final interpretation. Within limits, he concluded that no one interpretation can be fixed nor final: "The understanding of the text is never a definitive one; but rather remains open because the meaning of the Scriptures discloses itself anew in every future."[3] In other words, the understanding that one has of Scripture is always conditioned by one's social and cultural setting.

> Liberationists argue that no interpretation of a biblical text can escape being within a political context and worldview, since politics and ideology are inescapable.

Liberationists argue that no interpretation of a biblical text can escape being within a political context and worldview.[4] Politics and ideology are inescapable. José Miguez Bonino says, "Every interpretation of the texts which is offered to us (whether as exegesis or as systematic or as ethical interpretation) must be investigated in relation to the praxis out of which it comes."[5] Various liberation theologies are committed, as Elisabeth

Schüssler Fiorenza notes, to people who have been oppressed and ignored by history.[6] Pastoral theologians like Don Browning claim the essential role of experience when they argue for "thick description" in social research, narrative accounts that capture some of the feel of experience.[7]

Experience is not some jacket that can be taken off and left in a locker room until after textual interpretation is complete, though preachers were taught to do this when exegesis was conceived as an objective science (well into the 1970s and beyond). Rather, exegesis is an art that tries to follow some scientific principles. In fact, until only recently, exegesis, hermeneutics and homiletics were conceived as sequential steps, operating in a linear chain. The relationship could be compared to a relay race (or moving from one seminary classroom to another) in which the biblical scholar passes the baton to the theologian who passes it to the preacher.

A troubling aspect of this relay image is that preaching tends to get viewed as mere popularizing or dumbing-down. In fact, biblical and theological classes have their own goals and objectives (for example, writing academic essays), and given the scarcity of sermon assignments in many of those classes, proclamation of the Word may not be one of them. Homiletics has the responsibility of preaching the gospel, and thus it cannot blindly adopt the methods of those not specifically dedicated to it. Homiletics needs to tailor even the traditional exegetical exercises with its own theological exegesis in order to ensure that the gospel is located. It needs to find ways to speak simply and do theology using ideas, imagery, and experience.

When preaching is perceived as popularizing or dumbing-down, what does this say about the Word of God and the church? Rather, preaching needs to be upheld as having its own hermeneutical tasks from beginning to end that are geared to the gospel as well as having its own rhetorical goals to negotiate. In some ways preaching is the most difficult of assignments because it must end up being clear and simple—not an obvious requirement in some fields—yet that simplicity must come from having worked through what is complex each week.

Homiletics Past

I describe the typical understanding of homiletics as follows:

> These three terms [exegesis, hermeneutics, and homiletics] and the actions they represent traditionally were understood to be like three consecutive buses a preacher took between the Bible and the sermon in what

we might imagine to be Sermon City. Early in the week preachers used to board the Exegesis bus and travel up Bible Boulevard through the historical district of town where they would engage historical critical exegesis. They would then transfer to the Hermeneutics bus for the trip up the newer end of town to Today Street, during which they came to understand the significance of the text for today. At this point, biblical interpretation was effectively finished and the direction for the sermon was clear. Preachers got off the Hermeneutics bus and transferred to the Homiletics bus for the rest of the journey up to the church, during which they applied their understandings to the particularities of the congregation's life and work.[8]

Things have changed. Preachers automatically make personal connection with texts when they read them, and these cannot simply be ignored in the exegetical process. Connections to the specific life of the congregation need to be sought throughout the process. The interpretation of the text is the sermon, thus there is not first an interpretation that someone hands to the preacher and to which is added various sermon elements. Interpretation continues all the way through sermon composition and delivery.

Budgeting Preparation Time

Preachers used to be encouraged to spend most of the week on critical study of texts, an exercise that left little time for sermon composition, but that method did not seem to aid the process. Essential exegetical study can occupy perhaps only a third of the total preparation time available. Other "texts" having to do with contemporary experience also need research and analysis; moreover, composition needs time. The old formula for sermon time still holds for many preachers—an hour in the study for every minute in the pulpit. Jana Childers says that in her third decade as a preacher, "It takes me three or four two-hour blocks and two or three four-hour blocks to write a sermon."[9] That is between fourteen and twenty hours, close to the old rubric. Barbara Brown Taylor says, "After twenty years, I may spend an hour or two less than I used to, but I still come pretty close to the old advice about spending one hour . . . for every one minute."[10]

In my homiletical training, composition was left to the end of the week: students were typically taught to take notes during the week from various readings and to write on Saturday. I encourage students to skip the note-taking stage: write on a daily basis not in note form but in a form that can be imported to the sermon. Old notes are like yesterday's tea bag, they generate little flavor and only tint the water. It is far better to take the energy one receives from talking, seeing, and reading and convert it directly into material that potentially can be part of a sermon draft. Cutting can come later.

Homiletics Present

A more appropriate overall model for the preacher might be to conceive of a single bus filled with people who are huddled in conversation in three groupings:

> The first group is having a conversation about exegesis. Another group including Bible commentators, theologians and preachers is talking about hermeneutics. A third group is talking about homiletics, including people from the congregation, and from the preacher's own circle of family and acquaintances. These conversations happen simultaneously on the one bus. The circles of conversation are not clearly divided and sometimes people in one group turn to join another. The preacher fluidly moves back and forth from conversation to conversation as the bus makes its way along Bible Boulevard and Today Street up to the church. The weekly route may be the same but each journey is different, for different people are on board according to the specific text and contemporary events. In this model, homiletics shifts from being third-in-a-sequence to one element of a threefold parallel activity of exegesis, hermeneutics and homiletics.[11]

This revised model is perhaps more realistic of what actually happens, and it values what the preacher does and the central role of preaching for the church.[12]

Experience, of course, is not a uniform thing. When we speak of the role of contemporary experience in preaching, we speak mainly of three things: the experience of the congregation, the preacher, and society in general. We will address each one in turn, as each needs its own form of exegesis. In a later chapter we will turn to telling stories from experience.

CHAPTER SIX

EXEGESIS OF TODAY'S WORLD

E very preacher needs to be able to speak to the contemporary world. This involves understanding the congregation, understanding the self, and understanding social situations. Every congregation has an identity, shaped by past and present; every preacher has traits that are well suited to ministry and some that are less well suited; every social situation is complex and needs ethical and social analysis. Here we make a case for an exegesis of each of these key components that contribute to the contemporary world in preaching: the congregation, the preacher, and the social situation.

Exegesis of the Congregation

In *Preaching as Local Theology and Folk Art*, Leonora Tubbs Tisdale devised principles for doing exegesis of a congregation. Her idea was innovative; until then preachers thought of exegesis as confined to biblical texts. As she sees it, congregations have various subcultures. Preachers benefit from listening to the many "resident theologians" who "contribute to the questions, insights, struggles, and life situations which feed the formation of the Sunday sermon."[1] They help the preacher to preach in ways that are responsive to local contextual theology, grounded in the lives and experiences of the people.[2]

Preaching in multicultural settings presents need for exegesis. James R. Nieman and Thomas G. Rogers portray congregations using various "frames"—ethnicity, class, displacement, and beliefs. The sermon must "presume mutuality; in how meaning is constructed" and may be followed by a discussion where other voices and perspectives are heard.[3] These authors found that in such settings, preachers stress not differences but what people have in common, especially life in Jesus Christ, and sermons thus lead to a celebration of God as a trustworthy author of life and provider of all things.[4] The sermon form in itself signals "an encounter with God in which memory is reconstructed, experiences are affirmed, and dignity is conferred."[5]

If we were to draw up our own list of questions we might use to engage a congregation, they might include: How old is the church? What are its roots? What is its denominational history? How important is its history to it? In what year(s) did it have its biggest membership? What is the current size of the congregation? What is the racial and cultural mix? What percentage of those who attend are members? Roughly how many people are in each decade of age range? What is the average age of the members? Roughly how many people belong to the following family categories: single, married, divorced, widowed? Roughly how many people belong to the following economic categories: student, stay-at-home parent, employed, unemployed, disabled, retired? What is the average financial giving of church families? What percentage is involved in the church's mission work? pastoral care? administration? Bible study? other groups? Who are the key members of the church? Who have been key members but are not any more? Who has left the church in recent memory? What stories about its past does the church like to tell? What stories about its past does the church not like to tell? How does the church handle conflict? Who was ordained from this church and what candidates are there? What mission projects has the church supported? What projects in the church's outreach ministry continue to hold most pride? In the last searches for ministers, what aspects of ministry have been given the highest priority? Of course, the list could go on but one quickly gets a sense of how important Tisdale's type of exercise can be.

Tisdale encourages preachers to treat local events as signs and symbols, to treat them as "texts." Raw material can be drawn from stories and interviews, archival resources, demographics, architecture and visual arts, rituals, events and activities, and various people.[6] One then needs to analyze and interpret the cultural data with particular attention to how the congregation views the world (for example, views of God, humanity, creation, time or eschatology, church, mission) and what it values.[7] The sermon for her is imaginative "dance" or folk art in which the preacher discerns "fitting and faithful themes for proclamation." The preacher as folk artist seeks "symbols, forms, and movements that are capable of capturing and transforming the imaginations of a particular local community of faith."[8] This kind of community exegesis is not a weekly endeavor, yet preachers should mentally engage the results of such congregational exegesis each week in preparing sermons. In fact, as one goes about one's pastoral duties each week, one is naturally engaging in slight revisions of the congregational profile.

Student Assignment 8: Do an exegesis of your congregation or of the class to which you will preach using the above questions and/or your own.

Identifying a Congregational Need

Part of what congregational exegesis yields is congregational needs; in other words, preaching presumes pastoral care and social action. Harry Emerson Fosdick (1878–1969) of Riverside Church in New York was a great proponent of preaching to needs, which is why he advocated that preachers identify "an object to be achieved."[9] If he preached on the need for joy, he would explore the subject of joy theologically and then move to create it in the sermon.

In identifying congregational need on a weekly basis, preachers may look in three places. First they may look to the biblical text: check to see if obvious sparks are triggered with stories or specific incidents in the community. Second, preachers may determine

Identifying a Congregational Need
1. Let the biblical text lead you to a need.
2. Use a key event in community life to name the need.
3. Think of one individual who needs to hear the sermon.

that a situation in the congregation or world may be so large as to demand attention, like a church anniversary or tragic circumstance. Third, a preacher may use the major concern of the sermon (that is, the transposed version of the major concern of the text or theme sentence) to identify one person who needs to hear it. The sermon can be written for that person (though he or she would not be identified). If a preacher speaks authentically to the needs of one person, many will respond.

It is helpful to distinguish between the expressed need of the congregation, the congregation's actual need, and the preacher's need. The expressed need is what the congregation might say or has said that it needs, in its own words. A parallel situation exists in counseling situations, where parishioners identify a presenting issue or ostensible reason for the visit that may be different from the actual issue. A teenager might complain of having no friends (the presenting issue) when the actual need is lack of parental expression of love. A congregation might say it needs more youth, but the actual need may be its fear of change that prevents youth from coming.

The actual need is the need of the congregation as it is discerned scripturally and theologically and stated using Christian vocabulary. For example, the expressed need might be: we need fewer meetings. The actual need might thus be: we need to know God; or, we long for community.

> **Definitions:**
>
> **Expressed need**—The need the congregation identifies for itself, in its own words.
>
> **Actual need**—The need of the congregation as it is discerned with Scripture and theology and stated using Christian vocabulary.
>
> **Preacher's need**—Any agenda of the preacher that is unrelated to the needs of the congregation.

The actual need of a congregation is discerned with the help of the biblical text, listening for what God is saying to the particular situation. For instance, a text might say God seeks to be known; or, God establishes relationship. Once the theme sentence of the sermon is established, the preacher can consider what actual need it meets in the congregation (for example, we need to know God; or, we long for community). A preacher might even try to get back to the expressed need so that he or she is using the congregation's own words as part of the sermon. It is often helpful to move from the expressed need to the Scripture to the actual need in the course of the sermon itself.

We have been speaking of doing an exegesis of the congregation. It is also possible to *eisegete* the congregation's needs—that is, to impose the preacher's own predilections and perspectives onto one's understandings of the congregation—and hence, fail to see what the congregation's actual needs are. It may be important to do congregational exegesis with trusted members of the congregation so that eisegesis is avoided.

Involving the Congregation in Sermon Preparation

Several homileticians advocate that preachers incorporate members of the congregation in the sermon process, precisely to identify and meet needs. Lucy Rose thus refers to a "roundtable church"[10] and John McClure speaks of "the roundtable pulpit."[11] He advocates that preaching be the result of a collaborative process in which the preacher meets weekly with a congregational group (for no more than three months per group) to help bring various perspectives into the sermon. James R. Nieman and Thomas G. Rogers say that something like this is a must in multicultural settings; preaching needs to be collaborative, involving members of the congregation in Bible study and in choice of images or stories to ensure that diverse perspectives are represented.[12]

The Preacher's Need

When preachers avoid identifying congregational need, they are prone to act out of their own need, which is frequently unrelated to congregational need. The preacher may focus on what the preacher thinks the congregation ought to know, for instance, about a doctrine or the background of a biblical text, though it is unrelated to their daily lives. The preacher's need is not necessarily negative; it may even be prophetic. It is the task of the preacher, however, to express the congregation's actual need and meet it; the preacher needs to establish some legitimate connection between the material for presentation and what will be helpful for the people.

Exegesis of the Preacher

In addition to exegesis of the congregation, the preacher's self requires exegesis. Even as God initiates a relationship with the people through the sermon, they experience a relationship with the preacher. This can help or hinder what God is accomplishing through the sermon. In *Blue Like Jazz*, Donald Miller speaks of a friend he interviewed and that he names only as Penny; she tells of reading the Bible and becoming a Christian: "I really can't explain how freeing that was, to realize that if I met Jesus, He would like me. I never felt that about some Christians on the radio. I always thought that if I met those people they would yell at me."[13] Who the preacher is matters.

Stephen Farris has developed the idea of an exegesis of the self in which he asks questions about the preacher in relationship to the congregation. For example, I read what ..., and my congregation reads ...? His questions include age, gender, socioeconomic factors, theological stance, and so forth. Two of the most important questions concern what group of people the preacher has the most difficulty relating to and what pastoral situations the preacher is tempted to avoid.[14]

The preacher's character is an issue that goes right into the pulpit. Teresa L. Fry Brown uses self-exegesis as a means to prepare for actual sermon delivery:

> Prior to the preaching moment I have undergone a process of self-exegesis. Who's Teresa today? How do I feel? What have I noticed about myself? What is God saying in this time? Am I physically, emotionally, spiritually, psychologically equipped to deliver the sermon God has placed in my heart? I dream about delivery of the sermon. I see the faces of the people, hear my voice, feel how my body moves, hear God speaking, and even smell the anticipation of hope. There have been times when I have envisioned the angelic host within the congregation helping me preach. I think about all the women and men who were unable to preach due to social restrictions, and I am encouraged to preach with God's power. [15]

By this exercise Brown is reminded of the importance and privilege of preaching and is readied for the act.

If a community is not convinced of the integrity of a preacher, if they do not trust the relationship, no matter what is said or how well it is said, they may not listen. However, if a congregation senses that as preachers we believe what we are preaching, that we have faith, that we care about them, that we have help, that we stand with them under the Word, not against them and over the Word, then communication is, of course, enhanced.

> Student Assignment 9: Identify roughly a dozen probing questions and do an exegesis of yourself in relationship to your congregation or class.

Episcopal bishop Phillips Brooks (1832–93) believed character was so important that he made it part of the central feature of his homiletic. "Truth through Personality is our description of real preaching," Brooks said (subtly referring to both the preacher and the Trinity) in stating the theme of his 1877 Lyman Beecher Lectures.[16]

Of course everything that preachers say or do communicates something of who they are. It is common knowledge in employment interviews that within the first thirty seconds interviewers have made their decision about the candidate, and it rarely changes after that time. An argument can be made that since similar quick decisions are made about the preacher, there is little one can do to alter how one is received. We are who we are, and we cannot help communicating this. Besides, most people in the congregation already know our identity, not least by the quality of our pastoral care and administration.

Alternatively, one might argue that the preacher should stay out of the sermon. Karl Barth believed that any attention to ethos was interference with the Word.[17] He died before the preacher's role as nothing more than a conduit was exposed as false. People always speak from the limitations of their own self, time, and culture. Furthermore, God never intended the Word to be handled with sterile gloves, kept free from contact with anything human. If this had been the plan, Christ would not have come in human form. Preachers at best may hope to be translucent, allowing God's light to shine through their words and actions, but they can never be transparent, as though they do not speak from their humanity.

Ethos and Rhetoric

Rhetoric speaks of the character of a speaker as ethos or virtue. Ethos is not fixed; the way that we think of the character of a person is more or less fixed. Who the preacher is in absolute terms is not the primary issue but rather who the congregation perceives the preacher to be in the particular moment: Do I like him or her at this moment? Do I agree? Ethos changes in accordance with what is said and who is listening.[18]

Craig Loscalzo frames the issue in a helpful way:

> Who *you* are is not the issue, but who your hearers *perceive* you to be. We may not like the sound of that, but it is radically true. If people perceive you as a compassionate, caring person, they hear your words of compassion and care with their heads and hearts. But if your congregation considers you aloof and unapproachable, they will have trouble hearing and experiencing your message of compassion. Even if *you* feel you are warm and caring, the congregation's perception may be quite different.[19]

Still, ethos in the church is particular. The authority to preach is an office given by the church; it is not granted by the individual in the pew according to likes and dislikes in the moment. Further, faithful listeners overlook aspects of personality in order to listen for God's Word.

Why Preachers Attend to Ethos

Preachers cannot leave ethos simply to chance; listeners interpret ethos as intentional, a result of decisions the preacher makes. Everything the preacher says or does reflects choice. For example, a study showed that preachers in growing churches used "credibility devices": their language was personal, narrational, assured, and businesslike as opposed to folksy, with passive language constructions and less interesting words.[20] Preachers cause ethos, even though the listener finally evaluates and discerns it. It is commonly assessed through what listeners know of the preacher's moral, intellectual, spiritual, emotional, and personal habits.

Moral habits concern the preacher's overall moral character. Such habits include trustworthiness, an ability to make the right kinds of decisions in difficult circumstances, and respect of others with different opinions. Intellectual habits are demonstrated by being informed and getting correct facts, curiosity and interest in people and events, and a disciplined life of study, the fruits of which are clear. Spiritual habits are assessed, for example, by the preacher's knowledge of Scripture, willingness to talk about God, ability to talk about all manner of human situations in appropriate theological ways, depth of faith, and reliance upon God. Emotional habits are communicated through the preacher's concern for the congregation, demonstration of emotion appropriate to the subject matter, and ability to empathize with the suffering of others. Personal habits are assessed through grooming, dress, manners, and mannerisms.

> The preacher's character, as portrayed in the sermon, needs to be intentional, reflecting choices the preacher makes to build trust. Ethos is reflected in moral, intellectual, spiritual, emotional, and personal habits, as these are demonstrated in preaching.

We have spoken of ethos the way Aristotle spoke of it. But André Resner says that, for preaching, this is not enough. The preacher must center on God, and the character of the preacher must be shaped by the cross, by dying to the old self and rising to the new. The aspect of the preacher's character that matters most is the transformation effected by the cross that marks the beginning of a new age. The sermon is thus effective only by proclaiming the gospel for salvation.[21]

Practical Implications

These general truths about ethos translate into four practical guidelines for the preacher. First, ethos is of particular importance in the opening minutes of a sermon, when a relationship must be established or reestablished. Introductory material to the sermon thus should not be too demanding, for listeners are still trying to adjust to the preacher as a person.

Second, although preachers are usually the only ones to speak during the sermon, they need not monopolize the conversation, and their tone ought not to be authoritarian. Words can reflect conversations, actions, and concerns that preachers have seen or heard during the week that allow the congregation to identify with what is said.[22]

Third, ethos is determined not just by information and experience but by whether or not listeners agree or disagree. Thus, preachers need to reflect a variety of viewpoints, not just their own. This is especially the case with controversial issues; reflect countering positions that members might hold using what David Buttrick calls "contrapuntals."[23]

Fourth, ethos presumes that that the congregation's actual needs will be foremost.

A Story

A good preacher chooses to connect a biblical text to today's world. With Isaiah's call, a preacher might tell stories of similar kinds of experiences today. Sometimes (but not every week) the preacher will relate an autobiographical story, such as this from Barbara Brown Taylor concerning the call to ministry she experienced listening to her childhood minister-friend:

> One Sunday he asked me to sit up close to the pulpit. He wanted me to hear his sermon, he said, and as I listened to him talk about the beauty of God's creation and our duty to be awed by it, all of a sudden I heard him telling the congregation about a little girl who kept tadpoles in a birdbath so that she could watch over them as they turned into frogs, and how her care for those creatures was part of God's care for the whole world.
>
> It was as if someone had turned on all the lights—not only to hear myself spoken of in the church, but to hear that my life was part of God's life, and that something as ordinary as a tadpole connected the two.[24]

Stories like this bring yet other stories to mind that will help identify the meaning we are developing for today.

Pastoral Care

An aspect of the preacher's self is expressed in the sermon through pastoral care. Congregations listen to how preachers talk about people in the Bible or our world and they project from them to how the preacher will minister to themselves. G. Lee Ramsey offers three ways to measure pastoral care in sermons. First, how the preacher speaks of listeners as human beings: what does the sermon say about human nature and sin and human responsibility? Second, how the preacher speaks about what God provides: what does the sermon say about God's grace and human freedoms and limits? Third, how the preacher speaks about the church: what does the sermon say about the church as a pastoral community in the world? Ramsey uses this as a model for preachers for assessing the pastoral effectiveness of sermons.[25]

As a result, the preacher's words may often be quite intimate. Consider the last third of this sermon on Matthew 4:1-11, on the temptation of Christ:

> Innocence comes from Jesus Christ. It has already come for us. Our innocence dawned on that first Easter morning, in its radiant splendor, when God announced to the world: the power of death is broken. My love is ultimate. Our innocence washed over us in the waters of our baptism. Our innocence is the Spirit of Jesus Christ, who meets us in the stranger in the midst of the struggle, pain, joys, and temptations of daily life. Do not retreat from Christ by retreating from the world. He stands with his arms already enclosing you when the temptation to give up seems greatest. Even now, no one here is outside of God's love. No matter what you have done or what has been done to you, Christ gives you the power to walk the right path.

People are typically most loving when they experience themselves to be loved—it is not so much selfishness as human nature—so if you want your congregation to do something, love them into it.

Exegesis of Our Social Situation

In dealing with our world in the sermon, we have spoken of exegesis of the congregation and exegesis of the preacher, and now we turn to a third kind: exegesis of the wider social situation. Social situations require their own analysis on a frequent basis. One important way to do exegesis of our situation is through social analysis with a view to justice and ethical behavior. This is not something added to the gospel; it is part of it. Jesus preached about the kingdom or realm of God, the marks of which include justice, loving-kindness, and walking humbly with God (Micah 6:8). Jesus was committed to the poor, the sick, the homeless, and the needy. The only way Christians can ever ignore social justice is to retreat to a fractured view of the world.[26]

Because the facts need to be right—otherwise the preacher's ethos is in question—the preacher must read the newspapers, watch television, and stay informed. Situations must be described accurately. Don S. Browning calls this the descriptive task of theology: by examining the theory-laden practice of communities, questions arise that can then be addressed back to the biblical texts that shape the community.[27]

> ### Homiletical Method and Ethos
> 1. Pay attention to ethos throughout the sermon and particularly in the opening minutes.
> 2. Reflect conversations or attitudes of the congregation in preaching.
> 3. Present countering viewpoints to your own, particularly on controversial subjects.
> 4. Speak to the actual needs of the congregation.

Several writers help preachers gain a critical perspective of our situation. One way, says Christine M. Smith, is to name radical evil for what it is, seen for instance in what she calls handicappism, ageism, sexism, heterosexism, white racism, and classism. She proposes that preachers speak with people who suffer oppression such that they "*weep* and passionately feel," "*confess* the truth of the oppressions," and "evoke *resistance* and action."[28]

Charles L. Campbell is concerned that preachers take seriously the principalities and powers and the manner in which they penetrate social institutions, including the church.[29] He recommends asking of our individual churches, what do we resist? How have we accommodated ourselves to the powers that be? And how can we be more resistant and caring as a community?[30] All sermons have an ethical dimension and need to shape not only individuals but also communities of character.

Practical Matters

When we raise social justice or ethical issues in a sermon, we do not need to turn the whole sermon into an essay or a summary of facts and figures, the sort of exercise that may be part of a study program separate from worship. The goal is still to preach the gospel and to bring the good news precisely to those people in the worst kinds of situations. These issues can become part of the weekly vocabulary of preaching and thus part of the fabric of the congregation's conversations.

Some social data can be helpful to establish social realities, provided it is not overused; facts and figures can dehumanize the very people we want to treat with compassion by turning them into objects and numbers. One of the best ways to raise issues is to tell stories in the manner of Smith's own brief yet powerful reflection on the ageism shown to her dying uncle:

> I will never forget one visit. Several family members were present. He began to talk about dying, and each time he tried to speak someone quickly silenced him with reassurances that he was fine and that he would get better. This happened more than once, and finally he gave up trying to communicate to us his feelings about wanting to die. To this day I have regretted what happened there.[31]

By the end of the sermon, such situations should be addressed by the gospel such that God's help is named.

Strategies for Social Analysis

Too many sermons focus narrowly on the individual church, town, or region. Such focus encourages notions of a small God who is not concerned with all of humanity. William K. McElvaney says that the community for Christians is never the isolated community of family or circle of friends or even church. Rather, it is the global community, no part of God's creation excluded.[32]

Many pulpits focus only on the forgiveness of sins and the relationship of the individual soul to eternity. For Walter J. Burghardt, concern for the poor remains a head trip until it touches "the less fortunate images of Jesus, those who share far more of his crucifixion than of his resurrection."[33] He recommends that preaching employ four principles of social justice: (1) "A person is more precious for what he or she is than for what he or she has"; thus, we are to share rather than possess[34]; (2) we have a right only to as much of the earth's resources as we need "to live a human existence in union with God"[35]; (3) "The real presence of Christ [can be seen] in the unfortunate and underprivileged, in the impoverished and imprisoned, in the maimed and marginalized"[36]; and (4) community rather than isolationism.[37]

> Social analysis with a view to justice is not something added to the gospel; it is part of the gospel, something Jesus repeatedly demonstrated in his earthly ministry.

Arthur Van Seters recently devised an interconnected ethical web for preaching that stands as an excellent tool for ethical analysis. The web has Jesus Christ at the center. In relationship to an issue, a preacher asks, in turn, questions of faith (theology: how does this influence basic belief?), moral character (who are we called and enabled to be?), norms (God's requirements), situation and context (what are the particular details?), and authority (what guidance is given by Scripture, reason, tradition, and experience).[38]

One homiletician has drawn attention to preaching and disability. Kathy Black offers five excellent preaching guidelines: (1) avoid using disabilities as metaphors; instead, state clearly the intended message (for example, instead of "we are blind," say, "we do not understand who Jesus is"); (2) look at the situation of the person with the disability in the biblical text rather than focusing on the disability itself; (3) acknowledge the many cultural and social boundaries Jesus crossed in performing many of his healings; (4) emphasize the actions of the person with the disability in the text; (5) focus on the response of the crowds.[39]

Ronald J. Allen gives eighteen steps in preparation for topical preaching, but his approach is so balanced that it can serve as a model for responsible social or ethical analysis: (1) determine that the topic is of sufficient importance for the pulpit; (2) identify preassociations with the topic; (3) list everything you need to know about it; (4) search for biblical perspectives; (5) trace how the topic has been interpreted in the history of the church; (6) focus on two theologians on the topic; (7) bring out the denomination's position; (8) investigate other relevant dimensions of the topic; (9) inventory the congregation's experience with it; (10) imagine what it is like to be different persons in situations relative to the topic; (11) evaluate the topic theologically; (12) state your own position; (13) articulate viewpoints other than your own; (14) consider the mind-set and situation of the listeners; (15) locate the listeners in relation to your position on the

> ## Three Strategies for Social Exegesis
> 1. Smith: weep, confess, resist
> 2. Campbell: resistance as community character
> 3. McElvaney: awareness of the gospel's global claim
> 4. Burghardt: share resources equally
> 5. Van Seters: faith, moral character, norms, situation and context, authority
> 6. Black: honor people with disabilities
> 7. Allen: 18 steps for research

topic; (16) state what you want to say in the sermon; (17) decide what you hope will be the result of the listeners' hearing of the sermon; and (18) design the sermon so that it will have a good chance of accomplishing its purpose.[40]

In general, sermons do not have enough time to allow for detailed analysis of controversial issues. They are often best handled when the sermon relates to a study project in the church.

Student Assignment 10: Using one of the above strategies, do an exegesis of a social situation or issue relevant to preaching.

Practical Sources for Ethical Direction

A Caution in Preaching Social Justice

Much ethical and social justice preaching is of the "you do it" sort. Listeners are told what to do on their own resources: there is no help from God. Those who fail to do social justice are portrayed as lowly creatures when, in fact, they need the good news as much as anyone.

Ethical direction normally arises from the biblical text itself; it is what our preaching ancestors called the moral sense of Scripture. Ask of the text, what action is implied on the part of the hearer? Sometimes the action arises out of a principle like loving one's neighbor. Sometimes it arises out of imitating a practice observed in a text, for instance the faithfulness of the friends in carrying the paralytic to Jesus (Mark 2:1-12). Sometimes it arises out of God's actions because they have direct implication for human behavior, for instance God's generosity implies that we be generous to others.

Often the moral is to one side of a text; in other words, it is not in the primary direction of focus; this is the case with many of the difficult texts involving Jesus:

> Still, even in such [difficult] texts a moral can be discerned though not one involving direct imitation of Christ: Christ overturning the tables in the Temple (Mark 11:15-19) speaks of the need to avoid defiling the holy; his condemnation of the fig tree out of season (Mark 11:12-14) speaks to the urgent need for change; his command to tear out your own eye rather than sin (Matt. 5:29) speaks against judging others; his bringing of a sword and not peace (Matt. 10:34-36) speaks of full commitment to Christ; his rebuke of his mother (John 2:4) speaks against assuming that our agendas are God's; his delay for two days to respond to Lazarus's illness (John 11:6) speaks to the same thing; his condemnation of all the scribes and Pharisees (Matthew 23) speaks against presuming self-righteousness; his commending of the dishonest Steward (Luke 16:1-7) speaks of the need for Christ's followers to be shrewd; and his narrative treatment of the elder son (Luke 15:11-32) is a caution against works righteousness.[41]

A key guide can be this: the moral sense leads back to God, for the human action that God requires is the action God empowers. Social justice on its own is impotent and can seem like tedious ideology, a preacher playing politics. Social justice gains its power in preaching when set in relationship to God. Because God wills and empowers social justice, it will prevail. Preached this way there is a true sense of hope because God wills and equips people for their tasks.

Student Assignment 11: Identify in a sentence what is the moral sense of your text and write a paragraph that will help you employ it in your sermon.

Beginning to Compose the Sermon

Wednesday is a good day to start writing parts of the sermon. At the end of chapter 5, students were asked to choose two pairs of sentences to provide a possible structure for the sermon. There are other ways of proceeding, as we will see in chapter 8. (One does not always need to have the overall structure in mind in order to begin composing some parts of the sermon.) However, for purposes of discussing contemporary experience in the sermon, we may continue with the Isaiah example.

> Concern of the text: Isaiah was not good enough.

> Concern of the sermon: our world is not good enough.

> Major concern of the text: God gives Isaiah a new identity.

> Major concern of the sermon: God gives us a new identity (that is, in Christ).

Using these, one would deal with our world and thus experience when we deal with concerns of the sermon, namely, our world is not good enough (that is, trouble), and God gives us a new identity (that is, grace).

Below are a few examples of things to keep in mind when dealing with experience.

1. Develop situations and issues in ways that touch people where they are and mobilize them toward change rather than leave them frozen and immobilized by the immensity of the demand.

For example, when developing "our world is not good enough," a preacher might have occasion to tell people that "everything we buy goes back into the ground." This is to tell them the truth about pollution of the environment, but if left there it can create a sense of despair. The problem is too big. What can people do that will make any difference? The clue here may be to involve the congregation. For instance, help them see the positive consequences of even one small act of stewardship (like recycling bottles), repeated each day, starting with a few persons, working up to thousands, spreading across the nation, moving overseas over several years. Help them get a sense of the momentum of history and to remember also that human efforts on their own are never the whole story.

2. Enable social action by identifying what God is doing in relation to such situations. Listeners may be mobilized by injustice—they are not empowered by it. Thus later in the sermon, in dealing with "God gives us a new identity," we might speak of the ways God through the Spirit empowers change. Call upon God's resources. If using an emotionally difficult story in the first part of the sermon, an equally powerful good news story of God's action in the world is needed later to balance the sermon.

Example: the first half of a sermon I heard contained an account of a woman in a Nazi prison camp. It was a powerful story, a horrific account of the reality of human sin. Specific details of violence were mercifully and necessarily omitted. (There is no place in any sermon for details of violence; the barest facts are enough to bring terrible pictures to mind.) By the end of the sermon, however, listeners had still not encountered God doing anything active, which might leave the impression that God is not more powerful than the worst of human deeds. Such a story cannot be used unless one has something of equal or greater emotional and theological force to counter it.

3. If one lacks a strong story of good news to achieve the necessary counterbalance, as required, one may develop an idea with sufficient rhetorical passion and detail to provide the necessary balance.

In a sermon on John 12:9-21, Jesus entering Jerusalem to die on the cross, someone might choose as a major concern of the text "Christ opts for God's power," and the transposed major concern of the sermon might be "Christ rules in love." It is a good idea but it needs development and focus to become an event listeners can experience today. Here is one attempt to develop it; because it is a major concern of the sermon, that is, it is about experience today, no attempt is made to follow the text (that would have been done immediately prior to this when dealing with the major concern of the text):

> If Christ's love had nothing to do with us, it would be
> simply another abstract idea to stretch our minds
> around. There would be no power in his love to deal
> with all the sin and broken relations in the world. But
> this rule of Christ is personal, intimate, and caring. It is
> not something we need to read about in the morning
> paper or wait for the evening news to see. We may not
> have known Christ when we came here, but we may
> know Christ as we leave. Even in this brief time
> together, Christ has reestablished a relationship with
> you. When you leave the doors of this church today,
> you cannot leave him behind, for he is going ahead of
> you, and with you. There are no doors you will enter
> this week that he will not already have entered. There
> is no trouble you can get into that will keep him away.
> Our ruler is a close relative of ours. If God is his daddy
> (he called him Abba) and we are God's children, then

Christ is our brother, our sister, our closest of relatives,
and we are all one tight family. He is not a distant relative, like some cousin you see every few years, if it is
convenient, if you do not have to go out of your way.
Christ is the resurrected ruler who is ever present, in
the power of the Holy Spirit, when the sun is setting, in
the middle of the night, and in the blaze of the morning
light, still overcoming death, still seeing love through.

4. Create a sense of excitement about the wonderful things God will do
this week, both with and without human help. Hear the closing moments
of a sermon of the great Scottish preacher James S. Stewart:

It is true that he is here in this church at this moment,
and that if only we were not fast held behind the gates
of sense and flesh we should actually see Him here, face
to face, now. It is true that He can take our lives and
interpenetrate them with his own, to enable us to say, "I
live, yet not I, but Christ liveth in me." It is true that
one day we are going to see Him face to face without
any veil at all.

These things are true. And you believe them. But today
I am begging you not only to believe them—but to
imagine them, to visualize them, to see them, and to act
on the basis of them. For it is as we let the shining,
supercharged truth of them get hold of us, really take
possession of us, that like Simeon we shall meet Christ
reborn for us this Advent time.

And then? Why then, what does it matter whether life
be long or short? If it is to be a long day's strenuous
march, what joy, O Christ, to have Thy blessed com-
panionship all the way! If it is to be a brief moment and
a sudden call—"Lord, now lettest Thou Thy servant
depart in peace, for mine eyes have seen thy
salvation."[42]

We now turn in the next chapter to consider in more detailed ways the
important topic of the preacher's use of stories, images, and experiences.

CHAPTER SEVEN

THE USE OF STORIES, IMAGES, AND EXPERIENCES

Preachers are storytellers. Not only do they tell stories, but story-telling is an essential medium for preaching. People normally converse in story, and preaching strives to be conversational. Preachers tell Bible stories to bring them to life; even nonnarrative texts are more vital when portrayed through narrative and situated within a real-life setting. Preachers also tell stories from experience in order to bring the joys and struggles of life before the Word of God and find in the shadow of the cross the new creation breaking into their midst. Stories entertain, generate humor, cause people to feel, actually generate experience in the preaching moment, and bear salvation.

One objective of preachers can be to make a movie with words. David Buttrick has spoken of a field of consciousness coming into focus as in a camera,[1] yet the idea of motion pictures may even more readily communicate what the preacher is after. Others speak of the sermon proceeding in episodes, or vignettes. All of these are encouragements not to think of the sermon as static but dynamic, organic, having a life of its own. Compose it visually and aurally, offering something for the eyes to see and the ears to hear. It is advisable to present drama, as life itself is dramatic, and to offer humor and sorrow, echoing daily life. Show people doing things in life situations, whether talking about the text or about our situation, and you will be making movies. All in all, one needs to use stories, images, and experience to help communicate the gospel.

Telling the Truth

Excellent preachers re-create biblical stories or current events; they do not just report. Movie directors make essential decisions about all manner of things. The first thing listeners need in a story is where and who. Every new scene needs to be located immediately and its characters need to be shown in that setting. Suppose a preacher begins, "Sarah did not know which way to turn. She swung hard to the left and then to the right." In order to visualize, listeners depend solely on the speaker, and here they have no way to know if Sarah is on a swing, in a car or boat, or on a dance floor, much less whether she is five years old or ninety-five.

Of next importance is the principle of people doing things, so get to the action quickly. Long descriptions of a rising sun may work well in novels, but the narrative technique of preachers needs to be compressed. Bible accounts do not give all the details necessary to make a movie (for example, details about clothes, weather, or time of day) and the preacher must nonetheless make decisions based on research as much as possible, not pull things from midair. Creative license must never alter the heart of the text, making it say something else. For instance, if a preacher makes up a character, say a witness of the woman anointing Jesus with nard at Bethany (Mark 14:3), the text will be altered. The focus is in danger of shifting to the new narrator and away from the significance of what is happening between Jesus and the woman; she is anointing him for his death on the cross. Or to take another example, a preacher contemplated reflecting on her own experience of childbirth as a way of telling Mary's story in giving birth to Jesus. Whatever value this might have for the congregation, this makes the preacher of primary focus; Mary becomes of secondary focus, and Jesus gets third in line.

The preacher must never lie, claim something as fact that is fictional, say that something was a personal experience that was not, or disclose something that was told in confidence. At the same time, for legitimate pastoral reasons, preachers sometimes need to alter the details of a story (names, location, gender, age, and so on) in order to protect confidentiality or to be able to communicate experience effectively, pastorally, and confidentially.

Some fictionalizing is necessary, but it must always be in the service of truth. If asked about it later, the preacher must be able to say that the account is true but that details were altered for pastoral reasons. Humorist Garrison Keillor likes to tell the audience that he makes his living telling lies, but anyone who listens carefully knows he more frequently tells the truth. Theologian Julian N. Hartt says with appropriate subtlety and nuance: "A story may be truthful, that is authentic, whether or not it is factually accurate. Which is to say it may square with our perceptions and value structures even though it may be faulted by our memories or by some public instrument for ascertaining the facts."[2] Elizabeth Achtemeier is close to the heart of the matter in observing in *Preaching as Theology and Art* that "art allows the one seeing or hearing it to enter into a new experience . . . to participate in reality a new way."[3]

Plot and Characters

Stories carry theological implications for how people are to behave and believe. Stories need plot and characters. The number of basic "plots" in experience that touch people deeply are probably few in number. Most tragic stories have a plot that contains abandonment, betrayal, oppression, defeat, loss, injury, or illness. Most joyful stories, by contrast, have plots of courage, reconciliation, justice, accomplishment, discovery, healing, or recovery.

Plot and character in stories are related. People tend to think of plot as a series of events that happen to characters; that is a fairly static notion that informs "B" movies. Creative writers know that most plots, "can, do, and should evolve according to the qualities of their chief characters, the battles they face with reality, their responses."[4] That is why writer Anne Lamott humorously says that plot is "what people will up and do in spite of everything that tells them they shouldn't."[5] In fact, contrary to Aristotle, who held a static notion of character, plot is the result of character, not the other way around.[6]

Plot is the necessary outcome of some conflict within a character. It is this inner conflict that gives the verisimilitude preachers are after. Verisimilitude is the lifelike imitation of real life in art. Resist portraying any character in a sermon as a romantic ideal. The story of an ideal mother who never spoke an angry word in her life is generally less authentic and believable than the story of a mother in whom duty and longing occasionally conflict.

William Foster-Harris, a gifted teacher of creative writing during the 1940s, taught the value of contradiction in character portrayal (though for obvious reasons we would never do this with Jesus):

Do not hesitate for an instant to give your hero or heroine ... impulses to evil. ... For these dark powers, fused with their opposites—the will to good, the moral impulses, the powers of the spirit—make your central character. The real purpose of the story is to test the fused contradictions which we cannot see but know to exist.[7]

The conflict arises within a character, and the plot becomes its resolution. Biblical characters typically have conflict. The story of Abraham and Isaac, when told from Abraham's perspective, might be interpreted as the tension of piety versus parental love.[8] A good preacher will try to make that conflict evident. Listeners can discover a character's values, emotions, and motives through the action or through conversation.[9] Trust stories to say what they mean and listeners to get the point of stories on their own. Stories make points in their own ways. Simply supply sufficient interpretative material immediately before or after telling a story to link it to the theme. Usually, only one sentence is needed for this link. For example, a link to a story might be, "A single parent recently experienced the truth of this." Or a link back to the theme after a story might be, "She discovered the truth of what we have been saying: that God...."

> **Before or after telling a story in a sermon, link it usually with just one sentence to what came before or what follows.**

How to Tell a Story

Foster-Harris made the following recommendations for telling a story that preachers can keep in mind: (a) set the situation and characters in place with no flashbacks until the action is well under way, making sure that you start with action having already happened. (Focus on the events in your text and get the scene developed before filling in with events that occurred earlier.) (b) Develop some complication at the beginning arising from internal conflict that shows in the character's decisions and actions. Do not dwell on the emotions; show them in actions or appearance and create them, don't discuss them. (Focus on the developing conflict in your characters or in the reader as one reads about them.) (c) Move to a crisis in which the character makes a decision the way he or she always has, that is, for the good or for the bad. (d) Conclude with a climax or an answer or reward.[10]

Anne Lamott gives a similar formula for writing a story, which works well for preachers. Her formula is, "ABDCE, for Action, Background, Development, Climax and Ending."[11] (It is easy to miss noting that D and C are reversed in her sequence.) Even though preachers are normally just writing short vignettes, her ABDCE formula can be an excellent guide.

Using Stories Theologically

Stories can be categorized theologically as either trouble or grace. Whether or not a story is an explicitly religious story is not the issue; the preacher makes a story religious by telling it from the perspective of either trouble or grace. A story is trouble if it is bad news: the actions are sin, brokenness, or suffering. A story is grace if the preacher interprets God to be in the story providing the help that is needed. How stories can be used in the sermon depends on how they can function from a theological perspective. Stories need to be classified theologically, though not by doctrine, for that is often too restrictive. The categories that we identified as categories for concerns of the sermon automatically apply to stories in our world. Stories can serve as theological metaphors of:

TROUBLE
  1. God judging/commanding us
  2. The human condition after the fall/the old order
  3. God suffering (Christ's ongoing crucifixion in the world)
GRACE
  1. God forgiving/atonement
  2. God overturning the powers, principalities, and old norms
  3. God acting through people/the new creation

If one sees a story in daily experience, one should record it immediately. If one wants to discover how it might be used in a sermon, test the story from the perspective of each of these six categories; for example, one might ask, is this a story that demonstrates the kind of forgiveness we find in God, or is this a story that shows what it looks like when God suffers? The same story may be able to be told from different perspectives, thus which one is chosen will depend on the individual sermon. Each of the latter three categories in the list above can be linked to the cross; that is, the cross has obvious and important connections to each of the atonement, God in Christ overturning the powers of death, and the promise of the new creation.

> Test a story from the perspective of each of the six theological categories; for example, one might ask, is this a story that demonstrates the kind of forgiveness we find in God, or is this a story that shows what it looks like when God suffers? The same story may be able to be told from different perspectives.

Filing Stories

Preachers generally have no shortage of potential stories for homiletical use, but they do not know it because they cannot find them when they want them. When it comes to composing a sermon, stories often seem in short supply. Preachers suffer not from a shortage of stories but from an inability to see them when they happen, to isolate them from daily experience, or to harvest them when needed and to use them with theological effectiveness.

One answer to this inability to find appropriate stories when one needs them is to record stories and file them. Some preachers file stories by subject matter: mothers, fathers, children, work, play, summer, food, home, knitting, baseball—you know the list and the categories are unending. No wonder they cannot be found when needed. "Did I file it under dessert, Christmas, clothes, or teenager?" Preachers are theologians, therefore it makes sense to file stories using theology. One could do this by doctrines: creation, baptism, sanctification, communion—but again, the list goes on and on; precious time is wasted looking for what cannot be found.

It is simpler to organize according to trouble and grace. If you do not like filing, use only two categories: trouble and grace. Keep a journal of stories you read, hear, or see, but be sure to write in it. Barbara Lundblad says, "[I take] a notebook with me everywhere. I write things down so I'll remember things I'm sure I'll never forget!"[12] Such a simple (I hesitate to use the term *filing*) system also requires that one read it to find stories. By knowing the six potential theological functions of stories, they actually become easier to use in the sermon: you know how they might fit. To repeat, the same story might be told in different ways to meet different theological purposes. For instance, the story of a bully at school being shunned could be told as a metaphor or image of God's judgment, much in the manner that Jesus told of the plight of the rich man who ignored Lazarus on his doorstep (Luke 16:19-31). Alternatively, and perhaps better, it could be told as a metaphor of the human condition, the aloneness that results when we cut ourselves off from God and others.

Almost none of a preacher's grace stories are of the happily-ever-after variety. Try to avoid preaching fairy tales or stories with fairy-tale endings; as one of my professors once humorously said, "The Holy Spirit is not Casper the friendly ghost."[13] Christianity is not about making everything nice or tidy. For instance, one might conceivably tell a story of several youths out on a boat late at night when a storm comes up. Their families are worried and send for help. The youths see lights on the shore and make it to safety. Whatever power this story might have if properly told (it needs more detail) is lost if the purpose of telling it is to say simply that God is good. Listeners then ask, "Why wasn't God good when my friend drowned?" Such a story, if it is to be used, needs to be told to include the worst-case scenario. Thus a preacher could conclude: "What if safety had not been found? Even then, we know in faith that there is a love stronger even than death and someone stands on a distant shore inviting safe harbor, from whose love no one can be lost."

Do Stories Need to Be Explicitly Religious?

Preachers need not look for stories that are explicitly religious. If all our stories are mainly about religious people, God's relevance for the rest of humanity is diminished. Surprising as it may be, it does not matter whether the people in the story are Christian or even recognize God. What matters is that the preacher name God where God is seen and find the gospel in the midst of daily life.

Nor do preachers need to look only for stories with positive endings. Thomas G. Long gave an account from an August Wilson play, a heart-wrenching story of racial humiliation that ends with a prayer of desperation: "Where the hell is God? Come down, O God! Let justice roll down like the waters. Save us, O God! Come, quickly, Lord Jesus!" Long takes this plea to his biblical text concerning the wrath of God, and, in effect, turns it around such that the words of the characters echo God's own anger: "The problem," says Long, "with our understanding of the wrath of God is not that we have made too much of it, but precisely that we have made too little of it."[14] The story now functions as an image or metaphor of God's judgment, a mark of the old age that is put to death with Jesus on the cross.

Begin in the Middle

In telling any story, start with the action having already begun, the technical term for which is *in medias res*, Latin for "into the middle of things." Leading with the title of the movie or book can diminish attention. Instead, just begin your excerpt as though it is real life:

> Hard-hearted, fast-living Charlie was watching his Lamborghini business in Los Angeles go down the tubes when he received news that his father had died in Ohio. He flew there expecting to inherit the large estate, only to discover that he had a brother, Raymond, who had been living in institutional care all these years. Raymond had inherited the wealth.
>
> Charlie had no love for Raymond. He only took him on his trip back to Los Angeles to try to keep a hand on the wealth. But something happened along the way. We don't know whether it was that Raymond wouldn't fly or that he had to stop at exact intervals for cheese balls and apple juice snacks or that he would only wear K-Mart underwear. We don't know if it was because they had to stay in a motel an extra day since Raymond, the Rain Man, wouldn't go out in the rain. Whatever it was, it became apparent as they were driving across the Nevada desert, the sunset a blazing orange. Music was being sung a cappella in the background: "The hip bone

connected to the thigh bone / The thigh bone connected to the knee bone / The knee bone connected to
…"—and we knew before we got to the end of the song
that it could only be the work of the Lord. For it was
not just bone connected to bone, it was blood connected to blood and flesh connected to flesh and
brother connected to brother. "Now hear the name of
the Lord!"[15]

Conflict:	Charlie's greed versus his need for love.
Plot:	Reconciliation
Metaphor:	God acting through Raymond, a sign of the new creation
Theme of the sermon:	God heals relationships. "This morning, we had pancakes."

Finding Stories, Images, and Experiences in Real Life

In former days, big pulpit preachers had researchers who combed newspapers and books looking for illustrations on assigned topics. Perhaps
when sermons were mechanical, it was easier to insert such stories.
Nowadays, sermons tend to be more organic, and stories of experience are
often more valued. Sometimes stories come as one goes about chores.
Barbara Brown Taylor calls this her time of "'checking the nest.' During
this phase, I go about my business and let the sermon ideas incubate,
coming back periodically to see if an egg has appeared."[16]

Three common sources for stories about contemporary experience are
available to the preacher, and these are stories from personal life, the arts,
and the news.

Personal Stories

Personal stories afford intimate glimpses of people's lives, revealing
something beneath surface appearance. These stories may be about anyone, and they may be about the preacher from time to time, but they are
more properly centered on others. More than one story about a preacher's
own life in, say, every two sermons is often unwise, for listeners can be
very quick to assess "it's all about the preacher." Some preachers try to get
around this by telling a personal story as if it happened to someone else
("A friend of mine told me of an encounter he had. . . .") It is a feeble ploy

and most congregations have heard it enough to see through it. A better technique can be to drop unnecessary references to "I" and become an invisible narrator. Are you really crucial to the story, or is your relationship to it peripheral? Do you really need to say, "I once knew a woman in her eighties. ..." or would the story be hurt by simply saying, "A woman in her eighties ..."? Barbara Brown Taylor cautions that stories about the self may involve voyeurism, making the congregation more interested in the preacher's life than the biblical text. "My rule is to refrain from using 'I' material unless I think that my listeners can say 'me too.'"[17]

When one does tell an "I" story, spend a sentence shifting the attention back to the congregation (for example, "But we have all had similar experiences.") By deliberately moving the focus back to the people, a preacher may bring to a conscious level of awareness an experience in the mind of the listener, and the true purpose in telling the story is thus fulfilled: their experience is what matters. Richard L. Thulin provided excellent suggestions for appropriate use of autobiography in *The "I" of the Sermon* (Fortress Press, 1989).

The typical reason that preachers tell stories about themselves ought to be to deepen relationships with the congregation. Thus stories of the self ought to demonstrate some common human weakness (not a vice, and similarly not a strength or virtue that sets the preacher in a glowing light right next to Jesus). Avoid private stories of the sort one tells only a counselor or intimate friend, as well as any story that might damage the office of preacher. If ever you have any doubt about the suitability of a story, do not use it.

Susan May told the following story effectively in a sermon on God's love. She tells about a morning in which everything had gone wrong, from waking late to the children arguing over breakfast, until suddenly she broke. In terms of our discussion here, her daughter's action stands as a metaphor or image of Christ's action:

> I don't remember now whether it was that one more trip to the bathroom, or the spilled cup of juice, or the lunch box that broke open at the last minute. Something pushed me past the breaking point, and I began to yell. I yelled and screamed. Me, a college-educated, sophisticated, civilized, mature, training-for-effective-parenting me.
>
> I was horrified and embarrassed, completely aware that I was making a fool of myself. But I couldn't stop. Until my daughter came across the room, put her hand on my arm, and said, "Mom, maybe you forgot that we love you."[18]

Conflict:	Good versus stressed parent
Plot:	Losing control
Metaphor:	Christ acting through the daughter, a sign of the new creation.
Possible theme of the sermon:	God loves you.

In neither this case, nor the next, is there any question of the preacher's well-being in the pulpit as the story is related, for instance as may happen at a more obvious level if a preacher breaks into weeping. When there is such a question, it draws attention away from the Word, so that the preacher, not the congregation, becomes the object of pastoral focus. The pulpit is simply not the proper setting for this kind of self-focus.

Peter Vaught preached on the red dragon of Revelation 12:1-6, which represents the force of evil. He tells powerful and sad stories of the dragon in his childhood. They are important stories to hear, for, as he says, the vast majority of families are dysfunctional. People in the pews are dealing with similar stories of alcoholism, physical or sexual abuse, and neglect. He is explicit in using his story for mission purpose. One brief excerpt must suffice:

> I hope you came from a family where Mom and Dad did look out for you. I hope you came from a family where you were cared for and loved and protected. If you did, you were lucky.
>
> Most of the people I will come in contact with in my life were not so lucky. One of the most ugly faces of this mess is that most of the people I meet—people who have been raised in homes that did not work the way they were supposed to—have the biggest chance of doing the very same thing all over again to the people they love. Friends, the red dragon is a frightening face of evil.
>
> Both of my parents are dead now. I received an inheritance from them. I have inherited feelings of being responsible for everything that happens. I have inherited not trusting my feelings. I have inherited not trusting others. This is the legacy my parents have given me. My mom and dad were not evil. They were weak like the rest of us. They were misinformed about many things. Like the rest of us. The dragon was there knocking at the door.[19]

Vaught continued his sermon with a discussion of God saving the woman giving birth from the red dragon in Revelation. He ends with his own vision, a dream in which his dad calls him to the center of a family gathering to tell him of his love. His last line: "With this dream of rec-onciliation and peace, God brought this child out of the reach of the red dragon."[20]

Conflict:	Understanding of parents versus anger at them
Plot:	Betrayal
Metaphor:	The human condition, or God overturning suffering in the New Age of the cross
Theme of the sermon:	God disposes of the dragon.

Vaught demonstrates what can be a very important homiletical rule: he shows compassion for even the worst person he mentions. Whether this person (or group) is in a story that we tell or in the biblical text, always empathize with the worst person. This means "try to understand, try to empathize" not "try to sympathize, condone the actions." Someone in the congregation will always identify with that person, and that person needs God's love. Whenever a preacher dismisses anyone as unworthy of God's love, others are unintentionally dismissed as well.

The Arts

The arts include novels, poems, paintings, photographs, sculpture, architecture, dance, drama, movies, concerts, and the like.[21] Preachers do not need to live in large cultural centers to have access to art. Art is a part of every community; books of art can be found in every public library, and art reviews are given in newspapers, journals, and on television. The Internet provides excellent access, and we will discuss in the next chap-ter possible uses of art using technology in sermons. Here we concentrate on representing art only in words in the sermon.

There has been considerable conversation about the respective values of using stories from "high" versus "popular" art. Some people insist that if substantial numbers of folks in the congregation have not had some exposure to the work of art in question, then using it in a sermon bears less fruit than if it is something with which they are familiar. This is a good point. Unfortunately, it cuts out a great deal of religious art that can be of service in the pulpit. Moreover, preachers cannot safely assume with even popular art that it is known by everyone present. The rule with any work of art can be that the preacher's words must so re-create the work of art before the congregation; it is as though they are looking at the work, seeing it in front of their eyes. (The same principle applies in dealing with a biblical text: represent it before commenting on it.)

Preachers tell stories from the arts for at least three reasons. First, artists are good sources for stories. Second, art gives another person's perception of reality. Third, art and the news can help bind communities.

Preachers contemplating art are like journalists on the prowl, looking for a fresh angle. They may find their story:

In the artwork itself. Robert P. Waznak, in a Christmas homily, related a story by Truman Capote of a boy named Buddy (Capote himself) and his best friend, a woman in her sixties who lives with the family. On Christmas they are most pleased with the two kites they give each other as presents. They rush outside to fly them, and the woman ends up surveying the countryside and Buddy, and saying:

> My how foolish I am! You know what I've always thought? I've always thought a body would have to be sick and dying before they saw the Lord. And I imagined that when He came it would be like looking at a Baptist window: pretty as colored glass with the sun pouring through ... such a shine you don't know it's getting dark. And it's been a comfort to me to think of that shine—taking away all the spooky feeling. But I'll wager it never happens. I'll wager at the very end a body realizes the Lord has already shown Himself.... As for me, I could leave the world with today in my eyes.[22]

In the events that took place around the artwork. Mary Donovan Turner preached about Peter's need to speak his faith (Acts 4). She hinged her sermon on a few words she heard on National Public Radio; an author of a book on five famous musicians was asked if there was a message for his readers, to which he replied, "Don't die; don't die with your music still inside you."[23] The implication is that singing our faith is important; it is already the new creation in our midst, brought about even as we preach the cross. Charles L. Rice preached a sermon that was as much about the people around him in the movie theater as it was about the people in the movie, *Ordinary People.*

> Sitting next to us were two young people, fashionably dressed—in fact, downright chic. They supplied a second sound track; it was like seeing two movies, one on the screen and one filtered through their eyes.... "Boy, look at those cars, color coordinated brown and black. And all that loot!" In another scene.... "Look at those pants ..." And so it went. All the superficial stuff was the story for my neighbors, as if this

successful lawyer and his two-years grieving wife and his sleepless lean
son had it made.... But they need God.[24]

Treat Art as Though It Is Real Life

Art needs to be treated as though it is real life. Remember, a preacher
can usually only fruitfully make use of one episode or small aspect of plot
or subplot. I once attended a church where the minister would tell the
entire plot of a new movie the week it was released. The result was that
seeing the movie was spoiled, not enhanced, so some people were placed
in the awkward position of trying to beat the preacher to the movie theater. Steven Spielberg's Academy Award–winning movie *Schindler's List*
could conceivably be used in a sermon by focusing on shades of the color
red. As the color of the opening scene fades to black and white, pink is
the last color of the dying flame of the Sabbath candle. Red becomes the
color of righteousness, the only color we see in a black-and-white movie.
The little girl in the red coat is seen in the streets, then from above as
Schindler watches in horror the massacre in the ghetto, then hiding
under the bed. When the corpses are dug up, we glimpse the red coat
wheeled by on a cart. Like a symbol of God in the movie, the color could
not quite be snuffed out. And by the end of the movie, thanks largely to
Schindler's efforts, many survivors of the Holocaust, dressed in brilliant
colors against a summer sky, place stones on Schindler's monument.[25]

The same treat-as-though-real-life principle can be followed for a photograph. I remember a black-and-white photograph of the interior of the
Chartres Cathedral, on exhibit in Pittsburgh some years ago. It was taken
by Eugene Smith, the photographer who covered World War II for *Life*
magazine.

Some of you may know that during World War II Chartres Cathedral
in France was converted to a hospital ward. Now, if a church has to be
converted to something else, a hospital is a good choice. I saw a photograph of it recently. There were no pews. Instead there were cots, rows
and rows of cots, on either side of the central aisle. You could almost hear
the quick, echoing footsteps of the smartly starched nurse, in apparent
haste as she passed one of the stone pillars. In the foreground, set apart
from the other patients, was a lone soldier, lying on a lone cot, with his
head wrapped in cotton bandages. Just above his head, if he had been able
to see, he would have seen the fresh roll of bandages that had been placed
in the big dry well of the stone baptismal font. The amazing thing about

this picture is that the soldier may not have even known from where his healing was coming.

Conflict:	A church versus a hospital
Plot:	Healing
Metaphor:	God overturns the world, the new age is begun in Christ.
Central idea of the sermon:	God is the healer.

In recalling architecture, or other art, where the story may not jump out (as it does in some photographs), one can imagine the artist who created the work. Ask yourself, what would I have to be feeling to create this (that is, what might have just happened to the artist)? Who would respond well to this? How would this make different people feel (for example, someone without a friend, someone hungry, someone ill)? The story can be the response of people to the art, as we find increasingly with reader-response criticism.

The News

Too often sermons portray a small God. If preachers portray God acting only with regard to the local church, region, or even nation, they portray a small God, too small to be of help to most Christians who watch news or work or travel in the world and are concerned for it. A small God encourages small faith. If God is not interested in the suffering of a woman whose family was killed in a flood in India, how may a listener trust that same God to be concerned about matters close to home?

Preachers may look for a balanced range of experience of men and women; young and old; rich and poor; black, red, yellow, and white. For the fullest range, sermons ought to have stories in each of these categories: *personal, local, church,* and *world.* Perhaps a single sermon would not have each of these, but by every second sermon each can be covered. God's love knows no national borders; thus, preachers lean into the pain of the world and discover a grace, says William K. McElvaney, "that restores us as we are 'restoried' in the larger vision and work of God."[26] By taking preaching onto the global stage, preachers disclose the largeness of God's mercy and, amazingly, new ways to sing God's praise.

A preacher not long ago said that he had stopped reading the newspaper and had sold his television in adopting a simpler lifestyle. His actions may themselves be a luxury preachers can ill afford. What Barth told preachers needs updating: have the Bible in one hand, the newspaper in the other, and the television on in the background. The lives of our congregation members are shaped by media. Their thinking is affected by media. Their topics of discussion are, in part, provided by media.

In addition to reading the local newspapers, try at least once a week to read a leading newspaper online, such as the *New York Times* or *The Times* of London, partly because high quality reporting can be a source of excellent stories. The Reverend Fleming Routledge demonstrates this superbly with her own book of excellent sermons, *The Bible and the New York Times* (Grand Rapids, Mich.: Eerdmans, 1998).

Stories used from newspapers and television news should include a short direct quotation from someone involved in order to bring the story to life. In general, avoid extended dialogue; it is too difficult. Besides, for the length of stories in a sermon, short quotations are all that is needed. It might be the son's words as he left home; or the mother's words when asked about loss of the village's drinking water; or the child's words about the coming of the soldiers. Build the story around that person's actual words. Here is an example:

> CBS evening news ran a clip on Mike and Giona
> Sullivan. He is a physician, and she is a pharmacist.
> They gave up wealth and financial security and bought
> a mobile home, not for holidays, but to help poor
> Americans in the rural areas of Maryland and
> Pennsylvania, people who have no medical insurance
> and either from shame or lack of means will not seek
> medical help from normal channels. The two of them
> see as many as ninety patients a day, and everything
> they provide, from examinations to medical tests to pre-
> scriptions, is free. One of the patients said: "It's all love,
> it's just love." The Sullivans are devout Roman
> Catholics and believe that God has called them to this
> ministry. They have the words Mission of Mercy written
> in big letters across the front of their mobile medical
> clinic. Giona says, "We gave up financial security for
> this. But I wouldn't trade this for anything." We may
> not all be called the same way, but such are the words
> that spring from our mouths when [we] let Jesus guide
> our lives.[27]

Often the last line that a preacher uses for a story will be the most important, something that perhaps links the story to the life of Jesus or back to the biblical text at hand.

Things to Avoid

The goal in using stories from the news is to hold up individuals near and far as God's loved ones, to interpret their situations in light of the gospel, to help listeners recognize God in the midst of even the worst situations, and to preach so that the new creation is ushered in through our words. The purpose is not to turn the sermon into a terrible newscast or a social-justice tirade. In fact, one of the best ways of raising social justice or ethical issues in preaching is by telling a story of someone involved. Such stories involve the congregation at a personal level and tend to side-step barriers listeners might have set in place. Again, the preacher should avoid going into any detail about violence beyond the facts of it. Similarly, avoid repeating details of a story the people already know too well. Nonetheless, be like a reporter looking for a fresh angle and human interest. Use empathetic imagination (or what I call a horizontal treatment of trouble) rather than tell the story in judgmental ways (a vertical treatment of trouble), and thus allow the congregation to feel something of what might be the suffering or joy of others.[28]

Stories from the Global Stage

Here are two brief examples, along with one longer one, all from the international stage. In the first, I create an image or metaphor of God's judgment from the crushing of the democracy movement in Tiananmen Square, Beijing, China, on June 4, 1989:

> One scene from the carnage in Tiananmen Square may never be erased from the minds of those who watched its many replays on television. We only had to see it once to remember it. It was as though we were there. As far as one could see on this vast open square, there were thousands of people who had been supporting democracy. The army was holding them back, making a kind of street for a row of rolling military tanks. As we watched, suddenly a man in a white shirt broke loose from the crowd and ran directly into the path of an oncoming tank and stood there. We watched in horror, sure that as in other reported instances, the tank would

crush him. But in this case the tank first slowed, then stopped. The man still stood there. His head was moving back and forth. We could not hear him. But we knew he was saying something and we knew what he was saying. He was saying the only words he could be saying, "Not by might, nor by power, but by my Spirit, says the Lord!"

The scene does not have to be dramatic, however, as in this metaphor of Christ's suffering:

> It is the same kind of wonderful faith that was shown by Mary Robinson, the president of the Republic of Ireland. She was the first head of state of a Western country to visit Somalia. She was deeply, profoundly moved by what she saw. "I smelt, felt, touched the suffering. In Ireland we still carry with us the memory of starvation in the 1800s. I found it unacceptable as a mother to see other mothers having their children die beside them. I feel ashamed for our humanity. I feel ashamed as a European head of state. I am personally shamed and offended to sit with women and watch children die. What does it do to us as humans to have this going on?" She said on the *MacNeil/Lehrer Report* that she is on a crusade in faith that things can be different. She is calling for people to be committed and angry and determined to change a world order in which men have too often been found to leave a legacy of war and destruction.

Splitting Stories

Finally, this example can show how a story from the news may be split—the first portion being told in the first portion of the sermon as a metaphor of life as we experience it with one foot in the old creation, and the second portion as the conclusion to the sermon and as a metaphor of God's love:

In the first half of the sermon:

> How quickly we move from Easter. You could probably each tell a tale of the thief sneaking into the sheepfold.

Maybe for you it was a story like Serbian civilian target-
ing in Bosnia. The television news showed a mother in
a babushka and old winter coat arriving at a hospital
with her younger son in tow. They had managed to
arrive safely. She was probably around thirty, but her
hollow eyes, which said she had seen the worst, made
her look sixty. She had heard that her other son might
still be alive, although he had not come home for two
days. Sitting in blue flannel pajamas in one of the beds,
a bandage wrapped around his head, both eyes now possibly forever blind, sat her son Sayad. "Sayad," she
called from the doorway. "Where have you been?" he
said in response, his head turning only approximately in
her direction. He was not quite sure that he could again
trust that she was there, there for him. "Where have
you been?"

That may be our question of Jesus, these past weeks.
"Where have you been? You said you were the good
shepherd who would keep us safe from the thief." All of
the suffering is enough to make one want to rage
against the world, to push the resurrection far away, to
shut out hope that seems too foolish, impotent, and
weak to make a difference in a world awash with
despair.

Toward the end of the sermon:

If this morning we could gather around young blind
Sayad's bed in Bosnia, as in fact we do this moment in
prayer, we would pray with him in the power of the
Holy Spirit. We do not know by what name he or his
family know God. But we do know that the One we
know as Christ was present in Sayad's mother and
brother coming to him when he asked, "Where have
you been?" And we know that Christ was present even
when Sayad thought he was alone. Christ continues to
suffer, but a new age is dawned in Christ, and all the
power of eternity will bring good out of evil, and justice
even out of the pain in your life. And we also know
that on this day, when we name people in prayer,

ourselves or others like Sayad, that by the power of the
Holy Spirit the risen Christ will attend to their needs,
whether or not they recognize who it is that ministers
to them.

We have been talking about using stories and images from experience.
We have shown various sources of stories for preachers and how these stories may be used to theological advantage in service of the gospel. We
now turn to issues of overall sermon form. Once sermon composition is
underway, form becomes an issue.

Student Assignment 12: Using some of the above principles, write a portion of your sermon. For instance,
write about the biblical text using a concern of the text
or the major concern of the text to guide the paragraphs
or page you compose. You may also start to connect
with some experiences using a concern of the sermon to
guide your writing. This is a rough draft so expect to
refine it later, but it is good to get something down now
on the page.

For Further Reflection and Study Concerning Wednesday

1. In this section, we examined exegesis of today's world. In light of
exegesis of the congregation, what are the benefits and drawbacks of a
congregation being diverse or all the same? Which would you prefer?

2. To what group(s) do you expect you may feel greatest resistance in
ministry? Through the sermon how might you demonstrate care for those
people without overcompensating?

3. Ethos is said to change according to the subject a speaker discusses.
Do you think people will respond to you in different ways throughout
your sermon?

4. Ought sermons to raise social justice issues? Why? What guidelines
would you suggest to help preachers in doing so?

5. Are trouble and grace adequate to categorize stories or might something else work better as a way of filing?

6. A preacher takes a risk in claiming some action to be a sign of God. What if the person in the story might not agree? Does that make a difference? What if the preacher claims an action in a story to be God's action and then eventually in real life the story has a bad ending? Ought the preacher to avoid all stories where the ending is not known?

7. Some preachers are convinced that they are not creative and that they cannot tell stories. In your experience, is the ability to tell stories much different from relating events that happened in one's day?

8. When preachers use trouble and grace as categories with which to view experience, they train themselves to see God in the world. Is there a danger if preachers in the course of their ministry speak readily about God when, for some people, God seems absent?

9. Given the six theological categories of stories developed here, do you feel you might be able to use stories from contemporary experience in your preaching? from art?

Section IV

Thursday: What the Preacher Says

We come now to Thursday. By Thursday, the sermon ideally is well under way: the foundation work is done, the Bible passage has been studied, a theme is determined, possible bridges have been scouted, and some writing has begun. In order to put it together as a coherent whole, a preacher needs some sense of overall sermon form—what it might look like. At the end of chapter 5, we considered two pairs of concerns as one possible way of organizing the sermon, but there are other ways we need to lift up here. In the last century, scholars were particularly attentive to biblical form, and we now recognize that the form of a text influences its meaning, both in terms of content and rhetorical effect. Form can have various implications. Psalms are praise songs, thus their genre prevents them from providing much information about their background. Parables often surprise, so one looks for what is surprising in what they say. The Epistles are letters that were typically read aloud in worship as though they were sermons, thus one listens to them considering the effect of the words on those originally gathered.

Sermons also have forms, and these forms affect their meaning, content, and what they achieve. Sermon form may be considered at two levels: exterior or surface structure and deep structure. Surface structure includes the sermon body, introduction, and conclusion, as well as issues of sermon genre. Deep structure is like grammar in language; it has to do with theological issues such as, what does it mean to preach the gospel? Does the gospel also have structure that relates to its meaning, content, and effect? If so, does some of that structure need to be implemented in a sermon in order to communicate the content?

Composition of the sermon is the concluding step in what we are calling the preacher's hermeneutical circle. Monday was devoted to what the biblical text says (understanding); Tuesday was focused on what the text means (explanation); Wednesday was dedicated to understanding what experience says (application); and Thursday is devoted to what the preacher says (intention). This phase carries through to the end of sermon on Sunday, but on Thursday one is concerned with what words the sermon will use, to what shape, purpose, and effect.

People who are unfamiliar with the task of preaching might tend to think that biblical interpretation is an early phase of sermon preparation and that it is complete when exegesis is complete. Some scholars have this mistaken impression and may assume that preachers can simply take exegesis into the pulpit and preach it. In fact, there is so much more. Only in sermon delivery is the act of interpretation of the biblical text complete on the part of the preacher. The sermon is the interpretation; the interpretation does not first exist in some unwritten form in one's mind to which one then attaches current events. Rather, the events are selected as part of an emerging interpretation that gradually coalesces as one composes the sermon. Of course, even when the sermon is delivered, it is not finished. Through the Holy Spirit the congregation receives the Word and embodies and proclaims it in their life throughout the week. In a sense, the sermon is over not when the preacher sits down but rather in the course of the week as the people exercise their ministries feeding on the Word.

This fourth stage of the hermeneutical process—what the preacher says—is what takes the preacher through to the end of the worship service on Sunday.

SERMON FORM I: SURFACE STRUCTURES

Preachers speak and listeners listen with established conventions in mind. A person reads a detective story with different expectations and demands than those brought to a romance novel. Sermon forms similarly belong to certain conventions, and listeners hear these with certain expectations and demands. In this chapter, we are concerned with two categories of surface or exterior form: the body, introduction, and conclusion of the sermon and genres or shapes of the sermon as a whole.

The Body

A traditional way to discuss the body of the sermon is to speak of an arrangement of points and illustrations. The term *New Homiletic* refers to the revolution in homiletics that began roughly with H. Grady Davis in the late 1950s.[1] Since his time, one speaks commonly of a sermon that grows or of narrative plot or of the development of a key image or a sequence of "moves." Common to any sermon is development of a theme that answers the question, what was the sermon about?

Everything in the sermon is in some way related to the theme or what we have also called the major concern of the text (or its corresponding version, the major concern of the sermon), because it is the heart of the matter. Listeners hear the theme to be whatever is given greatest emphasis, repetition, and typical positioning, at least at the beginning, middle, and end of the sermon. One of the most difficult tasks for preaching students is to compose the entire sermon with a single focus, not two or ten, even though the sermon may develop several minor points, thoughts, moves, or images along the way.

At the same time, a sermon is a dialogue between the biblical text and our own situation. Michael J. Quicke says that a common complaint in the circles in which he moves is that sermons spend "over 90 percent of the time in the Bible world and less than 10 percent in the contemporary world"; as such, these sermons lack relevance.[2] Other preaching circles might demonstrate the opposite problem. Some kind of balance is needed so that the Bible and our world are each given adequate attention.

The biblical text needs central emphasis, although where one establishes it in the sermon can vary. How many times one moves into it and seeks to apply it to our times can also vary. Sermon form can be pictured in a variety of ways beyond points and subpoints. Eugene Lowry joins a descending curve and an ascending curve to form a pointed loop (or the Christian *ichthus*—fish symbol—turned on its nose) to sketch his "homiletical plot." Others use line graphs to highlight rising conflict and moments of emotional climax.

An image that depicts most approaches can be obtained by using a sine graph or curve, a device commonly used in science and math. Whether a preacher treats the biblical text or our situation, the central theme develops at the heart of what is said, explicitly or implicitly, throughout the sermon. When a biblical concern of the text is developed, it is represented by a complete curve on one side of the mean line, moving away and returning (that is, in and out of the text). In the same manner, on the other side of the mean line, the development of contemporary life with a concern of the sermon is portrayed (that is, in and out of contemporary experience). Partial developments can be indicated by smaller curves. Here are just a few basic possibilities:

1. Move once into the biblical text and apply it to our world. This is a standard exegesis-application format. On a smaller scale, it is a picture of one of David Buttrick's "moves" (a theological idea from the text is clearly stated; the idea is elaborated with an "analogy of experience" that anticipates congregational "blocks"; and the move is quickly concluded with a repetition of the main idea).

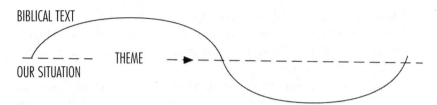

2. Move twice into the biblical text and our world: the first half is trouble, the second is grace.

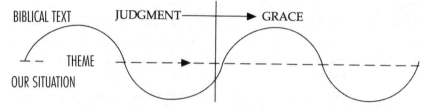

3. Move partly into the biblical text at the beginning of the sermon and complete the treatment of the text at the end. (The number of movements here may vary.)

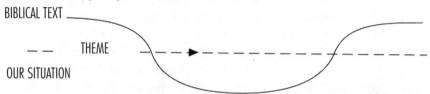

4. Move from an experience to the biblical text and conclude with an experience in light of the text. (If our situation explores the inverse of the good news in the text, this structure can be used to preach hope.)

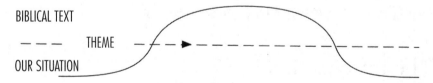

5. Move several times in complete movements.

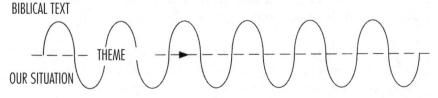

Students and accomplished preachers alike are encouraged not to switch too often between the biblical text and our situation, normally fewer times than in the illustration just given. Every time the preacher shifts from the Bible to today or back, the congregation must work extra hard. They have scenery in their minds, whole landscapes and characters too, and they have to put the stagehands of the mind to work to change the set and get the new actors in place. Frequent change can be just too demanding. Listening to such sermons is like trying to grab a housefly in midair—you think you have it, but it is gone.

However, if the preacher gets stuck in one location, the congregation will be bored. Think of the preacher as a guide taking listeners through God's mansion of many rooms. Take the guests into a room, seat them, talk about the room, allow them time to note its features, and move on only when it will not seem as if they are being rushed. But do not keep them in the sitting room while lunch is served on the porch.

In the body of the sermon a preacher needs to get to what Samuel J. Proctor called "the relevant question," namely "So what?" or "Therefore?" As he humorously says, "The 'relevant question' is already asked in the minds of the hearers—whether the preacher ever gets to it or not."[3] David Mains says that 80 percent of listeners are unable to say what the preacher was looking for.[4] For Proctor, the relevant question "is like saying, 'so far, so good; now where do we go from here? Does this break down into relevant application for my life, my family, my community, my country, my world, the church, the Christian community, or the whole human family?'"[5] Proctor is thinking broadly of application, and one hopes that has not been delayed until the very end. One can also think of the "So what?" as, what has to happen now? What can we now do with God's empowerment? We call this *mission* and say more on this later.

The Introduction

The introduction is commonly determined only after the theme sentence is decided, along with some plan for design sequence. Thomas G. Long offers excellent suggestions:

1. The introduction should promise something of what the sermon will be about (that is, some need or question, such as, why do we pray?).
2. What is promised should be of value to the congregation.

3. The language and tone of the introduction should create a fair expectation of the language and tone of the sermon.

4. Whereas the introduction should anticipate the whole sermon, it should also lead directly to the next step of the sermon.[6]

> **The introduction needs to promise some benefit to the hearer.**

Clearly the introduction must get the congregation's attention, yet also not immediately plunge them into the heart of the issue. Listeners need time to establish a relationship with the preacher. Some preachers try to make the first sentence a "grabber," such as, "Judith was driving her children to work when she noticed a wheel from her car rolling down the road beside her." By contrast, David Buttrick (who provides the most detailed contemporary study of sermon introductions and conclusions[7]) says people do not easily attend the first few sentences of a public address. When one shifts what one is looking at with a camera, a short time may be needed for the focus to become clear. He says the same thing happens in sermons, so the first two or three sentences in a sermon are fuzzy. The congregation must adjust to the syntactical patterns of the preacher.[8] This means that preachers need to be modest in their expectation of what can be accomplished in the opening minutes of conversation.

Buttrick also cautions against the "step down introduction," one that keeps shifting the focus or subject (for example, from the guest teacher to the trip to the first job, and finally, to what matters). Pick one focus and point of view and keep it.[9]

The simplest, though not necessarily the most imaginative, introduction may start directly with the biblical text. Perhaps paint the situation of a biblical character or writer. Quickly establish the setting. Try to create a movie in words. Ask yourself, if I were to make a movie of this text, what decisions would I need to make? (For example: is it night? Is there a breeze? Who is present? What are they doing? Is there something unusual? What sounds are there?) As in a movie, some of these items are background that the camera merely notes in panning; central action and characters are what the camera seeks.

If the introduction deals immediately with the biblical text, tell some of the text's story before making any observation or reflection based on it. For example, if preaching about the biblical Rachel, do not start the sermon by asking, "Who would have expected Rachel to do what she did?" or stating, "My own response to Rachel may be your own." First, re-create Rachel's story in the listeners' minds. Just because a biblical text was read prior to the sermon in worship does not mean that the congregation is now fully immersed in the text and its times, as though they have been studying it all week like the preacher.

> Introductions may start with:
>
> 1. a story related to the theme sentence
> 2. an image from the text or our world
> 3. a doctrine
> 4. an inversion of the theme sentence

At least four easy alternatives to opening with the biblical text are available. One is to repeat a contemporary conversation or to relate an event that is relevant to the theme sentence. Another is to use a central image, metaphor, or phrase from the biblical text or today that will figure in the sermon. Third, one may speak of either a doctrine or a topic of relevance to congregational life. For instance, around Christmas one might speak of the Incarnation; or during a congregational crisis one might speak of the need for forgiveness.

Finally, a preacher may employ inversion: tell a story that seems to deny or contradict the theme.[10] For instance, if the theme sentence is "God ministers to the needy," one might tell the story of someone in need who experienced God as absent. Or if preaching on "God answers prayer," one might speak of someone who prayed that her husband would be healed but whose prayer did not seem to be answered. By focusing on the inverse, one names how life is typically experienced, in other words, a real issue is named. One starts with where the people are, and through the sermon one moves to bring the gospel to bear on such situations. By the end of the sermon, presumably one would return to this particular story or one like it in light of the gospel. Where God seemed absent and remote is now shown to be the place of Christ's presence.

Although one does not plunge directly into the heart of issues in the introduction, one does need to point in the direction one is going, that is, to the theme sentence. The sermon is a bus, and its destination needs to be posted up front. Listeners need some signal as to where they might be headed. The preacher must help the listeners to hear what will be said; it is not enough eventually to say it once. The old formula for essays (and sermons) is not far off the mark: "Say what you are going to say, say it, and say what you have said." This needs to be finessed, however, for the sermon is not just ideas: merely state where the sermon is going rather than drive the congregation on a boring tour through the sermon's table of contents. Give them clues that will direct their access to one's purpose in the sermon.

The Conclusion

Even as the introduction points to where a preacher is going, the conclusion reminds folks where they have been. Less is needed than is often thought. One generally need not summarize the key points of what has been said (if points were used); this may have been more important when sermons were normally an hour long, in which case a summary could serve to bring the hour into sharp focus. With the shorter norm of sermons today, such review may seem silly. If the congregation does not grasp the content before the conclusion, it is time to rewrite the sermon, not write a summary.

Barbara K. Lundblad says how important it is for her to know how her sermon ends, "Once, I hope, not twice or three times." She avoids three-point sermons that lead her to say "thirdly" toward the end, because if she uses numbers, people only wait for "thirdly"; she also avoids saying "finally" or "Amen" because she wants the sermon "to continue in the minds and hearts of my partners."[11] Do not have people say of your sermon what I overheard someone saying of one of mine: "Quite a few stop signs were driven through."

David Buttrick raises a number of cautions about conclusions, including:

1. Avoid ending the sermon with a question (for example, will you or won't you bear witness to Jesus Christ?). A posed question "will neither be answered or remembered."

2. Avoid quotations in a conclusion that interfere with the direct discourse appropriate to a closing.

3. Avoid personal testimony, for in the conclusion it "will leave a congregation with a consciousness of the preacher rather than the gospel."

4. Use direct, simple, concrete language.[12]

There is no concensus on the style or tone of the conclusion. Buttrick is wary of the conclusion that passionately repeats the same structure in consecutive sentences (for example, We must go out into the world to ... We must go out into the world to ... We must go out into the world to ...). Buttrick might agree with James S. Stewart, who advocated the decisive ending and

Less is more.

"the quiet close": "You will never weaken the force of your final appeal by keeping it restrained."[13] However, one might agree with some African American and other traditions that are energized by passionate repetition and sophisticated use of rhetoric; Henry Mitchell speaks of "cultural roots which demand that a sermon end in a celebration," and this celebration leads into the world with new hope and confidence.[14] Cleophus J. LaRue encourages whatever suits the message.[15]

Most people do not know where to begin or end a story or a sermon. This common error is most easily addressed in both instances if one cuts the first and last few sentences, for these often consist of needless commentary. Less is more.

A number of additional principles may be kept in mind:

1. The conclusion should bring a sense of completeness to the sermon.

2. A return to an opening story almost always signals closure, so finish. Upon such a return, the opening story should be recast in terms of the gospel message.

3. The conclusion should point to where the sermon has been, using the theme sentence.

4. The conclusion should point to the world and the congregation's mission in it.

Sermon Genres

The emergence of the New Homiletic in the late 1950s meant the emergence of two parallel streams in homiletics. Propositional preaching (the established homiletic) emphasizes propositions and principles of logical thought. Narrative preaching (part of the New Homiletic) emphasizes story and principles of art. The recent revolution in homiletics had the issue of form as its catalyst and center—in particular the differences between propositional and narrative preaching.

Propositional Forms

The "propositional" or "propositional-discursive" label is sufficiently elastic to include most traditional sermon forms. Propositions are logical proposals, statements, or claims. *Discursive* comes from the Latin word meaning "to run about," implying an argument that moves from point to point, gradually building a strong, reasoned position. In much current theological thought proposition and propositional are terms laden with negative connotation. Anyone who defines truth in propositional terms is hopelessly out of touch with postmodern thought. Since readers may be hearing this message in other classes, it is important to acknowledge these negative connotations. However, use of the term here is descriptive rather than evaluative. Much of the Bible is propositions, and preachers are right to be critical of all ideologies, including postmodernism. The propositional sermon can still be an effective way of preaching.

Commonly referred to as the three-point or point-form sermon, propositional preaching, has many varieties (even as it can have many or few points). Common to all, in theory at least, is that several lesser propositions serve a greater one. This has been the bread-and-butter sermon of the church for the last eight hundred years, for it has great flexibility, versatility, and possible enduring potential. It came to prominence around 1200 with the recovery of Aristotle's works and thus of empirical evidence based in reason. Already in 1300, Robert of Basevorn commented with amusing candor, "Only three statements, or the equivalent of three, are used in the theme either from respect to the Trinity, or because a threefold cord is not easily broken, or because this method is mostly followed by Bernard [of Clairvaux], or, as I think more likely, because it is more convenient for the set time of the sermon."[16]

Propositional preaching has three key historical precedents:

It commonly exhibits an exegesis-application approach. This form dates back to the synagogue, if not to the time of building the Second Temple (see Nehemiah 8:1-8), where the norm was to read Scripture and comment upon it. Under Charlemagne, priests read the Latin New Testament and followed with a translation, an explanation of the text, and an application of it to the people's lives. The Puritan plain-style sermon (exposition, doctrine, application) was yet another modification.

Another precedent was the medieval disputation, followed by nearly all of the great teachers of the period. Teachers like Thomas Aquinas began with a question and moved to arguments against the position and then for it. This approach is more commonly known as Hegel's thesis, antithesis, synthesis. Its three-part movement was easily adapted to the point-form of preaching.

A third form from classical times has been the syllogism, the basic unit of ancient logic: if A, and B, then C.

One can already see that point-form seems to encourage an idea-centered approach. It can be excellent for the communication of information. Does this mean that propositional preaching must be identified with preaching as information? Probably not, but the tendency is there. For precisely this reason, it has drawn fire in recent decades for seemingly representing an authoritarian style of ministry, in which the preacher stands over the congregation rather than with them under the Word, using a lecturing style of proclamation.

Of course there were other reasons for change. Propositional preaching seemingly arose when the preacher was often the most educated person in the community, when the preacher was automatically granted considerable authority, when little distinction was made between the preacher's opinion and actual fact, when fewer things in society were open to interpretation, when church attendance was a social duty and congregations were a captive audience, and when, because of lack of formal education, congregations avidly sought information and learning (as opposed to now, when they may seek more for integration and shared perspective).

Many preachers used three points for every sermon. Points are not the problem: they can be helpful devices if there are three practical things to remember. They can easily be misused when the preacher's need for three points becomes imposed on a text or when points are chosen more to help the preacher get a sermon than to help the listener get a life. In such situations, the thought line of the preacher becomes the rule rather than our guide. The preacher's information becomes more important than the listener's process of reflection and identification.[17] The problem becomes acute when the listeners hear points and ask, "What is the point?" In practice, many homiletical points did not merit the attention they were given.

Narrative Forms

In 1970, Charles L. Rice argued for the use of imagination along with reason in preaching and suggested several story-based forms modeled from literature: he was against "the marshaling of arguments and neat regimentation of propositions. Life does not present itself in that form—life does not feel that way."[18] Stephen Crites, in a landmark essay in 1971, argued that narrative or story, far from being an abstraction from reality, is in fact the way in which we experience it.[19]

The revolution became full-blown in 1971 when Fred B. Craddock published *As One Without Authority*. He drew on ideas of William Edwin Sangster, who took readers through a preacher's thoughts during the week as a way to build the sermon,[20] as well as of H. Grady Davis, who explained "inductive continuity" as an "organizing principle."[21] Craddock modeled the sermon on the preacher's inductive probings; thus, sermons were to move through various experiences and narrow to a conclusion.[22] A deductive or traditional propositional sermon, by contrast, starts with its conclusion stated as a proposition and then widens to build a case to prove it. The conclusion is never in doubt from the beginning; in doubt is only the manner of proof.

Other factors came into play to make narrative of major importance. North Americans listening to jazz, blues, gospel, and Motown music became interested in its roots in the rhetorically sensitive, story-based, oral traditions of many African American churches. Authority that was so long under suspicion in race relations became socially widespread in the post-Watergate, post–Vietnam War era, after the president was seen to have lied to the American people. In scholarly circles, the parables were finally appreciated as central to Jesus' own preaching, and the Bible was recognized to be largely story. Language was no longer understood to be just information; it was expressive and based in metaphor. Perhaps as compelling as any of these changes, however, was the effect of television: its medium is mainly narrative in small bites, and it shapes the way viewers think when they go to church.

Narrative in one form or another had been present in the preaching of the early and medieval churches and by the 1900s was commonplace at least in sermons in the English-speaking world. It had minimal strength, however, being largely restricted to canned stories or merchandised illustrations that only served to make plain a point that had already been established with propositions. The stories were subservient to points and did not have anything to say by themselves. They were like metaphors in Aristotle, regarded largely as decorations. Only in African American and some regional churches with oral roots was the power of narrative to make its own points never lost. What is now sometimes called narrative preaching thus arose to meet the changing needs of re-forming congregations, many of whom were in search of narratives that would bind them together.

A narrative sermon uses principles from narrative and art to develop unity. A sermon might display a sense of completed action, growth, or emotional resolution. A narrative sermon is rarely just one long narrative, although it is sometimes characterized this way by preachers unfamiliar with homiletical literature. Narrative sermons might still use propositions, but they proceed as much by stories, images, and experiences that use plot, character, and emotion. The truth of such sermons is recognized not through logical reasoning and proofs but by its correspondence to both Scripture and life experience: "Does this reflect life as I know it in faith?"

> David Buttrick prefers speaking of narrative and propositional sermons as "preaching in the mode of immediacy" and "preaching in the reflective mode," that is, reflecting on experience.[23]

Narration implies flexible organic structure. Structure emerges out of the events of a story more than being imposed on them. Narration implies style as well as form: something is told, or related, in the conversational manner of life experience. The perceived model for language shifts from the essay or lecture to the novel and short story.

The chart on pages 145-48 lists common varieties of propositional and narrative sermons.

PROPOSITIONAL PREACHING
Types of Propositional Sermon

Exegetical Sermons: A biblical text is treated line by line or verse by verse to explain its meaning and relevance for today. Examples of this form are found from Cyprian (*On the Lord's Prayer*) to Karl Barth to today (that is, first this, then this, then this).

Expository Sermons: Preachers frequently begin with an introduction, exposit the biblical text (that is, explain and interpret a theme) in one lengthy exegetical section, move to some form of bridge to our own time and situation, apply the text to our own lives, and end with a conclusion, possibly including an exhortation to action (that is, because of this, this follows; or this is how they were, so this is how we are).

Topical or Thematic Sermons: A theme is developed from contemporary life or from pastoral experience. Harry Emerson Fosdick (1878–1969) and others used this form, often without reference to a specific biblical text, and perhaps unfairly earned for it the label "unbiblical." Preachers could progress up a *ladder* of points of increasing importance (that is, important as this is, consider this, and this) or could examine a single idea from many angles, as though it were a faceted *jewel* (that is, it could be this, or this, or this) or could begin with an emotionally powerful incident that would culminate in some spiritual insight, with appropriate lessons or ethical instruction for the congregation (that is, from this, we learn this or must do this).

Doctrinal Sermons: Similar to the topical sermon, the theme is a particular Christian doctrine, and often free use is made of theologians and Scripture.

Puritan Plain-style Sermon: This label originally identified a sermon that used plain imagery and minimal structural divisions and that was delivered in the plain style of rhetoric classically reserved for teaching (in contrast to the middle and grand styles for pleasure and persuasion, respectively). Although now perhaps disappearing, it evolved with Wesley and others to follow the pattern: exegesis of a biblical verse in a lengthy introduction; identification and development of a particular doctrine, which forms most of the body of the sermon (with reference to any Scripture); and eventual application and conclusion (that is, this means this in church teaching, and it breaks down into these points).

145

PROPOSITIONAL PREACHING
Typical Use of Points

Two or more points are taken from:

- one verse of Scripture: for example, John 1:1 "In the beginning was the Word, and the Word was with God, and the Word was God." Here the verse is a three-part verse. Preachers have sought to process verses through the lens of pastoral and prophetic need; hence the possibility: (1) God made all in the beginning; (2) the Christ we know was with God; (3) we may trust Christ eternally. This triad is modeled on syllo-paradigm to focus on God's action, instead of ours; thus, "Christ embraces us eternally."

- one long passage of Scripture: for example, Psalm 23 might be preached thus: (1) Our paths are dangerous; (2) the Lord is our Shepherd; (3) there is nothing to fear.

- several verses or passages, that is, using a Bible concordance to find a variety of texts to make related points: for example, (1) bear your burdens—Galatians 6:2; (2) bear one another's burdens—Galatians 6:5; (3) cast your burdens upon the Lord—Psalm 55:22.[24]

- traditional doctrinal understanding, largely outside the biblical text: for example, using 1 Thessalonians 1:5 ("Our message of the gospel came to you not in word only, but also in power and in the Holy Spirit and with full conviction"), we might discuss the doctrine of the Word. Here the divisions might come from our own understanding of the Word that would then be related to this text. Thus, (1) God dares to become known through word; (2) Human words differ from God's Word; (3) God's Word is action and power; (4) God's final, eternal Word is Christ.

NARRATIVE PREACHING
Types of Narrative Sermon

One-story formats (pure narration):
1. The biblical text retold in its time,[25] that is, there once was a ...
2. The biblical text retold in our time, that is, the other day ...
3. A story of our time is told that intersects with the biblical text in such an obvious manner that only minimal linking may be required somewhere in the sermon. H. Grady Davis anticipated these models.[26]

Multistory formats (pure narration):
Here are the simplest:
1. "One-two": one story of brokenness is countered by a second story of hope, the biblical text intersecting in obvious yet minimalist fashion.
2. "One-two-one": one story, broken midway by the biblical text, with the ending given to the first story in the final third.[27]
3. "One-two-three": The first story leads to the second story, usually the biblical text, and is followed by a third story that counters the first.

Hybrid formats (mixed narration):
Preachers employ narrative principles and varying amounts of narrative. The varieties are too numerous to categorize helpfully, for the sermons include anything combining narrative with nonnarrative material.[28] Eugene Lowry's "homiletical plot" may be considered in this category:
1. Upset the equilibrium by posing a problem in the "felt needs" of the hearers.
2. Analyze the discrepancy.
3. Disclose the key to resolution from the gospel.
4. Experience the gospel in the lives of the hearers.
5. Anticipate the consequences.[29]

NARRATIVE PREACHING
Sample Uses of Stories

Retelling the biblical story in its own time (a one-story format):
Ella P. Mitchell preached on Esther, amplifying a sense of God's call that is hidden behind the original story more than it is central to it. Her sermon used the following moves:
1. Esther's background,
2. Esther's dilemma,
3. Esther's action,
4. celebration of God's work through Esther.[30]

Telling a contemporary story (one-story format):
Thomas H. Troeger preached a wedding sermon on the wedding vows. He told the story of a couple who, each year, on their wedding anniversary, donned their wedding clothes and had their picture taken in their front room. He pictured them on their fifth anniversary and the meaning of "poorer"; on their fifteenth and the meaning of "worse"; and on their forty-seventh, discovering the rich delight in having kept promises and in meditating on "in sickness ... until death."[31]

Using a multistory format:
Fred Craddock preached a sermon on Galatians 1:11-24 in which he asked the congregation to envision a face when he said the word "bitter." He told five stories (each introduced with, "Do you see a face? I see the face ...") before turning to Paul in the same vein and identifying the bitterness with which Paul himself is struggling.[32]

Being Flexible with Forms

Students rightly want to try many of the above sermon forms. However, the exercise is less satisfying than they hope because they discover considerable fluidity among the varieties: start to write a doctrinal sermon and one may end up expositing a biblical text. A point-form sermon may have a lengthy narrative portion. If an inductive sermon identifies its conclusion at the beginning (in the manner of deduction), does it cease to be inductive, even though its thought everywhere else proceeds in an inductive manner? Eugene Lowry once suggested that preachers should see their task "as shaping rather than organizing sermons." As if to underline the fluidity he found in notions of form, he defined a sermon as "an ordered form of moving time."[33]

What is important for students is not absolute loyalty to exterior forms, for they do not allow that kind of rigidity or clear distinction. What they do offer is a facility to stimulate creativity, variety, and interest in serving the gospel. Listen to Barbara Lundblad reflect on how she determines sermon form once she has a focus for the sermon.

> I try to see the shape. Sometimes the shape follows the shape of the scripture text—a biblical narrative retold conversing with the community text, a biblical image reflected in city streets, a parable at the playground. The shape determines how the sermon moves: straight ahead in linear fashion, weaving back and forth between biblical text and community text, going around and around to look at an image from different angles. Sometimes I paint three pictures, trying to touch people in different life situations. Sometimes I hear a refrain or a question that returns again and again, tying the sermon together. Sometimes the end is clear as I begin, but often the ending emerges only in the process of writing.[34]

There is no one right exterior form of preaching. Preaching can be authoritarian in any form. Propositional preaching can make listeners slaves to the preacher's reasoning; narrative preaching can make listeners slaves to the sound and light show of a preacher's use of images. Weak content is a liability for any form. Moreover, any form can be flawed.

Flawed Forms

For example, the single-story sermon (from the Bible or today) can be as flawed—for different reasons—as the propositional sermon that forces a biblical text into rhyming points (for example, "God works by finding, minding, and binding"). When a single story is used, unless the preacher is very skilled indeed (as some like John C. Holbert are),[35] the congregation can be left struggling to make some direct, substantial connections with God in their lives. These connections should become conscious in listeners' minds, not left in the subconscious.

The single narrative is probably the most difficult sermon for anyone to pull off effectively, and probably should be used sparingly.[36] One can act out a story, and it may teach effectively and get good response, but as with a teaching sermon, does it get to the gospel? If the story is told in biblical time the congregation may wonder how it connects with them. If it is told in contemporary time, the congregation may wonder how it connects with the Bible.

If the point of the story is revealed only at the end, people might not get it. The point of the sermon is not a surprise at the end; ideally listeners should be clear about the import of the sermon at least by midway, if not from the start, such that they are already applying it to their lives by the end. Identification with a character in the gospel story is often not sufficient to make the gospel explicit or conscious. Recognizing a familiar situation as described in a story does not necessarily mean listeners will make the connections the preacher makes or desires them to make with their own lives. In many cases, as listeners, interpretation of a single narrative sermon gets stuck at stage two of the hermeneutical circle, with listeners asking, what does this mean? The "So what?" never gets answered. (The same thing is true of propositional sermons that exclude experience.) Even appreciation of this type of sermon by a congregation on the church steps after a service may not mean that they met God.

The norm for most preachers may be hybrid forms, indeed, forms that largely evolve in composition. One is free, after all, to use whatever form facilitates proclamation of the gospel.

Newer Forms

Within the last fifteen years or so, some new sermon forms have emerged, often building on or reviving what went before. Eugene L. Lowry's *How to Preach a Parable*, although specifically arguing for narrative, articulates how sermons that are not necessarily narratives can nonetheless employ narrative principles.[37] Both Christine M. Smith and

Carol M. Norén have shown how feminist concerns move sermon form away from models that stress authority and toward models reflecting relationships.[38]

Powerpoint and Video Images

One of the new forms is the use of PowerPoint and video images. In fact, one of the pioneers of this form might be said to be Aimee Semple McPherson (1890–1944), an independent Pentecostal evangelist who (like many in her time) used a chart sermon that involved presenting the outline of her sermon as an illustrated chart. Preaching on the good Samaritan (Luke 10:30-35) she pictured the events of the story on the chart and led the listeners verse by verse and detail by detail through the text using the chart. She led them in stages: "A certain man went down ... From Jerusalem to Jericho ... And fell ... Among Thieves [and so on]"[39] Perhaps the chart sermon was the inspiration for the flannel board in many Sunday schools of recent decades, on which cutout characters, animals, and elements of landscape made of felt were placed in order to depict Bible stories.

The strengths and weaknesses of PowerPoint at one level are the strengths and weaknesses of propositions. It can add clarity and structure to a message. However, it gears a sermon toward information and teaching and away from what we will later deal with as proclamation. Some congregational members are very attentive to PowerPoint because it gives them something to look at. Other people find less reason to bother listening when everything is previewed or summarized on a screen. High school students regularly exposed to PowerPoint tend to say that they find it boring.

The use of pictures on a screen, either moving or stills, perhaps accompanied by music, is also common for sermons. In general the use of screens in worship can free people from bulletins and hymnbooks and free them to move or clap to the music. In the sermon, pictures can be a way to focus attention. For instance, Capernaum is a place on the northern shore of the Sea of Galilee where Jesus based much of his ministry. If a preacher is able to show photographs or a video clip of the region, people have a sense of being there. To this end, thousands of images of biblical sites are available free online at http://holylandphotos.org or for purchase at www.bibleplaces.com.

The Reverend Ed Grimenstein uses something similar to the old chart sermon: he sketches in very rough form (stick figures) the different phases of a biblical text in order to make the abstract concrete and to give movement and visualization. He considers this to be a form of incarnation of the text.[40]

Some of Jesus' teachings, when used as a voice-over to various biblical or contemporary pictures, gain added significance from the juxtaposition of words and images. For instance, if a picture of a homeless person on the sidewalk is juxtaposed with "blessed are the poor," a person in church might connect what Jesus said with real homeless people outside.

Yet another way of using video is found in going to the website, The Text This Week (www.textweek.com). This lectionary-based resource provides a valuable art concordance geared to Bible texts. Biblical stories in art are indexed for preachers to access and download. The Reverend Tim Bauer once preached on the healing of the "paralytic" in Mark 2:1-12, and throughout the sermon a Dutch painting of the text from the 1600s was projected onto a screen.[41] Bauer commented on the painting throughout the sermon and drew listener attention to details that otherwise might have been missed, all the while developing the text and applying it to today.

The use of technology in sermons is controversial. Some say it goes against Calvinist principles that ban visual icons. Some say that it distracts from the Word. If a screen is used throughout, the preacher tends to disappear and, with this, the possibility of proclamation may diminish. This much is clear: use of technology will probably increase, and if it is going to be used, it needs to be used well. It requires a considerable financial investment in equipment (around $9,000 as I write). It also requires technicians: this can be a bonus because it can provide a ministry for young people. The biggest danger is that preachers spend time trying to provide fresh visual images when they need to be discerning God's Word and composing a sermon.

Other Recent Forms

Other recent forms of sermon are more conventional. Barbara Brown Taylor uses a method she says she got from her teacher, Fred Craddock: orientation, disorientation, reorientation—O, D, R. Orientation is what we think we know about a text, some shared perspective on the text. Disorientation is whatever shifts one's perspective on the text, what upsets the balance and causes new interest. Reorientation is some revelational insight that shows movement from the original perspective.[42] Her O, D, R is a pleasing update of thesis, antithesis, synthesis. Samuel Proctor has a similar five-stage adaptation: Proposition (and subject), Antithesis, Thesis, Relevant question, Synthesis.[43]

Catherine Gunsalus González suggests a method for preaching tough texts, or texts that listeners might find tough to hear, for instance Proverbs 30:7-9 in relation to our consumer society. First, voice as many reasons as one can think of as to why the text is wrong or does not apply. Then bring in other biblical texts to give perspective. Next deal with the text in depth. Finally apply the text to today.[44] (Is this a new order: antithesis-synthesis-thesis?)

Thomas G. Long and Mike Graves approach the sermon through the literary forms of the Bible. Biblical texts come in many genres: aphorisms, psalms, proverbs, miracle stories, parables, prophetic oracles, short stories, vice and virtue lists, and more. Long recommends that a sermon imitate some feature of the form and function of a biblical text so that the sermon, in a new setting, can say and do what the text says and does in its setting.[45] A psalm might "[swivel] the universe on the hinges of a single image"[46]; a sermon on 1 Corinthians 12:31–14:1 might move from Paul's challenges to a vision of unity.[47] Graves speaks broadly of sermons that are "form sensitive."[48] Presumably a sermon on the diatribe form in Romans 6 might adopt the role of an interlocutor, as Paul has done.

Robert G. Hughes and Robert Kysar offer three forms: two opposites in a theological paradox; a question with three answers, the last of which is the best gospel answer; and problem-solution.[49]

Evans Crawford describes a call-and-response format in some African American congregations: Help 'em Lord! ("The search is on for connections, and we start out in need of prayer"); Well? ("You're hinting to the witness with a chantable refrain or 'riff'"); That's all right! ("There are Good News and gospel possibilities; the sermon is becoming persuasive"); Amen! ("The truth is affirmed and the pitch is right for the people and Scripture passage"); and Glory Hallelujah! ("The point of loudest praise, highest joy, and praise to God").[50] This may be an updated version of the venerable, "Start low, rise high, strike fire. Sit down in a storm."[51]

Ronald J. Allen revives a variety of intriguing possibilities for topical preachers:

> 1. Deductive form of description, evaluation, and application—(a) introduction: 5-15% of the length, (b)

statement of the main point: 5%, (c) description of the topic: 15-25%, (d) theological evaluation of the topic: 15-25%, (e) application: 15-25%, (f) conclusion: 5-15%

2. Methodist quadrilateral—(a) introduction, (b) the Bible: 15-20%, (c) the tradition: 15-20%, (d) experience: 15-20%, (e) reason (that is, learnings): 15-20%, (f) synthesis: 20-25%, (g) conclusion: 5-10%

3. Practical moral reasoning—(a) experiences of the topic in the congregation: 10%, (b) listening to (that is, learnings from) the experiences: 20%, (c) critical analysis: 30-50%, (d) decision and strategy: 20-30%

4. General inductive—(a) preacher's story of becoming aware of the issue, (b) connection to the congregation, (c) exploration of the issues together, (d) resolution

5. Structure as praxis (inspired by David Buttrick)— four to six moves of four minutes each, each composed of a three-sentence focus, the move itself, and a three-sentence closure: for example, (a) introductory framework, (b) critical examination and analysis, (c) reevaluation or interpretation in light of Christian vision, (d) new understanding and revisioning of the future

6. Focus on mind, heart, and will—(a) introduction, (b) statement of the claim of the sermon, (c) focus on the mind (that is, what must we know?), (d) focus on emotion, (e) focus on the will, (f) conclusion.[52]

David Buttrick uses the term *moves* in a manner to emphasize "a movement in language," as opposed to static "points."[53] He suggests, as we have just glimpsed in Allen's fifth form, that the sermon is composed of a variety of these moves. They consist of (1) a theological idea from the biblical text (our "concerns of the text") and (2) analogies of experience (our "concerns of the sermon"), developed in anticipation of congregational blocks (our expressed and actual needs of the congregation).[54] A sermon in this manner will have many movements in and out of a text.

In my own work I offer a four-page sermon model in which each so-called page is really a metaphor for a quarter of a sermon:

Page One: Trouble in the Bible
Page Two: Trouble in Our World
Page Three: Grace in the Bible
Page Four: Grace in Our World

In this model the pages may be reshuffled, but this order stands as a basic norm. If there is a short introduction dealing with our world, it is considered to be prior to Page One.[55] The purpose of these pages when used as a model is to provide some flexible guidelines for preachers.

Barbara Brown Taylor, like many preachers, sometimes intuitively preaches this model. Her videotaped sermon for *The Great Preacher Series*, though chopped by the video editors, is published in its full form in an accompanying insert. Preaching on Paul's prayer in Ephesians 1:15-23, she introduces the sermon with a report of a trip to Turkey in which she found a ruined church that is now a sheep pen and that has the remains of a portrait of Christ blessing the world. Page One explores; Paul's church is broken. Page Two speaks of signs of ruin in contemporary denominations. Page Three is Christ blessing the world—in a kind of tiered fountain that Taylor traces in her text. Page Four is Christ still blessing the church today.[56]

Newer Forms:
PowerPoint and Video Images
Literary Forms of the Bible
Two Opposites; Three Questions; Problem-Solution
Dealing with Tough Texts
Call and Response
Topical Variations
Moves
Four Pages

These four pages constitute more than a model; they are the grammar of the gospel, and whether a preacher is aware of them or not, they work in any sermon at the level of deep structure of the sermon. They provide for the possibility of the gospel to be preached. To them we now turn in the next chapter.

CHAPTER NINE

SERMON FORM II: THE DEEP STRUCTURE

In this Thursday section we have spoken of exterior sermon form that functions at surface levels: introduction, body, conclusion; propositional sermons, narrative sermons, and recent innovations; points, verse-by-verse progression, development of a dominant image—all of these are evident at the surface. Sermons also have a deep structure that functions like grammar in language: it functions to enable the gospel to be proclaimed. Because of this, in many ways, it is more significant than surface structure. Even with automobiles, how well they run is more important on a trip than the style. The same is true for sermons, what matters most is how they perform the gospel, what they do theologically, and this has to do with deep structure.

For most of history, teachers of homiletics have taught their subject as though surface form is all there is. Preachers commonly assume the gospel is proclaimed when the Bible is preached. We spoke earlier of the Grand Canyon in homiletics today between those who seemingly advocate preach-the-text and those who advocate preach-the-gospel. Current textbooks in preaching pay almost no attention to how students are to preach the gospel. Preach-the-text operates uncritically on the assumption that text yields the Word of God and that this Word is the gospel. In fact, the gospel has identifiable content and shape and many biblical texts do not necessarily contain it, thus texts must be treated in a manner that leads to it. When the Bible is read as the church's book, texts point to the gospel, the gospel is their rhetorical purpose, and individual texts authorize it. Thus we arrive at a place of decision. There may have been a time in which students were so well trained in theology and so steeped in their traditions that it was unnecessary to spend much time in preaching class on something so obvious as "What is the gospel?" Discussion of the theological underpinnings of a sermon was unnecessary because churches were thriving and people had confidence that the gospel was being proclaimed. Perhaps that still is the case in some places, but if there is to be any hope for the church in the future, it will arise from being faithful to its calling to preach and thereby live the gospel. The church has no other reason to exist and all else flows from it: pastoral care, social justice, mission outreach. Nurturing faith is primary because, as Christ said, "Apart from me you can do nothing" (John 15:5).

> A basic test of the gospel is that it is hopeful: Jesus Christ is risen. The power of death is broken. A new age has begun.

However, it is also true that we live in a postmodern world in which even favorite assumptions need to be critically examined and tested. Hope is the basic test of the gospel: Jesus Christ is risen. He is alive. We have met him. We are loved. The power of death is broken. In the Holy Spirit he has given us his power. The future is changed; indeed, the past is changed and a new creation begins even as we preach the cross. These are key notions of hope.

A Crisis in Preaching

With regard to the gospel, there is a crisis in preaching. It is quickly highlighted when one picks up anthologies of contemporary sermons. Such sermons are normally chosen for their excellence, so one assumes they provide a better-than-average litmus test of preaching. In fact, there are dozens of sermon anthologies in libraries with the words *Best Sermons* in the title, including the annual anthology series that boldly and brashly claimed in its titles *The Best Sermons of* followed by the year.

Analysis of two particular contemporary volumes is fascinating, though analysis of nearly any anthology yields similar results. These two volumes were selected because the preachers were from a wide range of denominations. I examined each sermon for what it offered by way of God's help. Of twenty sermons in one volume, six offered no hope, seven made only brief passing reference to it, and seven spoke substantially about it, though typically for only one-tenth of the entire length. The other volume had forty-one sermons: eighteen offered no hope, ten had only brief passing reference, and thirteen had substantial hope, occasionally up to half the sermon. In both volumes, hope was preached only when texts obviously spoke of it (for example, the lost is found), yet many texts that spoke obviously of hope yielded none in the sermon.[1] Of the many sermon anthologies I have read, this rough pattern is consistent. Moreover, if one examines even the sermons that speak of hope for what they say of the gospel as the source of that hope, the numbers drop further still.

> If people find the Christian message irrelevant, it may be that God is hard to find in many sermons, hope is not created, and the gospel is not proclaimed. Too frequently we humans are the subject of the sermon and our actions are the focus. God is either left out or communicated as a remote or feckless onlooker who does little.

If these results are an indication of preaching in North America, early warning bells ought to be going off all along the homiletical fault line. Something is wrong. The results indicate that the gospel is not a dominant factor in most sermons. Even when biblical texts are good news, they are often turned into something else. Something about the way in which preaching is being done—and indeed how it has been assessed and taught—needs urgent remedy. As an indication of the depth of the problem and how deeply it has penetrated the church and academy, many homiletics books (and books in other theological disciplines) that are designed to assist preachers substantially leave God out.

Whatever reasons one gives for the decline of membership in many denominations in recent decades, this much seems clear: people leaving the church seem not to have heard the gospel in a way that facilitates faith-filled lives in these difficult times. These folks leave church walking in the old creation, and if there is a new creation begun in preaching, they have not experienced it. The shadow of the cross did not fall across their pew, and the dawn of a new era did not illuminate their paths. Most worrisome is the thought that the next generation is not receiving the faith as the previous one did. If people find the Christian message irrelevant, it could be that God is hard to find in many sermons, and the gospel has gone missing. It is hard to proclaim the gospel if God is not in the program. How does one preach the gospel?

Trouble and Grace as the Grammar of the Gospel

Christian hope springs from the Easter event. In an earlier chapter we noted that the gospel has a polar quality to it: sin and redemption, judgment and atonement, trouble and grace, cross and empty tomb, old age and new creation. The movement from the one to the other is the signature movement of the gospel. Here we claim that trouble and grace are the basic grammar of the gospel, the basic structure that facilitates communication of the gospel. When the gospel provides the intentional deep grammar of the sermon, the sermon is better able to proclaim it. Here are some steps toward that claim:

1. The gospel is polar. Joseph R. Jeter Jr. and Ronald J. Allen speak of it as "an ellipse with two centers: the promise of the unconditional love of God for each and all, and the command of God for justice for each and all."[2] Cultural optimism says, "Be positive." To preach authentic hope, the polar nature of the gospel is needed: something is wrong and God in Christ has set it right. This polarity is evident in what Linda Clader says: "My faith tells me that God is always beautiful, no matter what kind of

word God is communicating to me. If I operate on that assumption, I will be able to receive a word of judgment because behind it, I will be able to hear the more fundamental word of love."[3]

2. Trouble or law puts the burden on us: the sermon needs to discuss what is wrong in the world. At the simplest level, trouble places the burden to act upon humanity. Again, trouble has three expressions: God judging/commanding us; the human condition after the fall/the old order; God suffering (that is, Christ's ongoing crucifixion in the world).

3. Grace and gospel puts the burden on God: the sermon also needs to point to what it is in the nature and person of God that allows us to trust God to be in charge. At the simplest level, grace puts the burden of responsibility on God to act, and the good news is that God has accepted that burden in Christ. Grace may also be conceived or represented in three ways that find their expression in the cross: God forgiving/atonement; God overturning the powers, principalities, and old norms; God acting through people/the new creation.

> **Trouble puts the burden on humans, emphasizing what we must do. Grace puts the burden on God to act, and the good news is that God has accepted that burden in Christ.**

4. In order for the sermon to express the gospel, it needs to generate tension between trouble and grace. This tension already exists, it is not something the preacher manufactures but captures. Both poles are necessary. Clearly hope cannot be found just in judgment; judgment is our condemnation, and sin is the ongoing expression of the old world order that culminates in the crucifixion of Christ. Grace is what God offers against the background of sin and has to do with forgiveness, empowerment, faith, and promise; it is rooted in the gospel, what God did in Christ for our salvation. Grace without cost is a fiction; it is what Bonhoeffer called cheap grace.

John Wesley called the preaching of both judgment and grace in every sermon "the scriptural way, the Methodist way, the true way."[4] Charles H.

Spurgeon (1834–92), the famous Baptist preacher of Southwark, London, taught his preaching students: "The grandest discourse ever delivered is an ostentatious failure if the doctrine of the grace of God be absent from it; it sweeps over [our] heads like a cloud, but it distributes no rain upon the thirsty earth; and therefore the remembrance of it to souls taught wisdom by an experience of pressing need is one of disappointment, or worse."[5]

5. Move overall from trouble to grace in the sermon. One could argue at least three ways for this as the underlying overall movement for the sermon. First, since the gospel is what God does to save, it needs to be heard in relation to trouble; trouble needs to precede grace in the sermon. "From what does God save us?" needs to come first. Second, this movement mirrors the movement of the faith from the Exodus to the promised land, Good Friday to Easter, the crucifixion to the resurrection, from the old creation to the new creation, expulsion from Eden in Genesis to entry to the New Jerusalem in Revelation, despair to hope—not the other way around, and not back and forth like two parts of a hinge gradually wearing each other out. One can find in the Bible other movements (for example, the goodness of creation in Genesis to the fall; righteousness to sin), but these are the movements of sin, not the gospel, and sin is not the defining movement of the Bible as a whole. Third, gospel is treated by many as though it is just content. In fact, it has form that relates to its content: its form is trouble to grace, law to gospel, cross to resurrection.

The Gospel Has Form

Homileticians made a key discovery in recent decades: the gospel is not just content, it has a form and effect. It is the story of what happened at the turn of time in the life, death, resurrection, and ascension of Jesus Christ. It continues to happen in power whenever we preach these events. Stories have structure and can be told in various ways, but the key elements remain the same. Psalms, hymns, parables, letters—they all have basic structural and stylistic features that mark them as separate genres. The same is true of gospel; it has structure and form, which is the definition of a genre. It moves from trouble to grace, from Good Friday to Easter. It may be told and retold in many different ways—from the various perspectives offered by countless individual biblical texts and doctrines—but the basic story, the underlying movement, the final outcome remains the same. Luther claimed that the heart of the gospel is Romans

3:28, "For we hold that a person is justified by faith apart from works prescribed by the law." Others might name the heart of the gospel pointing
to different Bible verses, but if we speak of the gospel of Jesus Christ, such
verses necessarily point to and invite some form of narration of the gospel
story (that is, justification by faith in whom?). A new age has dawned
that exists alongside the remnants of the old, yet we participate already
in the new, and the end is already in sight.

Of course the gospel is not the gospel until it addresses the particular
circumstances of an individual or community life, thus the expression of
the gospel will vary from situation to situation. However, the basic content of the gospel that meets the present has some degree of consistency
given by the personhood of Jesus Christ in the Holy Spirit and the nature
and character of his life, ministry, and unity with God.

The scholarly battle has already been won that determined that the
meaning of a text is affected by its form; form, content, and rhetorical
effect are intimately related. Another battle remains to be won, however.
Some homileticians have now claimed that the same arguments that were
applied to literary genres of the Bible apply to the gospel genre at the
heart of the faith. The gospel has a form, its movement from crucifixion
to resurrection is related to its content, and these contribute toward its
rhetorical and spiritual effect. To deny that the gospel has a form can only
be at the expense of communicating the gospel effectively. Gerhard O.
Forde was getting at the form of the gospel when he said the preacher's
words "have the form of the cross, presuppose it, drive inexorably to it,
and flow from it ... cut[ting] in upon our lives to end the old and begin
the new."[6] Because the gospel has content, form, and effect, the implications for the sermon are large.

It became clear that to preach the gospel was not just a matter of
adding some gospel words to a sermon, the way people add pepper to soup
to enhance flavor. Gospel is not just a surface matter of sprinkling a few
references to Christ here and there. The sermon needs something of the
bold plot, movement, and shape of the gospel, not to mention the language, imagery, and emotion of the cross and empty tomb. It needs some
of the cross's way of putting the old norms to death as well as some of the
resurrection's way of inaugurating a new era. A sermon that fails to communicate joy and hope, even in the midst of suffering, may be said to
have failed to communicate the gospel.

We have seen that sermons have many varieties of exterior form. Most
of them function well as potential vehicles for the gospel and most of

them can be employed to display a movement from trouble to grace, because most of them are concerned with exterior form. The argument made here is that the content, form, and effect of the gospel provide the sermon with deep structure, a grammar, and movement. In other words, to preach the gospel does not reduce the number of sermon forms available; it enhances what each is able to express with them. This is said with at least one exception: the single exposition/application format tends to predispose the sermon to either trouble or grace; thus, at least in its overall structure, it seems to have the least gospel potential.

> To preach the gospel means that the sermon needs something of the plot, movement, and shape of the gospel. The sermon needs to provide an experience of what it is to move from death to life in the name of Jesus Christ and through the power of the Holy Spirit.

Voices Past

To argue that sermons should move from trouble to grace is relatively recent. An Episcopalean, Milton Crum, seems have been the first to suggest it clearly in 1977, though there were hints at it in the decades before.[7] Of course the ideas go back to Paul's notions of law and gospel, and Luther argued that only when people are awakened to their sin may they find safety and security in Christ. Progression seems to be implied. However, neither Luther nor his significant nineteenth-century homiletical commentator, C. F. W. Walthers, conceived of law and gospel homiletically, that is, as providing movement and structure of the sermon. For them, law and gospel were mechanical and static in structure (as were sermons), the necessary poles of theology in general. One jumped back and forth between them in a somewhat haphazard manner. In the sermon itself, one preached law to the sinner and gospel to the repentant soul, and listeners were to have no confusion about what applied to whom.[8]

John Wesley argued that law and gospel may be preached, "in their turns," or "both at once"; they are "the scriptural way, the Methodist way, the true way" to preach Christ.[9] Karl Barth affirmed law to gospel not so much in the sermon as in the preacher's preparation of it:

> The preacher, having thoroughly prepared himself, comes before his congregation, first and foremost, as a man who has been pierced by the Word of God and has been led to repentance in the face of divine judgement; but also as a man who has received with thankfulness the Gospel of forgiveness and is able to rejoice in it. Only in this progression through judgement and grace can preaching become genuinely original.[10]

Thus, for Barth, the sermon reflects the preacher's spiritual discipline throughout the week in preparation for Sunday.

Recent Voices

Even to speak of law and gospel has become problematic in some circles, largely because of the way it has been used—ever since Luther himself—as a tool of anti-Semitism. Law tends to be identified with Old Testament and gospel with New, when, in fact, law and gospel can be found in both Testaments. It is precisely for this reason that one looks for other less-loaded terms like trouble and grace, though even here there is inadequacy, for grace is not necessarily gospel. Grace finds its fullest expression in Jesus Christ, and it could be argued that until the individual knows how to appropriate that grace for herself or himself (that is, through faith), the gospel has not been proclaimed.

What was wrong with leaving law and gospel as poles that found their expression at will within theology? Why did they become perceived as the potential deep structure of sermons? A key factor here was the New Homiletic. It emphasized providing experience, not just information, and in order for trouble and grace to be experienced, each needs its own deliberate focus and time. The New Homiletic stressed that form affects content and effect, and the gospel has all three. It stressed plot and organic structure rather than static mechanical form, and gospel has a plot that needs to grow in relation to the contemporary situation. It stressed that language and metaphor are tensive, generating meaning through an underlying polar structure, and gospel is similarly tensive holding Good Friday and Easter as one. Metaphor says that two poles brought together generate new meaning; thus, with the metaphor love is a red rose, the meaning has something to do with the beauty, tenderness, and nurture required for love, not to mention the association of the color red with the heart. Tension between poles is built into all language systems; for instance, one cannot conceive of bad without conceiving of good, or of justice without injustice. When poles are properly linked, like trouble and grace, with the help of the Holy Spirit they generate new meaning and communicate the faith and life of the gospel. Neither one of the poles expresses it on its own, but held adjacent to each other in the sermon moment, something of the electrical dynamism of the gospel is experienced.

From Trouble to Grace

Starting with Crum, the case was made for sermons to move from trouble to grace. For Richard Lischer, the sermon moves from "the primal unity in God" through "one or more of the following sets of antitheses: chaos to order, bondage to deliverance, rebellion to vindication, despair to hope, guilt to justification, debt to forgiveness, separation to reconciliation, wrath to love, judgment to righteousness, defeat to victory, death to life."[11]

As we saw earlier, Eugene Lowry worked with a similar understanding when he developed his enormously significant *The Homiletical Plot*, in which he proposed that the sermon move to experiencing the gospel and anticipating the consequences.[12] The sermon moves to what Henry H. Mitchell calls "celebration" and "contagion" of joy in many African American churches.[13] James Harris speaks of preaching in the context of oppression with a view toward liberation and transformation.[14] Numerous voices have contributed to make trouble to grace one of the largest yet least frequently discussed schools in contemporary homiletics.[15]

The chart below concerns two deep-structural parts of the sermon. It may help students understand the implications of this distinction in the composition of the sermon.

VARIETIES OF GOSPEL MOVEMENT	
Trouble (or judgment or law) may be broadly conceived in various ways, all of which find us—the church, our neighborhood,	**Grace** (or good news) may be conceived in various ways, all of which depend on a portrayal of God *doing the acting*. The evi-

or our world—falling short of God's intention. The emphasis here is upon what we must do or fail to do at God's urging.	dence that we offer, in addition to the biblical text and tradition, is that found in the cross and resurrection, the true source of Christian hope.
From:	*To:*
Condemnation	Forgiveness
The opposite of the hope we will proclaim from the biblical text	Christian hope as found first in the biblical text (and larger gospel story)
A true reflection of who we are in the brokenness of our life before God; our masks removed, our sins exposed	A description of the manner in which God has already met us, embraced us, and given us the the strength to continue
A development of the judgment in the biblical text and its application to our lives	A development of the grace in the biblical text and its application to our lives, complete with mission possibilities
A focus on the manner in which Christ continues to be crucified today, or in which the exodus is today's story	A focus on Christ's resurrection power today, of the inbreaking of the realm of God in our midst
Our doubts concerning God (or God's actions in the biblical text); Identification of our real needs, as opposed to our conceived needs	The certainty that is ours in faith that takes account of doubt; God's meeting of our real needs
A problem in the world boldly confronted (for example, poverty or violence)	A portrait of God's action in meeting the needs of this world (for example, for hopelessness there is now hope; for despair there is faith; for anxiety there is comfort; for war there is a God who is acting for peace; for homelessness there is a mighty God, willing that a home be found)
The world's values (for example, the manner in which what passes for love or success lets us down)	Christ's overturning of the world's values (for example, strength is found in weakness)

Our "no" to God (and God's "no" to us)	God's "yes" to us
Our "no" to the world; a deepening sense of our distance from God	God's "yes" through us; a mounting sense of God having closed the distance between us
The ways in which the burden of responsibility for what is wrong lies with us	The ways in which God in Christ has accepted the burden and acted to enable us to meet the demands
Dependence on our own resources	Dependence on God
The apparent absence, unfaithfulness, fickleness of God	The steadfast presence, faithfulness, and certainty of God
It is too late	It is not too late
The old creation	The new creation

Listener Experience

The listener's experience is also important in determining the order of judgment and grace. Can a sermon produce hope if it does not end in hope? I suspect it can be done; I just have not heard it. If Buttrick is right, it takes three to four minutes for an idea to take shape in the minds of listeners, and that long spent on trouble will leave an impression.[16]

Still, sermons can be delivered that are only trouble; they are arguably just not the norm. Stephen Farris offers several conditions that apply: "We may preach sermons that are primarily challenge if: (1) the text is primarily challenge, (2) we have searched for the grace that is the basis for the challenge, (3) the people to whom we are preaching are analogically similar to the people to whom the challenge first came, (4) we remember that the challenge itself is more gift than burden."[17]

Some preachers are tempted to swing on trouble and grace like an old gate, back and forth. Several factors are against this. It wears the congregation out. Neither trouble nor grace comes into proper focus. Listeners just start to experience trouble and are rushed on to grace; the implication of each is lost, and they begin to experience numbness. They become caught in a repeating cycle of having the same wound probed and bandaged and probed and bandaged. Or they begin to hear grace and are shifted back to how bad the world is. To switch metaphors, trouble and grace are like two kinds of tea, and each needs time to steep. The experience of first the one and then the other is a mark not only of the gospel but also of God's encounter; trouble and grace are who Christ is. Judgment on its own produces moralism, instructions about behavior, encouragement not to hope too much. Grace on its own (a contradiction in terms since grace is found only in relationship to trouble) sounds like optimistic answers and pious helps. In succession, they offer the demand and promise of God.

Mission and Hope

Some preachers protest that grace cannot be the final note of the sermon. Sermons need to end with mission and lives of faithful service. As Samuel Proctor said, sermons need a So what? or Therefore?, or in the traditional language of the Bible, every sermon needs to answer for itself Micah's question, what does the Lord require of us? (Micah 6:8).

All of this is true, yet preaching effects a transformation of the world by the Word, the same transformation

> Might a sermon create hope for the listener that in its overall progression does not end in hope? It is possible, though unlikely. Trouble places a burden on people. Grace puts the burden on God, and God in Christ has accepted that burden.

from the old age to the new creation that occurs in preaching the cross. Even mission is transformed by the new creation. Obedience is required, yet God gives everything to meet the demand. Various missions—feed the poor, visit the sick, care for shut-ins, take action for justice—in light of the gospel become ministries in which Christ promises to be found empowering faithful disciples. His promise to provide what is needed is what matters. This is Calvin's third use of the law as an excitement to obedience, which is really grace, for as Paul said, "It is God who is at work in you, enabling you both to will and to work for his good pleasure" (Philippians 2:13). Mission itself is transformed from an onerous, even impossible, task to something that has no power to defeat.

Thus, by the end of the sermon, barriers to mission have been overcome by Jesus' death on the cross. The gospel transforms the nature of mission. Exhortations to mission are no longer *commandments*; they are *invitations* to encounter the risen Christ in the power of a new era begun even in the preaching of the gospel. Presented in this light, people ideally reach for their ministry, want it, need it as the essential response to God. Response becomes a delight and privilege.[18] The result of all of this is that even though there are tasks, people are sent away from church with hope and all of the resources grace provides.

Two Kinds of Trouble, Two Kinds of Grace

People naturally tend to think of judgment along a vertical (or transcendent) axis, with God above and us down below, being judged for our failure to keep God's commandments. Judgment in this sense awakens the guilty conscience, for as Herman G. Stuempfle has said, it hits us like a hammer and brings us to our knees asking for forgiveness. This is a very important understanding of judgment, inspired by many places in the Bible, not least the Garden of Eden and Christ on the cross.

> Mission situations thus become a form of both invitation and assurance. They are places of labor but also promises of places up ahead in which people will encounter the empowerment of the risen Christ.

Anne Lamott invokes a vertical understanding when she describes her high school notion of God: "God as high school principal in a gray suit who never remembered your name but is always leafing unhappily through your files."[19]

However, there is another biblical understanding that Stuempfle has developed in a helpful way for preachers.[20] One may use judgment on a horizontal (or immanent) axis that is even more important for contemporary preachers. It can free one from moral finger wagging and pulpit thumping of the sort that can communicate a hierarchical understanding of ministry in which the preacher is at the center as the one in authority and control.

Using this second kind of judgment, one holds a mirror up to the world as it truly is, not as we like to pretend it is, and we find ourselves judged accordingly. Stuempfle called this second understanding of judgment a "mirror of existence." This mirror reflects conditions after the biblical fall: accidents, illness, natural disasters, lack of meaning, anxiety, despair. This mirror also reflects our communal and individual responsibility in relation to situations around us; some people call this systemic evil (evil that resides in human systems). We become conscious of living in wealth while millions of neighbors in other parts of the world are dying in poverty, or of failing to root out what breeds violence, or of misusing the earth's resources in ways that will hurt future generations. Theologians like Juan Luis Segundo, James Cone, Beverly Harrison, and Dorothee Sölle joined many throughout the centuries in naming poverty, injustice, inequality, and oppression as theological concerns.

The term *judgment* implies, for most of us, someone who is doing the judging. The conception we are using here is that judgment is a way of naming the conditions of human life lived under the reality of sin. To speak of oppression and suffering as judgment, then, is not to say that they are the direct results of some specific sin on the part of those who experience them; rather, they are the tragic realities of a world defined by human fallenness. Reinhold Niebuhr understood the human situation as tragic and pitiable as implied in Jesus' words, "weep for yourselves" (Luke 23:28). Niebuhr also said that Christianity was beyond tragedy, that once we weep in repentance, salvation and hope become possible.[21]

A practical implication for the sermon is this: employ good news appropriate to the judgment. If one uses the vertical, transcendent understanding of judgment (the "hammer" variety that finds us at fault with a guilty conscience before God's throne) one will proclaim grace as forgiveness, new life, and fresh opportunity to begin again.

By contrast, if one uses a horizontal, immanent understanding of judgment (that mirrors life as we know it in the fallen world of the old creation), one will proclaim grace as that which overturns the powers of this world and reveals God's saving work in our midst. Stuempfle called this gospel "antiphon [that is, sounding back] to existence."

TWO KINDS OF JUDGMENT AND GRACE		
	Vertical Axis/Transcendent Judgment (hammer)	Horizontal Axis/Immanent Judgment (mirror)
experience:	a guilty conscience	consciousness of suffering
result:	request forgiveness	desire for action
	Grace (vertical)	Grace (horizontal)
experience:	forgiveness	overturning the world
result:	a new beginning	justice, peace, and so on

The right kind of grace matches each kind of judgment. For example, the primary word of grace to the lonely person is not, "You are forgiven." Rather, where there is loneliness one proclaims community. Where there is despair one proclaims new hope. Where there is hunger one proclaims nurture. Where there is war one proclaims peace. One does so because these are all rooted in what the cross has accomplished.

Many of my students have no difficulty preaching vertica l trouble, because it comes fairly easily in this world. It is and sounds judgmental and thus is harder to hear on the part of listeners because it often sounds like a critical parent. (Still, there is a difference: one needs revelation through the Bible to help one know what needs judging from the pulpit.) Horizontal trouble is much more attuned to the contemporary postmodern mind-set, and students often need practice in learning how to convert vertical to horizontal. In other words, if a sermon sounds too heavy-handed, chances are it uses trouble on a vertical axis of judgment. The whole draft does not need to be discarded if one knows how to do the conversion.

The key difference between the two is clear: the vertical judges and condemns; the horizontal tries to empathize, helps folks understand, and leads the congregation to deeper awareness without ever condoning. Vertical treatment of our consumer society condemns it as greedy; horizontal treatment helps people understand that we are afraid that there will not be enough, or we are afraid that others will think less of us if we do not own something. Empathy is key.

Culture today tends to resist authority and thus tends to hear horizontal trouble better than vertical. (There is a time and place for each.)

Vertical trouble sounds like a critical parent. Horizontal trouble sounds like an understanding friend. Preachers need to know how to convert vertical trouble—which comes all too naturally for most of us—into horizontal trouble in a sermon draft. The following statements of vertical trouble are converted into statements of horizontal trouble. Remember that empathy is the key:

1. Vertical: We are greedy in our consumption of goods.
    Horizontal: We are afraid there will not be enough for us.
2. Vertical: Those people are wrong to take drugs.
    Horizontal: They are looking for God in the wrong places.
3. Vertical: That man's behavior is obnoxious.
    Horizontal: That man does not know he is loved.
4. Vertical: They should pray and go to church.
    Horizontal: They have lost hope that there is anything beyond the present moment.
5. Vertical: We must change our ways.
    Horizontal: We have tried to change on our own and failed too often.

Student Assignment 13: Make your own list of five situations that represent vertical trouble and convert them to horizontal. Find a paragraph in the sermon you are working on (or some other sermon, perhaps from a book) that deals with our world using vertical trouble. Rewrite the paragraph using horizontal trouble.

The Sermon in Two Theological Parts

Trouble and grace are present in all preaching, often without the preacher being aware or in control. A movement from trouble to grace can function as a homiletical norm because it functions at the level of deep structure or grammar. In other words, for the most part it need not be limited by what surface forms one might employ.

From a deep theological perspective at least, the sermon may be conceived in two roughly equal parts, each of which gains strength and influence from the presence of the other. The first part is trouble and serves to make listeners aware of their or others' sin (vertical) or brokenness and suffering (horizontal). It represents the old order and puts the burden on humanity to change. The second part is grace and declares that God accepts the burden for that change in and through Jesus Christ. The cross, in being proclaimed, makes a difference, brings in the new age. By the end of the sermon, trouble is not forgotten; it is not erased. Rather, it exists in tension with grace, and grace is the dominant note because it is God's final word. Between the two, people "work out [their] own salvation in fear and trembling" (Philippians 2:12).

The Sermon in Four Pages

Once the sermon is conceived in two parts of roughly equal length, one is not far from what I have called the four pages of the sermon.[22] These pages are not literal; they are metaphors for four different theological functions that each form a quarter of the sermon.

The Word arises from biblical texts, and biblical texts need application to our time. Trouble is the movement from the biblical text (Page One) to our situation (Page Two). The grace of the second half is the movement from grace in the biblical text (Page Three) to grace in our situation (Page Four). We already saw these pages earlier in this book when we selected from the Isaiah passage a concern of the text, a concern of the sermon, a major concern of the text, and a major concern of the sermon. If just a short paragraph or so of material is used from today to introduce the entire sermon, it is not considered to be one of the pages. These pages are not inventions in the sense that sermons talk about either human actions or God's, in the Bible or today, in ways that are trouble or grace. In other words, these pages already exist in sermons, although often unconsciously or without control.

At one level, these four pages may be conceived as a model: the pages can be rearranged, for instance, for a shorter sermon or for speaking with youth or children. There is beautiful simplicity in Two-One-Three-Four. Numerous other variations are possible—for instance, one-two, one-two, three-four—provided that the overall division between trouble and grace remains roughly equal.

Sermons can be analyzed using these four pages. Students automatically know where each kind of material will be placed. For instance, a joyful story about someone finding God's help on a plane belongs on Page Four. An account of Paul lamenting the state of the church in Corinth belongs on Page One of a sermon on Corinthians. AIDS in Africa is Page

Two. A sad story with a positive ending can be split between Pages Two and Four. Students wanting greater detail with ample examples can turn to my *Four Pages of the Sermon* and my *Broken Words*.[23]

Why Four Pages Now?

Previous ages were perhaps more gospel centered; people knew their Bibles and lives were focused on the church. Sermons typically lasted more than an hour. Preachers were not attentive to trouble and grace (as we noted, they called them law and gospel) because in their method of meandering through Scripture, they were bound to cover both in the allotted time. Moreover, they preached key theological doctrines, and most of these contain gospel at the core.

Today's preachers have a largely different understanding from their forebears of what is a preaching text and what it means to preach it. Our ancestors' notion of text seemed both smaller and larger than a complete unit of Scripture: smaller in that they often chose just a few words, a part of a verse, and found a doctrine in it; larger because they felt free to roam at will in the sermon through Scripture with their doctrine as a guide, as though the entire Bible was the legitimate and appropriate text.

> The four pages are four theological functions of any sermon. Sermons can either talk about human actions or God's, in the Bible or today, in ways that are trouble or grace. Page One is trouble in the text; Page Two is trouble in our world; Page Three is grace in the text; Page Four is grace in our world.

Most preachers today do not feel it legitimate simply to go to a passage and extract a doctrine; rather, they try to treat the text with historical integrity. Sermon time in worship typically is greatly reduced from previous centuries and attention spans are shortened by television and other media. People do not know their Bibles. Biblical scholars are geared to historical criticism and the academy and seemingly less geared to the church. Many theologians have their own pursuits that are not centered on the church. In other words, the resources preachers depend on may not have the best interests of the pulpit in mind. All of these factors contribute to the need for preachers to preach the gospel.

Determining the Pages

One danger in conceiving sermons in two halves is ending up with two sermons instead of one. In order to avoid this, the trouble and the grace need to fit each other like hand and glove. At one level, this means that if vertical trouble (that is, guilt) is dominant on Pages One and Two, vertical grace (that is, forgiveness) needs to be dominant in the second half. At a more basic level, it means that one chooses as a theme sentence a statement of grace with God (in one of the persons of the Trinity) as the subject. This will be the theme of the entire sermon and will be the specific subject of the entire Page Three dealing with grace in the Bible. Page Four will be its transposed version, the major concern of the sermon.

Starting with that theme sentence, work backward to determine a concern of the text to use for Page One. It will be a statement of trouble and will indicate why God deemed it necessary to act in the manner indicated. For example, in one text it might be that Israel was hard-hearted; in another, the woman was bleeding; or yet another, the people were oppressed. In this manner of using simple inversion, Pages One and Two lead naturally to Pages Three and Four, and sermon unity begins to be built-in.

For example, return for a moment to the call of Isaiah and a possible layout of the Four Pages. Page One: Isaiah was not good enough. Page Two: Our world is not good enough. Page Three: God gives Isaiah a new identity. Page Four: God gives us a new identity (that is, in Christ).

Another example is from John 10:11-18. Page One: Many people follow false shepherds. Page Two: Many people unknowingly choose death. Page Three: Jesus Christ is the good shepherd. Page Four: Christ gives life.

A final example may serve from the Epistles, namely 1 Corinthians 1:17-25. Page One: The cross sounds like foolishness. Page Two: Many today dismiss the church. Page Three: God's power is in the cross. Page Four: Our power is in weakness. Or, our power is to preach Christ.

In terms of actual practice, once one sets out potential pages in this fashion, preachers will start to interact with their sentences for each page. They will say things to themselves like, "That isn't true all the time," or, "That seems too bold," or, "But what about this?" Do not let these responses cause you to reject what the text is inviting you to say. Rather, the sermon is starting to write itself. Build your resistance, exceptions, qualifications, and nuances into the sermon. Something is happening. You have something to say. If you have resistance to a text, find the path that will allow you and others to affirm what the text means.

> **Work backward from the theme sentence (Page Three) to determine the themes of Page One and Two: Why did God act in the manner indicated? What was wrong?**

A special word is needed about Page Four. As on Page Two, use stories of modern life. Use speech that pictures God acting in the midst of human affairs, phrases that allow others to hear Christ's approaching footstep or to feel the wetness of his saliva on their eyes or to experience the firmness of his healing touch. One might say something like this: "The woman, lying in her hospital bed, drew great comfort in hearing her daughter's distinct footsteps approaching from down the hall. Those same footsteps reminded her of footsteps she had heard many times in her life, the footsteps of Christ drawing near."

Sometimes stories are hard to find for Page Four. If you are ever desperate, do not hesitate to use some of the positive biblical stories as Page-Four stories, even though, strictly speaking, they are not. They can nonetheless function as though they are in an emergency. They can function as stories of people who were encountered and empowered by a saving God. Normally, however, we ought to be able to hold up people from our own time, for God is alive and active in our world.

The Difference Between Grace and Gospel

A small caution may be needed at this point. We have been talking about the need for grace to be present with trouble in order for the gospel to be experienced and proclaimed. Yet grace often needs something more to bring it home as gospel: grace is not gospel until it is experienced and received, as Luther said, *pro me*, for me. The listener needs to know—or be reminded of—the way that grace is his or hers. One can know that God is love and still feel shut out from that love because one is unlove-able. Grace becomes gospel through faith in the One who died on the cross for us and who rose to offer new life. Grace becomes gospel when one knows that the power of the old ways has been defeated and that new life is already begun in Christ. Grace becomes gospel when people hear and understand the truth of Paul's words in Romans 8:38-39, "For I am convinced that neither death, nor life, nor angels, nor rulers, nor things present, nor things to come, nor powers, nor height, nor depth, nor any-thing else in all creation, will be able to separate us from the love of God in Christ Jesus our Lord." In other words, the grace in the text needs to be linked to the person of Jesus Christ such that the text is seen as an anticipation or extension of the cross and resurrection. This, after all, is the starting and renewal point of faith. In other words, gospel is Christ-specific. We will return to this matter of linking texts and the gospel later.

Review

The following review is designed to provide a checklist for students who want to try a sermon using the grammar of the Four Pages.

1. The biblical text, as the normal source for what one says, needs to be treated at least twice in the sermon, using a concern of the text or major concern of the text as a guide. (Beginning students are advised to stick to only two substantial developments of the text, each perhaps around two hundred words, especially if, for class purposes, a limit of, say, ten minutes is allotted for the entire sermon.) The first encounter with the text develops judgment and the second develops grace.

2. After each biblical treatment (Pages One and Three), make some form of application to today (Pages Two and Four), using the transposed concern of the sermon or major concern of the sermon as a guide, remain-ing true to the judgment or grace of the section. For example, do not go from trouble in the text to grace in our world or from grace in the text to

trouble in our world. Use stories of modern life on these pages; do not get caught up in long abstract discourse.

3. Maintain the integrity of each Page: in dealing with the Bible, generally stick with the context of Bible times. Keep trouble mainly in the trouble section and grace in the grace section. Brief references to trouble are appropriate in the grace section and vice versa; the theme sentence is appropriate to be stated and restated anywhere in the sermon as often as may be helpful. Ten times may not be too much with the exact wording, and other ways of restating it can complement that.

4. Avoid making vertical judgmental trouble the consistent norm; rather, learn to employ the empathetic horizontal form. Try to keep the same form dominant in both halves.

5. If you tell a story of contemporary experience that implies both trouble and grace, split the story (in the same manner that we did the biblical text). Tell the trouble part in the trouble section and the grace part in the grace section. When returning to a former story in the grace section, this should be near the end of the sermon, for it almost always signals closure to the listeners.

> ## Homiletical Method
> 1. Move from trouble to grace.
> 2. Use each of the Four Pages.
> 3. Maintain the integrity of each Page.
> 4. Be consistent in terms of dominant vertical or horizontal trouble and grace.
> 5. Split contemporary stories if necessary.

Responses to Critics: Questions and Answers

Numerous criticisms can be made of the approach presented in this chapter—some from others, some of my own; some anticipate responses of students. Let me try to answer as many of them as possible here as a way to continue the conversation and clarify any confusion.

Question: Are the Four Pages not just one model among many?

Answer: No. Its primary significance is as a grammar for all sermons, and the Pages operate to varying degrees of efficiency in all sermons. Trouble and grace represent the grammar and movement of the gospel. They are the character of the gospel, the character of Jesus Christ, his life, work, and realm.

Question: Is trouble-grace not just a fancy way of talking about problem-solution?

Answer: There are a couple of responses here. First, in spite of superficial similarities, I doubt if one would ever think of problem-solution as an adequate way to speak of the crucifixion and resurrection (problem: Jesus died; solution: Jesus rose) or of the turn from the old age to the new creation, yet these events provide the form, content, and effect of trouble-grace. Second, problem-solution is static, mechanical, and modern. An answer is provided—over and done; trouble and grace is a dynamic relationship that retains the identities of the two poles while generating a third new meaning. Trouble is not gospel on its own, nor is grace, but rightly harnessed, gospel and faith are the result. Moreover, trouble is not forgotten once the gospel is proclaimed, the way a problem is answered and dispensed with; trouble and grace are both retained in the listener's mind and heart, and out of the tension, gospel is experienced, hence comes faith.

Question: Biblical texts do not necessarily move from law to gospel, so why should the sermon?

Answer: True, texts do not all move this way but the gospel that is the goal of preaching moves in this manner and the sermon need not follow the chronology of the text in order to represent the text or the gospel faithfully. Again, is the goal of the preacher primarily to preach the text or the gospel?

Question: Are not trouble and grace actually interwoven?

Answer: Yes, trouble and grace cannot be separated easily; trouble is sometimes grace and the gospel is often troubling. Stephen Farris speaks of struggling in futility to assemble a grill without the instructions, and, upon being handed the instructions, discovering what a gift commandments can be.[24] For preaching, one merely tries to separate trouble and grace as much as possible in the time available in order that the listener may experience the full weight of each in the same manner that Good

Friday and Easter, though one event, are separated and need to be experienced on their own.

Question: Is predictability not an issue? Will trouble-grace give sermons a predictable quality and form?

Answer: Yes and no. There is something predictable about the gospel message, and there should be; the listeners do not need to be anxious in every sermon about whether or not Jesus will rise from the dead this week, as may seem to be the case in some sermons. The exterior form however need not be predictable. Because trouble-grace functions at a deep structural level, the congregation is not aware of it any more than they concentrate on the lead in looking at stained glass. They listen at the surface level to comprehend and interact with what is said.

Question: Is trouble-grace in danger of reducing Christian theology to one doctrine, for example the doctrine of redemption?

Answer: Trouble-grace is not the doctrine one preaches each week, for that is determined largely by the theme sentence arising out of the biblical text. Rather, trouble-grace is the tenor of the gospel; it is what the gospel sounds like, heard from the perspective of various texts and doctrines. (A later chapter will explore the range of important doctrines a preacher needs to address using trouble and grace.) In this regard, doctrines are like the biblical texts from which they arise: they give perspectives on the cross, even as they can be lenses through which people receive God's light.

Question: Not all doctrines move from trouble to grace. What about doctrines like creation or the sovereignty of God? Does trouble-grace not threaten to compromise such doctrines?

Answer: First, even the creation account moves from chaos ("a formless void and darkness," Genesis 1:2) to order. Every Christian doctrine has a human dimension: the creation of Adam and Eve with free will anticipates the fall; God's providence (understood either as foreseeing or providing) implies human failure to trust; God's sovereignty contrasts human attempts to be in control. The human dimension of Christian doctrine is typically trouble, and the divine dimension is grace. Trouble-grace actually enhances our ability to teach doctrines effectively; it provides a responsible way of doing theology.

Question: Might fewer sermon forms be available with trouble-grace? For instance, can one preach the gospel and still preach the literary forms of the Bible?

Answer: Advocates of that approach rarely say that sermons on the Epistles should be letters, that sermons on the Psalms should be sung, or that sermons on the Beatitudes should be lists. Nor do they say that the order or chronology of the text must be the chronology of the sermon. Perhaps if they did, there might be a problem. Rather, what Mike Graves calls form-sensitivity is advocated:[25] some aspect of a text's form is to be imitated in the sermon, perhaps an image or rhetorical device. Since that imitated form is largely a surface form, trouble to grace can still function at a deep level.

Question: Doesn't the gospel require many forms?

Answer: Some preachers seem to resist the idea that the gospel is polar, that it is cruciform and that something of this form needs to be present in its communication. Since biblical form is a necessary part of a text's meaning, it follows that the form of the gospel is important for it as well. Some scholars are committed both to preaching the gospel and to respecting the integration of form, content, and rhetorical effect of biblical texts, yet they deny that the gospel has a form.[26] They are right in saying that many sermon forms are needed in order to communicate the gospel, yet they are thinking of exterior form not deep structure or grammar. Sermons do need variety, yet we need to be willing to examine our assumptions and not simply presume that the gospel is present when we preach a text. Critics who make this assumption need to discuss the gospel in a significant manner in their textbooks and not just assume it, explain what they mean by it, show in what ways it operates in their homiletic, indicate how it is present in any of the forms they use or recommend, and give guidance to help students get to the gospel in their preaching. Instead, nearly all of us teaching homiletics have been silent on these matters; we have been schooled in preach-the-text and are more complacent than we should be in matters of preach-the-gospel.

Biblical criticism has exercised a dominant influence over homiletics, and perhaps rightly so, as long as its goals were the pulpit. The New Homiletic trusted this relationship implicitly, yet this trust may no longer be warranted. For all of the continuing centrality of biblical studies for the pulpit, and for all of the ongoing need for preachers to do careful exegesis for the pulpit, the field of biblical studies in general has failed to account for either the Bible as revelation or how biblical texts are the gospel. This may be the real proof of a hermeneutical method; does it engage how the Word of God then is the Word of God now? The New Homiletic is focused on other issues and is perhaps too closely wed to biblical studies to depart from it significantly. In any case, preachers need to learn from the New Homiletic and move ahead. One important step is to reclaim in a modern way some of the theological ground of past preachers, without making their mistakes. What is needed is the ability to proclaim the gospel.

Student Assignment 14: Choose a sermon form from either this or the preceding chapter and complete a first draft of your sermon. Try using trouble and grace as the deep structure whatever exterior form you choose.

For Further Reflection and Response Concerning Thursday

1. Many of the exterior forms for the overall sermon are like molds into which one pours sermon thoughts. The New Homiletic argues that sermons are not just content looking for a form; form is organic. Thus, to a considerable extent, form happens through writing. Is the one an old approach and the other new, or is there some validity in each? How do you best compose, with a predetermined surface form or with one that evolves?

2. So many things are wrong with the world. Do you think that preachers can really afford to spend as little as a quarter of the sermon analyzing the world's problems (that is, Page Two)? Might preaching the gospel steer sermons toward faith and away from social ills?

3. To suggest that biblical texts do not necessarily contain the gospel seems like a big departure from what is common. Even to look for God in texts seems like a big step. Do these steps seem too big or radical?

4. Is there a difference between finding the Word of God in a text and finding the gospel, or are they necessarily the same? Can the Word of God not be the gospel?

Section V

Friday: Matters of Style and Substance

W e are in the final stage of the preacher's hermeneutical circle, "What the preacher says." This book has laid out the week day by day to encourage beginning preachers to spread out the tasks as much as possible, recognizing that an individual preacher's week will vary. However, once one arrives at the tasks assigned here for Friday and Saturday, there is no particular order to them, and their assignment to particular days here is somewhat arbitrary: any of the tasks laid out for these days could be a part of composition on Thursday or revision on Saturday.

The tasks in this Friday section attend to matters of style—in particular oral style, or writing for the ear, and substance—ensuring that the sermon is persuasive. In the Saturday section, we will return to matters of preaching the gospel.

CHAPTER TEN

SPEAKING FOR THE EAR

God's Word is spoken, and preaching is an oral event. Such an obvious point may seem scarcely worth pausing to consider. Yet there is more to it than may at first strike the eye, or ear. How the sermon is composed—the choice of words, the way thought is constructed—are all affected by the fact that sermons are meant to be spoken and heard. Linda Clader says that the final stage of her sermon composition is revising her sermon into an oral manuscript. "I try to find a style that is colloquial and truly oral (short, sometimes incomplete sentences; lots of images; a certain amount of repetition; simple transitions), but still dignified. If I find that I am trying to say something that won't go into oral style, I prune ruthlessly to get rid of it."[1] Why is this important? Some might say that surely it is the substance of what a preacher says that matters.

Suppose we were to attend a church service where the preacher was well prepared but became ill. Copies of a fully written manuscript of the sermon that was to have been preached are distributed for silent reading at the appropriate time during the service. Whereas this unusual exercise might be of benefit, we would not experience it to the same extent as a personal spoken address by the preacher who composed it. Listeners depend on personal expression, tone, gesture, emphasis, and pace to communicate the preacher's intent. In written form, these are absent.

Suppose the unfortunate preacher is able to send a DVD of the sermon to be played in the service. Would that suffice? Is the solution to insufficient numbers of preachers video links? or satellite television? or even three-dimensional holograms? Whatever value these may have in themselves, the event nature of preaching would still suffer. Preaching is personal communication that uses eye contact and is based in this time and place, in the personal and social needs of this hour, as preacher and congregation experience God's Word together. Though preaching needs extensive preparation, there is nonetheless an element of spontaneity to it. Preachers are moved by the Holy Spirit to make certain emphases, or proceed in a different direction, even as they preach, and listeners likewise are moved by the Spirit to understand.

The office of preacher is important. Preachers are set apart by the church for the particular office of Word, Sacrament, and pastoral care. The preacher not only represents the authority of the church, the one who the church has set aside for this function, he or she is also the one Christ uses in a particular way to speak God's Word. In becoming preachers, we agree to place the congregation's welfare before our own personal wants. This covenantal relationship of trust and love is embodied in the preacher, and for this there is no disembodied technological substitute. One of the problems of religion in America, says Charles L. Rice, is the "disembodiment of the Word."[2] The fact that the pastor preaches is important for how preaching is heard.

Sermons are spoken; this is essential to their nature, not incidental. The church has always insisted that the sermon is a spoken word.[3] The Word is not silent—or where it is silent, as in the case of signing for the deaf, it is still eventful. Theological libraries have large collections of sermons that gain their name by having first been preached. Sermons are events in time: God's Word addressed to particular congregations in particular contexts. For this reason Luther claimed that the gospel "should not be written but shouted" and that "the church is not a pen-house but a mouth-house."[4]

Herein lies a problem: in Luther's day (and in some local communities and regions today) writing imitated speech. We can see this even in ancient Hebrew, Greek, and Latin manuscripts where individual words and sentences run together, just as they do in actual speech, without punctuation or even capitalization to mark sentences. With the tremendous influence of radio, television, videophones, and the music and film industries, much of our conversation imitates speech that we hear.

However, in theology this is generally not the case. Seminary training is largely geared to the page, namely, the essay and the written exam. Until the mid-1800s, rhetoric (the classical oral art of persuasion) was at the heart of education, and examinations in schools and universities were oral, which meant that speaking was part of one's training in most subjects. By the late 1800s, education switched from oral to written exams, an economical development that improved writing but ultimately eroded the oral skills, not least of preachers-in-training. By the 1900s, rhetoric was in such decline that poet T. S. Eliot said it had become "merely a vague term of abuse for any style that is bad."[5]

Unfortunately, the pendulum has swung so far in the other direction that training in speech is rare. Often after eighteen years of academic training, most of it for the page, theological writers tend not to imitate speech; rather, our theological speech normally imitates writing. Speech that imitates academic writing often sounds like a lecture or an essay. Using it, one repeats the theological language and jargon of articles one has read; one probably stays in one's "head" and does not move into one's "heart." Experience is kept at arm's length.

Simple direct speech is important. Cyprian (200–258) said preachers are to use "not clever but weighty words, not decked up to charm a popular audience with cultivated rhetoric, but simple and fitted by their unvarnished truthfulness for the proclamation of divine mercy" (*Letter to Donatus*, 2). Luther said sermons should speak to the heart of the people "as simply and childishly and as popularly and as commonly" as possible.[6] Karl Barth echoed them: "Let [preachers] be simple . . . follow the path on which the Bible leads them [and] see things as they are and as they unfold in actual experience. This will preserve them from displays of doctrinal erudition which are of no great importance."[7]

Simpler speech is one of the things that distinguishes spoken from written communication, but the distinction is richer than that. Additional knowledge about words is needed, particularly knowledge of how our choice of words can actually assist God in preaching. Once we conceive of preaching as an oral event, we begin to shift our ways of thinking. Instead of composing with the eye for the page, we begin to compose with the ear for oral delivery and aural reception.

Words Heard

How may we compose sermons for the ear? Numerous scholars, like Jesuit priest Walter J. Ong, suggested for years that this is not just a matter of composing aloud and using words that sound good to the ear. A different way of thinking is involved. The differences are similar to those between a highly oral culture and a highly literate one.

We can get a sense of this by looking at the Bible. The biblical world was predominantly oral. Whereas biblical records obviously come from skilled ancient writers, the writer's world was highly specialized, not the norm for most people. Even those ancient writers were saturated with oral ways of thought.[8] We often assume incorrectly that rural biblical communities were literate in our sense of the word and that the biblical writers thought of writing the way we do. In fact, in the ancient world, writing was a skilled technology, and markings on the page were more like musical notes that needed to be sounded in order to be understood.[9] Thus we miss the significance of much of what we read. For example, we have already seen that we would be closer to biblical understandings of God's Word if we used terms such as the Sound of God, the Speaking of God, God's Voice, the Action of God, or the Event of God.

It would be easy for us, along with many scholars, to dismiss such expressions of thought negatively as unlearned, prelogical or prerational, belonging to "primitive" societies that lived by myths that no longer correspond to a reasonable worldview (for example, Bultmann and his followers). However, scholars now wisely avoid comparisons that lead to calling such societies "primitive" and appreciate their sophistication.

> Theological speech tends to imitate writing. To preach for the ear involves not just a shift of a few words, but a shift in thought from abstract to concrete and from literary to oral.

Only with struggle do we recover their more vibrant ways of thinking and speaking for the pulpit. One feature of language in oral cultures worth imitating in preaching is that this language was "attentive to the sensory (the concrete) and was more disposed to describing actions than to creating abstractions because people hearing what was said or sung could feel and follow concrete actions."[10]

New Perspectives on Oral Ways of Thought

"An arranged mind is resistant to seeing," says Eduard R. Riegert about the need for imagination: "The preacher is constantly at work trying to unarrange minds and lives."[11] The fascinating research results of Russian scholar Aleksandr Luria into peasant culture in the first half of the twentieth century may serve to awaken the imagination to alternative ways of thought. He discovered that people in truly oral cultures (people who have never been exposed to education) think in their own ways:

- They named individual colors not with abstract terms but according to things: tobacco, liver, wine, lake, sky, decayed teeth, and so on.[12] It is interesting how few colors are in the Bible.

- They were highly practical. When shown a picture of three adults and one child and asked, "Which one does not belong?" they answered, "They all belong. They were all working and the child was needed to fetch things."[13]

- Syllogisms were not used to infer new understanding. For example, precious metals do not rust. Gold is a precious metal. Does it rust? Respondents to this type of question would say they did not know. It had not been part of their experience.[14]

- They described who they were in terms of physical characteristics and appealed to what others might say about them. There was no abstract sense of self.[15]

- These responses do not indicate lack of intelligence. They indicate a different use of intelligence, an alternate way of thinking.

Preaching is oral; our sermons are heard aurally; and our rhetoric must reflect our medium. *Write for the ear, not for the eye,* is the frequent homiletical maxim. This is no small task as Charles Bartow, G. Robert Jacks, Jana Childers, Richard Ward, and numerous others tell us. A shift in consciousness is needed in how we use language.

Words in Aid of God's Event

Why should we care about words when we communicate God? Why not just speak and leave the rest to the Holy Spirit? These are good questions. Faith can be strengthened or diminished by the language we use to understand it. Many of the good words we use for God—words like eternal, immortal, immutable, omniscient, omnipresent, all-perfect, all-powerful, and a host of others—if used in excess can imply that God is impersonal and remote. Often preachers are simply unaware of the words and images they use for God. A preacher may say, "God's immutable and eternal will may be discerned to oppose injustice in the world," instead of just saying, "God fights injustice." Preachers need to speak with deep simplicity and concrete clarity about God's action in people's lives.

A preacher's words can also assist the event of God's encounter in the sermon. Biblical understandings of words are different from our own, in part because Hebrew and Koine Greek are not languages of abstraction.[16] We know abstract language, for it is the sort that dominates theological education; yet concrete language, rooted in the world we experience around us, is necessary for the pulpit.

This difference can be illustrated. The following discussion of the inspiration of Scripture by Owen Thomas is abstract in a manner appropriate for systematic theology:

> This theory of verbal inspiration and of revelation as the communication of propositional truths from God to humanity does not fit the facts of the Bible. It makes the words of the Bible the locus of revelation rather than the events described in the Bible. The words of the Bible are the record of events and the interpretation of them as events in which God is acting. Faith, or the reception of revelation in the Bible is clearly not the acceptance of supernaturally communicated propositions but rather trust in and obedience to the living God who confronts humanity in the events of the Bible.[17]

Whereas this is a good use of language for its scholarly and written rhetorical purpose, if used from the pulpit it will not be effective in most congregations. None of the physical senses is awakened; no emotion is addressed; nothing personal is communicated about God. For preaching, we might try something more concrete:

> When the Bible was written, God did not decide to lie
> down in lines on a page and squeeze into particular
> words lined up on that page, which we could then dust
> off and lift up and have them turn back into God's
> truth. God always has been found where the action is
> happening, in the midst of human affairs, particularly

where people are in despair and needing help that is beyond themselves. The Bible records crucial events, but it is the living God who speaks through them and the words of the Bible illumining the events of all times. It is God who in this manner shows us who God is, and it is this God who meets us now and gives us all the faith to carry on.

Concrete language such as this (you may have a better example) enables clear communication with the hearer.

> Student Assignment 15: Make a list of as many metaphors and names for God as you might typically draw upon for a sermon. After doing this, go to a source like *The New Interpreter's Dictionary of the Bible* (Nashville: Abingdon Press, 2006—check under "God, names of," "God, metaphors for," and "Jesus, metaphors for") and make a list of all the metaphors and names for God that the Bible uses. Compare your two lists and identify ways of speaking of God that you might want to employ more in preaching and prayer. One might pay particular attention to lifting up feminine images of God.

Abstract language is important and preachers cannot, and need not, eliminate it from preaching. A problem arises only if too much of our pulpit language is abstract: listening to it is hard. Communication is likely to suffer, and people are likely to drift in their minds unless use of it is limited.

The Bible as Model for Concrete Language

Preachers use biblical texts to influence the form and content of what they say. They might also use words the way the Bible uses words as an aid to be more concrete in theological expression. Augustine was the first to recommend this when he wrote the first preaching textbook, *On Christian Doctrine.* He had been a formidable teacher of classical rhetoric and now, as a bishop, when students wanted him to teach them about rhetoric, he replied that they did not need all of this formal training; they needed only to imitate what they found in Scripture.

For practical purposes, students might imitate any of the following biblical models, remembering that the ability to speak concretely can be a lifelong goal:

1. *God's Word as Event:* Instead of speaking of God's Word as an abstract thing (like our idea of word), we could speak of God's Word doing what God speaks. Isaiah spoke this way:

> so shall my word be that goes out from my mouth;
>   it shall not return to me empty,
> but it shall accomplish that which I purpose,
>   and succeed in the thing for which I sent it. (Isaiah 55:11)

Example: God's Word is misunderstood if we think of it as last month's unopened mail. It is not something we can push to one side or trample underfoot. It is more like a fax in the machine, a phone call coming through, a speeding train in a tunnel, a plane taking off, a planet spinning into a new day that will not be stopped.

2. *God Speaking Now:* The most important Hebrew and Greek words for *word* (including *dabar* and *logos*) share a common root (meaning "say," "speak," "tell," and so on) that communicate something happening now, in the manner of "Thus says the Lord."

Example: "Do you not hear God's voice right now, whispering in your ear?" or, "Listen for what God is saying to us now," or, "Christ is calling each of you by name, Mary, Bill, Tom, Sarah. (Put in your own name.) You can hear it."

3. *The Word as Creating:* Here we remember both the Genesis creation account and Psalm 33:6, in which God's Word is the agent of creation: "By the word of the LORD the Heavens were made, / and all their host by the breath of his mouth."

Example: We may be sitting here thinking, "This is all well and good, but when I leave this place, everything is just going to be the same as it was." Well that isn't true. While we have been here listening to God, God has been busy with the clay of our lives, molding a new future filled with new possibility and promise. With God creating our future, how can we dwell on our past?

4. *The Word as Command:* God's law carries an ongoing promise of fulfillment. We may speak of this command affectionately, warmly, and inti-

mately, as though we make no distinction between it and God, who uttered it. The psalmist spoke in this manner:

> I treasure your word in my heart,
> so that I may not sin against you.
> Blessed are you, O LORD;
> teach me your statutes.
> With my lips I declare
> all the ordinances of your mouth.
> I delight in the way of your decrees,
> as much as in all riches. (Psalm 119:11-14)

Example: How certain are the words God utters, for they fly to their destination without delay or detour, arriving at the same moment they are sent, healing those who are wounded, feeding those who are hungry, visiting those who are alone.

5. *Personify Attributes of the Word*: Personification of the attributes of God (for example, wisdom, love, and power) can help communicate a personal God whose actions may be seen in this world:

> Does not wisdom call,
> and does not understanding raise her voice?
> On the heights, beside the way,
> at the crossroads she takes her stand;
> beside the gates in front of the town,
> at the entrance of the portals she cries out.
> (Proverbs 8:1-3)

Example: God's love does not mope around the apartment, moving from fridge to TV and from TV to fridge, occasionally looking out to see if anything is happening. God's love does not know enough places to go and cannot get there soon enough.

6. *The Word as Objects in Action*: Our model here can be some of the startling imagery of the Bible that pictures God's Word in surprising ways. Thus in Zechariah, the words of God's curse upon the thief materialize as a "flying scroll," measuring thirty feet by fifteen feet: "It shall enter the house of the thief . . . and it shall abide in that house and consume it, both timber and stones" (5:1, 4). Elsewhere God's Word becomes a substance to eat: "Your words were found, and I ate them, / and your words became

to me a joy / and the delight of my heart" (Jeremiah 15:16); and, "'Eat this scroll, and go, speak to the house of Israel.' . . . Then I ate it; and in my mouth it was as sweet as honey" (Ezekiel 3:1-3); and, "So I went to the angel and told him to give me the little scroll; and he said to me, 'Take it, and eat; it will be bitter to your stomach, but sweet as honey in your mouth'" (Revelation 10:9).

Example: Take this word of hope that you have been given this morning, climb in it, and drive it home. Let everyone see you driving it, and wave to all you see. Go up and down Main Boulevard honking all the way along, so that everyone will hear. Park it outside your place in some conspicuous spot, maybe with a yellow line, and to everyone who asks, "Whose is that?" just say, "It belongs to Christ."

> God's Word may be variously portrayed as: event, speaking, creating, command, personified action, objects in action, power given to us, and one of the three persons of the Trinity.

7. *The Word as Power Given to Us*: Christ commissioned us to speak with his power (Mark 16:15ff; Matthew 26:18ff). Paul spoke this way: "My speech [logos] and my proclamation [kerygma] were not with plausible words of wisdom, but with a demonstration of the Spirit and of power, so that your faith might rest not on human wisdom but on the power of God" (1 Corinthians 2:4-5). This was the way with the exorcisms of the disciples. This is the way with us.

Example: These words flow ahead of us this morning. A great tide of mercy has been poured freely upon the land. Wherever you see it needed, just say the word, and you will see it, trickling at first, making a tiny rivulet on the hardened earth, then soaking the soil, and rising to cover even the hard-to-reach places. There can be no despair in a land that is awash with mercy.

8. *The Word as Trinity*: Of course there is no more personal, concrete, or active way for Christians to speak about God than to speak of the per-

sons of the Trinity. The Trinity affords opportunities to speak of God in many ways in any sermon. Here examples from the Bible and our world may be too obvious to cite, except to encourage sermon references to each of the persons of the Trinity.

> Student Assignment 16: Using at least two of the above examples of concrete oral speech for the word of God, write two examples of your own.

General Principles for Oral Composition

Probably no current book assists the preacher with oral composition better than G. Robert Jacks's *Just Say the Word: Writing for the Ear*. For example, among his rules for writing for the ear are the following: active voice is more alive than passive; don't use a fifty-cent word when a five-cent word will do; remove unnecessary occurrences of *that* and *which*; remove unnecessary or assumable information and get to the point; use dialogue for added interest.[18] Here I offer some of my own principles and examples:[19]

Do What You Speak About. If preaching on forgiveness, proclaim God forgiving in the present:

> Right now in your silent confession, God receives your confession and reaches to you in forgiveness.

or:

> Even before you dare to turn again to God, God has already granted your forgiveness that you might get on with loving others in the present and not be preoccupied with unloving in the past.

Show, Don't Tell. Instead of discussing peace abstractly, show its practice, as in this sermon fragment:

> What a difference it would make to how we view the world if we were to identify God around us. Strolling through the flower gardens at the park, a mother stops the stroller and goes over to the fountain where her two children are fighting over whose turn it is to have a drink. The ice cream of one falls on the shirt of the other. Both start to cry. "Peace," she says to them as

they start in again, blaming each other. She tells them a
story of when she was a girl as she cleans off the T-shirt
of the one with fountain water and a tissue. Then she
lifts them, one at a time, to the fountain. The peace of
God is like this.

When we say and enact "Peace," it does not always
happen quickly. But it always begins, and it will happen. It happens as surely as seed planted in the ground
and watered will sprout. As surely as we prayed all those
years for peace between the West and the old Soviet
block, those prayers eventually blossomed, and their
blooming had more power than all the guns of armies.
The sound of the blossoming prayers in the lives of the
people of the East drowned out the sound on a falling
iron curtain. The action of God. Even the newspapers
caught the signs of the God who made it all happen.

Accumulate Thought. Allow some material to be simply accumulated,
rather than analyzed, sorted, and subordinated. (Ong cites the use of nine
introductory "ands" in the creation account of Genesis 1:1-5.) Thus to
establish that people today are afraid, one need not turn the sermon into
a research paper; rather, one can accumulate a few quick simple situations
from the news media or elsewhere to make it concrete.

A young mother comes home with her preschool child,
closes the door, turns the lock, pushes the deadbolt and
sets the chain, secure at last. A man was in his mid-
forties with a family and mortgage eases off on the gas
pedal of his pickup as the factory comes into view, and
he wonders, "Will this be the day I get my notice?" A
new resident in the home sees the sunlit newspaper in
the lounge lying open to the obituaries page and picks it
up fearfully. We all live in fear of one thing or another.

Repeat for Emphasis. Excellent preachers help the listeners hear what is
being said through artful use of repetition. Ancient storytellers used this
to ensure that the listeners stayed on track. Rhetoric calls this the use of
copia (hence our word *copious*). In a written essay, copia is not valued, but
in preaching, by contrast, one has not said something until it is heard, and
often it is not heard until one has said it several times. Repetition of

key ideas and images is not only helpful but also essential if people are to understand one's meaning. The preacher is responsible not only for what is said but also, to a large extent, for what is heard as well.

Laura Sinclair, in an excellent paragraph of oral thought, demonstrates how repetition of one simple idea can be done without it seeming to be clumsy. The idea that "we once had compassion" is hinted at in the first line and restated in different words in each subsequent sentence. She is preaching from Ezekiel:

> As a community, we lack compassion for one another. Years ago, we as a Black race did not have orphanages, shelter homes, and foster homes filled with our children. We had what are called today "extended families." If a relative died and left children, we took them into our homes and raised them as our own. If there was no family, close friends took them into their homes and raised them. We cared about one another's children. We were interested in their growth. Our parents and grandparents didn't find themselves in nursing homes. We provided for them and cared for them in the warmth of our homes, where they knew that they were being loved and cared for. We didn't leave our responsibilities to the state or the federal government. The church and community took care of their own. I wonder, *Can our community's bones live?*[20]

Build Trust. Establish a good relationship with the people before asking them to entertain new ideas, especially in the introduction. They need trust (*ethos*) to be developed. Consider how quickly Fred B. Craddock wins our interest and respect in the following example. In this instance he does so primarily by naming one of our own possible responses to Romans 16:1-16 as his own response. Here is the opening paragraph of his Thanksgiving sermon entitled "When the Roll is Called Down Here":

> I hope you will not feel guilty if your heart was not all aflutter during the reading of the text. Its not very interesting. It's a list of names, a list of strange names. I always tell my students in preaching class, "When you're preaching from biblical texts, avoid the lists. They're deadly. Don't preach from the lists." It seems that Paul is calling the roll. That's a strange thing in itself. I have never worshipped in a church in which anyone got up and called the roll. It could be very dull.[21]

He then goes on to speak of the ways in which a list can be interesting, and he has the congregation's attention.

Connect to Real-life Experience. One can often best connect to the lives of people by speaking of relationships. Thus, the stories that one seeks are primarily those dealing with people interacting: real-life events, not fantasies; conversations between people, not interior monologues; purposeful thought and action, not the preacher's freely associated train of thought; and stories about humans in preference to animals or sunsets. For instance, rather than talk in abstract ways about alcoholism and faith's response to it, Ronald J. Allen quickly and vividly paints a picture of an alcoholic (note how some preachers like Allen arrange their words on the page to facilitate oral speech):

> The woman wakes up in the morning,
>   her life as shattered as the bottle
>   she threw against the wall
>   before she passed out.
> But the name of Jesus
>   is above the name alcoholic
>   and those who are in him
>   know that booze does not have the final word.[22]

Use the Present Tense and Active Voice. Instead of treating Bible events in the past tense with passive voice, like we would history in a written essay, speaking of them in the present tense with active voice helps make them vivid.

Poor—The past as history:

> The gospel of John tells us that on the night of Jesus'
> appearance to Mary in the garden, the disciples had
> been afraid of the religious authorities who might be
> looking for them. The commentaries suggest that the
> house where they had hid belonged to a rich person: it
> had doors that could be locked. The fact that Jesus
> appeared to the disciples in spite of the locked doors
> tells us that Jesus appeared in a manner other than his
> earthly body, which was fully human and suffered the
> limitations of our bodies.

Better—Emphasis on the present tense and active voice:

> The disciples tried to shut out hope. After Mary
> Magdalene had told them she had seen Jesus alive in
> the garden and talked with him, the disciples went to a

rich person's house where there were doors—doors they could lock and be alone in their fear of the police. The risen Christ would have none of it. He comes to them as he comes to us. As they are gathered on that first Easter Sunday night, he appears in their midst and says to them, "Peace be with you." He shows them his hands and side in the same manner that he would have us know that he is the same one as was put to death. He would not have his followers focus on the past.

Use Action Words. Words do things, like the utterance of "peace" in Luke 10:5-6. God creates with words in Genesis in the same way that God often saves with words like "I love you, you are mine." Consider all of the action words that Ola Irene Harrison uses in this poignant reflection on her own attempts to minister, preaching on the bittersweet scroll that John ate in Revelation 10:9:

> How is it that judicatory leaders verbally embrace
> women in ministry
> But I hold in my file a letter saying
> "Yes, they felt you were better qualified,
> But they believe the pastor should really be a man"?
> John's sweet but bitter scroll
> Is common food for many in ministry
> (And not only women)
> But for all those who have been called to speak
> A difficult word on behalf of Jesus Christ
> All pastors who struggle to speak both the comfort
> and the challenge of the gospel
> All those who champion causes that conflict with
> "the way things have always been"
> Called to preach for the sake of
> Christ's church and for the sake of God's creation
> Not only ministers but all Christians seeking to witness
> to God's presence in this world
> Speaking hope when there is no hope
> peace when there is no peace
> light when all you can see is utter darkness.[23]

Compose for Memory and Oral Delivery. In addition to writing for the ear, one needs to write for memory, so that one does not have to rely heavily on a written manuscript. One way is to line out thought, as

Allen and Harrison have each done above. Some people use felt pens to color thought units in the manuscript, so they can find the next unit of thought immediately upon looking down. Some preachers write out their sermons and take only notes from the completed manuscript into the pulpit. Another technique is to memorize the order of one's paragraphs and once one is able to recite their order, to memorize only the linking sentences (usually the last or first sentences of paragraphs) and recite them.

> ## Oral Practices:
> ## Accumulate Thought
> ## Repeat for Emphasis
> ## Build Trust
> ## Connect to Real Life
> ## Use the Present Tense and Active Voice
> ## Use Action Words
> ## Compose For Memory and Oral Delivery

Whatever route, it is wise to go over the sermon manuscript as many as eight to ten times, and to do so aloud, alone. Beginning preachers might try to do this while looking in a mirror to establish eye contact and to test gestures. Some preachers prepare for delivery of the sermon by recording it, then listening to it (perhaps while driving to make economical use of time), and repeating the process again, as often as is necessary to gain confidence and emphasis for delivery.

Preachers need considerable freedom from manuscripts. Only when preachers are familiar with their material, with its location on the page, and with its sound and rhythm, can they be sufficiently free of their manuscript to be more fully present, talking to their people and not to the page, and thinking what they are saying, not reading it. The ideal today is a conversational manner of speaking, not lecturing.

Rehearsing a sermon by reading it silently is not nearly as effective in assisting the memory of most people. One way to remember lengthy material involves intentional use of regular rhythm and sound in language, including parallel phrases and other similar language devices. Some preachers even compose by speaking aloud to ensure that their words sound right. In other words, putting some parts of the sermon to memory is not simply by rote mental exercise. It involves the senses and movement of the body in the same way that athletes are sometimes said to have a kind of kinesthetic (body) memory that assists them in performance. One can see this in the rocking movement of Orthodox Jews reciting prayers at the Wailing Wall in Jerusalem or in the dance moves of rappers.

One reason the King James Version of the Bible is beautiful to the ear is that it was composed for the ear, designed to employ the natural rhythms of voice, even though its English was intended to be slightly archaic even for Jacobean ears. (For reason of its imitation of natural speech rhythm, a colleague in drama uses it as the best tool

Rehearsing for Delivery: It is wise to go over the sermon manuscript as many as eight to ten times, and to do so aloud, alone, and perhaps looking in a mirror to establish eye contact and to test gestures.

for helping students discover the natural power of their voices.) Henry H. Mitchell uses sensory and other data in encouraging what he calls a "holistic encounter" with the biblical text.[24] Linda Clader speaks of the value of the body in rehearsal helping the memory: she is a "mediocre but happy pianist" and after years away from it she was surprised to discover that her fingers seemed to remember some of the Chopin and Scott Joplin she used to play. The same principle carries over to the sermon; rehearsal "is about hearing my own voice say the words that I have put down, letting my ears ring and my very bones vibrate with the sermon. I am teaching my body the music, so that when the time comes, I can sing it confidently."[25]

Students might experiment to discover what devices help them remember: is the material sensory? imagistic? ideational? Does it involve patterns of thought? plot? sound? rhythm? layout on the page? If in rehearsal you always forget a certain paragraph, drop it, or rewrite it, building in patterns that help the memory. Memory patterns that assist delivery generally also assist listener comprehension.

Delivery

We run ahead of ourselves if we talk about delivery when sermon composition is still underway, but we can jump ahead to it here because composition and delivery are related. This topic, like so many, is too large for the written pages of books; it needs to be engaged through performance. Charles L. Bartow defines revelation as "a felt action upon and within us mediated by human speech," and he says that what happens in the sermon is the meeting of two performances, what people do and what God does by way of self-attestation and self-disclosure: "Where *homo performans* meets *actio divina* there is a conflagration of love. We call it preaching."[26] Along with Bartow, others, such as Jana Childers and Richard Ward, have written outstanding contributions on performance.[27]

The pulpit requires a heightened sense of the natural self. Small gestures, like the turn of a hand, or frequent gestures that might be quite appropriate in conversation around a coffee table become ineffectual and distracting in the pulpit. Gestures must be deliberate and big enough to make a statement yet seem perfectly natural. To have a special pulpit voice sounds, and is, false. As a child, the first time I heard a distant relative preach, I was startled because somehow upon his arrival in the pulpit he acquired a Scottish brogue, as some preachers of that generation did almost as though it was a gift of the Spirit (that era often valued British accents as the proper way to speak). Preaching requires one's normal voice, yet louder than one would use for normal speaking. Even when using a microphone, one must still project one's voice to be heard in the farthest corner of the room.

In many seminaries, voice training is all but neglected, but at one time, most had full-time instructors of public speaking (in addition to homiletics instructors). Voice is one of the first things people notice, and it can mean the difference between people listening or not. Even reading of Scripture should capture attention; James Forbes says, "A preacher who doesn't respect the word enough to strive for excellence in leading the congregation to hear it doesn't deserve the opportunity to present his or her manuscript as if such words are somehow more important than the Bible."[28]

Voice involves posture, gesture, pauses, emphasis, pace, volume, tone, breathing, and a host of other essential elements. Those who teach what today is called speech communication no longer pursue one universal

BBC standard of good speech. Speakers are now advised to draw on their own experience, to find their own "inner voice" and a natural style that "embodies" the truth. Richard Ward notes: "The authentic sound that a preacher makes comes from the interrupted cries within the unexplored recesses of the preacher's own experience."[29]

Nonetheless, timeless practices still need to be learned, like breathing from the lower abdomen (a heavy book, placed on the stomach while you are lying down, should move up with each breath in), learning to use the lower registers of one's voice, and proper projection. An excellent guide, complete with practical exercises, is Patsy Rodenburg, *The Right to Speak: Working with the Voice* (London: Methuen, 1992). Make use of any occasion to read aloud, particularly to children or with a partner. Listening to recordings of your own preaching, perhaps with a musician who can give helpful coaching.

Sermon Exercise

In composing an oral manuscript try:

- speaking what can be seen (for example, his lip trembled as he spoke.)
- speaking what can be heard (for example, her voice grated against the night.)
- speaking what can be tasted (for example, some of these ideas have soured.)
- speaking what can be smelled (for example, there is an odor of Lazarus here.)
- speaking what can be touched (for example, these are prickly remarks.)

Developing the voice, like becoming an excellent preacher overall, takes many years of work.

Perhaps the single most important lesson any beginning preacher can learn is to slow down. When one is anxious one wants to finish soon. Moreover in the act of preaching one's sense of time is frequently distorted. As one speaks, one can hear voices speaking from the choir loft of one's mind saying various things, like, *Oh, I missed that paragraph*, or, *That person seems to be falling asleep*, or, *Why didn't I spend more time preparing this?* All of this is to say that one rarely goes wrong slowing down to a pace that may seem almost painful. Chances are it is just right for the congregation to get the sense of your words. Chances are that it is also the right pace for you: one should speak at a speed that allows one to think through and feel what one says as one says it (that is, not just read or recite). Try to visualize yourself speaking to someone in pastoral need, in which case you would never just rattle things off.

> Passion in the pulpit can be argued to be a theological issue before it is an emotional one. One should be excited for a reason, and that reason is the gospel.

Passion

John Mason Stapleton identifies passion as an important pulpit issue: "Passion is evoked as the gospel is yet reapprehended, reexperienced, and reunderstood—in a word, *rediscovered*."[30] Robin R. Meyers says that "We do not necessarily need a rhetorical strategy to arouse emotion in others so much as we need a rhetorical strategy to exhibit the authentic emotions in ourselves."[31]

Perhaps another angle can be taken on this. Many preachers would like to be more passionate, and they confuse passion with emotion and being emotive. Rather, passion in the pulpit can be argued to be a theological issue before it is one of emotion. There is no point being excited for nothing. However, if one is preaching the gospel, if one is offering true life, there is then reason to be excited, and that passion will show in one's preaching. Celebration in much African American preaching is both passionate and infectious and can powerfully assist proclamation of the gospel. However, one occasionally hears attempts at celebration in various traditions without getting to God's grace—what is the point of that?

Of course, sentence structure, rhythm, emphasis, and pace can be used to augment and express one's excitement. Read the sermons of great preachers through all ages and learn to spot passages that were delivered with passion; they often display parallelism, repetition, and short clauses and sentences. Augustine followed Cicero in identifying three styles of speaking in a sermon: subdued, for teaching; temperate, for pleasure; and grand, for emotional persuasion.[32] Read sermons of our own times for passages that signal passion, as in this excerpt from Jini Robinson:

> The fact is that the overwhelming love of God causes us to love ourselves and our neighbors as ourselves. The fact is that love brings us togetherness. The fact is that Jesus saves, strengthens, and preserves. He lifts up the brokenhearted; he restores the lost. Jesus befriends the lonely. He comforts the despairing. The fact is that I wouldn't want to live without Jesus. I don't know how I could make it from day to day without him. I believe my story would have a tragic ending without the love of the Savior. The fact is that Jesus is all the world to me, my life, my joy, my all. No feeling can overcome the fact of Jesus' presence. This is my story! Church, is this your story? Jesus is my reality! He is my strength from day to day. He is the fact, hallelujah! Praise the Lord![33]

We have been talking about preaching as an oral event through which God encounters people. We have explored how the oral nature of preaching affects pulpit language and practice. We now turn to rhetoric to learn how better to construct sermon thought to assist the eventful nature of God's encounter.

CHAPTER ELEVEN

COMPOSING TO PERSUADE

I t is not enough for preachers to speak in oral ways that address the senses. Preachers need to be convincing, they need to persuade. Since long before Jesus, persuasive speech has been known as the art of rhetoric. Augustine, himself a teacher of rhetoric prior to becoming a Christian, said that preaching should teach, delight, and persuade (*On Christian Doctrine*, IV, 9-12). One might think that persuasion in the pulpit means logical appeal of the sort amply demonstrated in systematic theology. Preachers, of course, need to be the best theologians they can be. However, rhetoric teaches that persuasion (or identification in contemporary rhetoric) results from different kinds of appeal in the pulpit, and attention to these affects how one does theology in the pulpit.[1]

Ancient teachers spoke not of one way but of three ways in which listeners may be persuaded. Any one of them might primarily account for someone's particular response:

• reasons of *logos* or logical appeal of arguments and facts

• reasons of *ethos* or ethical appeal (that is, character and integrity) of the speaker

• reasons of *pathos* or emotional appeal

Aristotle explained that, "[ethos] depends on the personal character of the speaker; [pathos] on putting the audience into a certain frame of mind; [logos] on the proof, or apparent proof, provided by the words of the speech itself."[2]

Without addressing rhetoric, seminaries have tended to concentrate on logos, typically ignoring the other modes of persuasion. The importance of knowledge and doctrine is plain and evident; thoughts need to be clear and well organized. Clearly, a sermon that is a kaleidoscope of imagery and feelings (pathos) is no substitute for the gospel, and similarly, an enthusiastic presence of the speaker (ethos) is no substitute for lack of preparation. However, the influence of logos in the theological community, at times, may be too great, particularly when conceived as logic and propositional information. Theological truth depends on narrative and poetic expression as well.

Persuasion and Preaching

One could protest, "Rhetoric is persuasion. Persuasion is manipulation. Christians have no business manipulating others." Lucy Lind Hogan and Richard Lischer recently have taken countering positions on precisely this topic.[3] Some people would add, with Luther and Calvin, that it is our business to proclaim, not to persuade; only the Holy Spirit can do that. Finally, some might say that the logical appeal or logos of Christian preaching, in a strict sense, is Christ (the *Logos* or Word of John 1:1), and preachers need only to attend to him.

Lucy Lind Hogan and Robert Reid have written *Connecting with the Congregation: Rhetoric and the Art of Preaching*, which makes the strongest recent case for the importance of rhetoric in the pulpit.[4] Henry H. Mitchell advocates that preachers choose material for an "affective purpose" as opposed to solely a "cognitive purpose." His approach is holistic, synthesizing what he calls the "logic of emotive consciousness" and "the logic of human reason." The entire being of the preacher embodies the message to the whole person in the pew. Nonetheless, he says it is "emotional logic" that must prevail, for the sermon must happen as celebration in the lives of the people.[5]

Robin Meyers advances the idea of "self-persuasion" as a goal for preachers. The listener must be persuaded by reasons the self provides (not the sermon)—yet as a response to the sermon. Self-persuasive preaching, in contrast to message-centered preaching, is "about getting [people] to talk to themselves in specific ways about specific things."[6] This happens through vicarious identification with the emotional states of others.[7] His basic advice is important: do not preach a sermon that does not first persuade you.

To be persuasive, preaching needs to appeal to all three levels: logos, pathos, and ethos. Pulpit theology needs to be relational, inviting response rather than shutting it down. Several things must be in place. The congregation must experience that which the preacher says arises out of the preacher's: (1) vital relationship with God; (2) vital relationships with the congregation—addressing how they relate to God and others; voicing their understandings, needs,

> **Homiletical Method**
> In composing your sermon, learn to vary your primary means of persuasion such that what you say at times appeals:
> to logic
> to ethos (fostering relationships)
> to emotion

concerns, and responses;[8] and (3) an integration of head, heart, and soul (or loosely: logos, pathos, and ethos). To achieve these goals today, the approach probably needs to be conversational and dialogical in tone and style rather than assertive or authoritarian.

Theology and Rhetoric

What it comes down to is this: preachers need to have reasons if they are to persuade others of the truth of Jesus Christ. This is why rhetorician Gerard A. Hauser has claimed: "In speaking and writing, you can use marvelous language, tell great stories, provide exciting metaphors, speak in enthralling tones, and even use your reputation to advantage, but what it comes down to is that you must speak to your audience with reasons they understand."[9] Theology provides many of the reasons listeners need to hear for understanding their faith.

Generally speaking, systematic or constructive theology needs to inform what is said but cannot be imported directly to the pulpit. Several reasons are obvious: it is written for the page, not composed for oral delivery. It is addressed to scholars, not the average person in the pew. It has its own particular technical language, referring to schools of thought and arguments of others, which is not readily accessible to the layperson. It addresses topics that do not always have a practical application. It may attempt to exclude experience. It typically seeks to establish its truths exclusively through propositions. It may refer less directly to Scripture than to the work of other scholars. It is usually more concerned with examining and explaining the faith than with proclaiming it; indeed, it sees itself arising out of preaching in a mediating position between the teaching of the church and the sermon itself. Further, as G. Robert Jacks would say, it is filled with fifty-cent words. All of this is natural and to be expected. Each theological discipline, including homiletics, conforms to its own established norms and rhetorical goals.

Preaching as Faithful Persuasion

Nonetheless, some theologians now see even theology as a form of rhetoric.[10] David S. Cunningham maintains:

> Theologians are involved not in the exchange of propositions, nor even in edifying "conversations," but in debates, disputes, and arguments. Theologians are always seeking to persuade others—and to persuade themselves—of a particular understanding of the Christian faith. The goal of Christian theology, then, is faithful persuasion.[11]

Preachers similarly gear speech to be persuasive. Because persuasion is based not just in fact and logic, one bears tremendous responsibility. One cannot simply trot out truths and claim they are objective any more than one can avoid the presence of bias. Preaching is a form of "faithful persuasion" that in the minds and hearts of hearers competes with other worldviews and philosophies.

David Lose wisely speaks of the need for preaching in a postmodern world to function as a form of testimony or confession: "Christianity exists solely by confession, the conviction and assertion of revealed truth apart from any appeal to another criterion; we live, that is, always by faith alone."[12] The purpose of confession is to say fresh words that allow the biblical text to be actualized and appropriated through the power of the

Holy Spirit.[13] Bruce E. Shields speaks of something similar when he says that preachers should actualize the gospel, not conceptualize it.[14]

For Lose, Cunningham, and others such as Rebecca Chopp and Lucy Rose,[15] theology is a dialogical, open-ended, organic process of communication that resists closure and cannot achieve the certainty for which many of us long. Rather than claim that truth is our possession, Cunningham would have us rely on truth that is akin to the event of revelation: "In other words, truth can once again become something that *comes to us*—rather than something that we grasp and manipulate how we will."[16]

An Advantage of Reading Theology

Excellent preachers keep reading systematic or constructive theology throughout their ministries, to sharpen thought and deepen understanding. Reading a few pages a week or until one discovers a fresh understanding will make an enormous contribution to sermons and ministry over the years. One does not have to be able to trace the direct and immediate benefit to a particular sermon, although that is often possible. What the systematic theologians say should inform what we say as preachers, even if perhaps we rarely invite theologians to speak on our behalf directly. Homiletical theology has a different identity from its systematic cousin, and hand-me-downs in either direction frequently make an uncomfortable fit. The relationship is nonetheless to be treasured.[17]

> The medium is the message. Theology cannot be narrowly conceived as a portion of the sermon. The parts relate to the whole and need to be composed or considered in the context of the whole, even as the whole is altered by the loss or alteration of any of its parts.

Form and Content

Systematic theology is not simply a content wandering through the seminary lecture halls looking for a form. It has a form already that both helps determine and is determined by its content. For systematic theology to find a home in the sermon, it needs to be modified. Conversely, a sermon is not simply a form looking for content, an empty genre waiting to be filled. Sermon content is related to many things: organization, surface and deep structure, style, oral expression and delivery, as well as anticipated response by the hearer. The medium is the message. The form is content. The structure is meaning. The rhetorical strategy has shape. The meaning is effect.

Everything a preacher says in a sermon has theological implications. Theology cannot be narrowly conceived as a portion of the sermon to be added to or taken away from the whole, though there are some portions that are more explicitly theological than others. Theology is expressed through propositions, metaphors, images, stories, symbols, and emotions. The parts relate to the whole and need to be composed or considered in the context of the whole, even as the whole is altered by the loss or alteration of any of its parts.

As a student, one moves from systematic theology and Bible classes down the hall to the homiletics class, perhaps in the mistaken assumption that one is looking for a sermon outline and homiletical application for theology. Instead, preachers must comment in their own way on the Bible, tradition, and all the various demands of daily faith and life. Moreover, they are to do so in ways that strengthen faith and nurture community. They are to use a style that is caring, without cynicism or mockery, that demonstrates love for their people. Often students end up scrounging for rhetorical tools that can compensate for lack of integration in their classes between (a) congregational and seminary needs and (b) an education geared toward essays and a vocation geared to speech. The fact remains that most churches with vacancies list strong preaching as the greatest need.

All thinking and speaking of God is theology. The type we do in systematic theology classrooms is important and helps us sharpen the theology we do elsewhere, but it is no more theological than the speaking of God that happens in the pulpit or, for that matter, at the dinner table (hence Luther's Table Talks, which he considered to be theology alongside his written tomes). The sermon, in a sense, is the completion of theology, made complete through Christ speaking it and constituting the church through it.

The Sermon as a Persuasive Event

Systematic or constructive theology is essential for preachers because it helps explain the faith; in Anselm's words, it is "faith seeking understanding." Each time one prepares a sermon, one must ask, So what? Why should the congregation believe what I say? What reasons can I provide?

Probably the most persuasive thing any preacher can do is introduce those present to Jesus Christ, who is found in Scripture, in the sacraments and ministry of the church, and in people everywhere through the Holy Spirit. There may be no way to introduce Christ to our people apart from the cross and resurrection. This is who Jesus Christ is; this is his character; he is both the One who died their death for them, and he is the One God raised up from the dead in righteousness to glory on their behalf. The cross and resurrection are a barrier and a stumbling block, and yet they collectively remain the doorway to Christian faith. Preaching on the resurrection is not just preaching on the past: it is making plain the significance of the resurrection in the present. As O. Wesley Allen says, "Any time preachers proclaim the Easter story, their role is to offer their congregations a glimpse of a concrete, real aspect of what cannot be seen fully at one time."[18] He adds, "Our story of the resurrection can be found repeating itself in our midst all the time."[19]

> Introduce those present to Jesus Christ, who is found in Scripture, in the sacraments and ministry of the church, and in people everywhere through the Holy Spirit. There may be no way to introduce Christ to our people apart from the cross and resurrection.

André Resner notes that some people would do away with the cross; they have been wounded by life and the cross is experienced as something that compounds individual suffering. Nonetheless, he says, the cross "is that power of God which renders evil as evil and which orients one to survive as an agent of redemption in a world 'not yet' fully inhabited by

God's shalom, yet one in which it is promised and guaranteed in Jesus' death and resurrection."[20] The Christ of Scripture encounters people now in the depth of their sin and brokenness and claims them as his own. Knowing Christ in this manner, is there any power in this world or the next of which people need to continue to harbor fear?

The Cross and Persuasion

> Until preachers take people to the central event of the faith, where they may again make a commitment of faith in confessing Jesus of Nazareth as the Christ, the anointed and risen one of God, they are without the firmest foundation possible for believing the preacher. In avoiding the difficulties of the cross and resurrection, ironically preachers make their message more difficult to accept.

One of the biggest blocks to the cross being persuasive today is the doctrine of the atonement, especially in its penal, substitutive version. This says that God demands a price for our sin and sacrificed God's own son. Numerous biblical texts seem to support this reading, but that is not the only way in which these texts can be interpreted nor is it most helpful in our day and age. Numerous other options are available that help explain the true meaning of Jesus' death, not least that human sin is responsible inasmuch as it leads us to kill the innocent. We cannot solve here the question of how to understand the atonement, and every systematic theology textbook provides alternatives. What we can do here is flag the importance of overcoming damaging or simplistic understandings in order that what really happened on the cross may be proclaimed. Christ took our sin upon himself that in his death he died our death and in rising he offers us his eternal life.

Any number of theological questions and themes are secondary to the cross and resurrection. Jesus Christ rose from the dead and meets us today. When people are taken to the central event of the faith, they have the opportunity again to make a commitment of faith in confessing Jesus of Nazareth as the Christ, the anointed One of God. This is the firmest foundation possible for preaching and the best reason for listeners to believe what is said. Without it, they can remain at a safe distance from making a leap of faith, safely debating such intellectual issues as, did Jesus perform miracles? or does God love me? A leap of faith needs to be made at a place near the border of reason where one faces head-on the contradiction of the cross. This is the place to which reason can lead, yet it can go no further; it can only point beyond to faith. If people are going to hesitate or stumble, as may be appropriate, it is good that they do so in the right place, which is at the empty tomb, where something more than just the outcome of an intellectual debate is at stake. Ironically, in avoiding the difficulties of the cross and resurrection, preachers make their message more difficult to accept.

It is fair to say that not every student may feel comfortable speaking about the cross and resurrection in such a direct manner, and there may be a variety of reasons why such a position can be faithful and have integrity, particularly in a time of vocational discernment.

Preachers may try to avoid the cross and resurrection, thinking perhaps that the subject, however briefly addressed, is too difficult for their people or themselves to struggle with this week. The sacraments, hymns, prayers, Scriptures, symbols, banners, and windows that surround people in worship all speak of Jesus as the Christ; is that not enough? Still, until this profound mystery is addressed in some manner from the pulpit, however succinctly, even through just pointing, until it becomes a conscious focus in listeners' minds, the cross and resurrection effectively stand as a barrier to what is said. The great unanswered and perhaps subconscious question of worship is, what does this matter? or why should I believe?

A preacher might tell people that Jesus was a great moral teacher whose teachings are to be trusted; yet he or she might not tell them that we follow his teachings because of who he is as the Son of God and that his identity is decisively revealed through the cross and resurrection. The reasons the preacher offers in support of what is said in this case are like life preservers cast on the surface of the water, yet none has sufficient buoyancy in itself to keep afloat those who are in need.

When members of the congregation have reasons to believe that are grounded in the gospel, they respond in gratitude and faith.[21] Only at the point where the nonsense and foolishness of the cross make sense of our troubled world is true conviction nurtured. Without proclaiming death of the old ways and the life of the new, we can never be sure that we have done what we could to enable the work of the Holy Spirit.

Allowing for Mystery and Contradiction

Being persuasive does not mean trying to answer all of the questions listeners may have. In fact, one of the most persuasive moves a preacher can make is to say, "I do not know" or "I do not fully understand." Many of the central Christian teachings are contradictions. Horace Bushnell, in the 1800s, once said, "Accordingly, we never come so near to a truly well rounded view of any truth, as when it is offered paradoxically; that is under contradictions."[22] He was talking about the importance of understanding that language itself is metaphoric, that is, it has a polar structure.

Here are some of the central tenets of our faith that may sound contradictory to seekers:

> Creation is out of nothing.
> God is Three in One.
> God became human.
> God is with us.
> Jesus was born of a virgin.
> Christ is fully human and fully divine.
> Christ died that we might have life.
> Christ is no king and king.
> Christ has come and is coming.
> We must die to have life.
> We must lose self to find self.
> We must be born again.
> In wealth we are poor.
> By giving we receive.
> In loving we participate in eternity.
> Love is stronger than violence.

Blessed are those who mourn.
The only certain knowledge is the knowledge of faith.
For the unreconcilable there is reconciliation.
We who are many are one in Christ.
The first will be last and the last will be first.
The obedience God demands is the obedience God supplies.

Preaching is most persuasive if it does not ignore these seeming contradictions, pasting wallpaper over them in the hope they will not be noticed. Rather, highlight them as part of the trouble of the sermon. Like Jesus' parables, which also have a yes and no to them, people must participate in these truths to make sense of them. They can be doors to faith. Their resolution is found near the center of faith in the knowledge that Jesus died yet is alive. Mystery remains; allowing for the apparent contradiction permits the cross to do its reconciling work.

The Cross and the Old Testament

What about preaching the Old Testament? Again, preachers should avoid doing what some early Christians did: avoid crudely reading Christ back into the Scriptures, as though they were about Jesus all along and the Jews had it wrong. There is prophecy in the Old Testament, yet even those passages (for example, the servant will be a light to the Nations—Isaiah 42) were not historically understood exactly as Christians now read them. Gardner C. Taylor offered a good perspective when he preached that many such passages are "Not clear and conscious prophecies of Christ...but conclusions from gazing in the direction of the everlasting God."[23]

It was clumsy preaching of the other sort that may have contributed to the rise of anti-Semitism and the Holocaust. Some of its roots may be found in the New Testament Scriptures themselves, and Clark M. Williamson and

> Denying a christological center to the Old Testament, one may still affirm a christological center to preaching.

Ronald J. Allen give preachers helpful pointers to avoid it.[24] The same God speaks in both Scriptures. Rather, preachers may find the message of God's salvation in the Old Testament text before them and develop it within its own historical context. They may then move to proclaim the resonance of that message with the truth known in Jesus Christ. Denying a christological center to the Old Testament, one may still affirm a christological center to preaching. Christians do not suddenly become Unitarian when they preach the Old Testament.

Let me offer an example. A student preached on Moses and the burning bush. The discussion of holy ground was weak because (a) the action of God, who alone is holy, was ignored; (b) places of congregational experience of the risen Christ were ignored; and (c) listeners were not led to anticipate events where they might expect to be encountered again by God in the future. The key event lay only in the past. Christian experience cannot effectively be reduced to history or separated from Christ. Preaching is strengthened by being solidly rooted in the depth and breadth of listeners' experience.

The Cross and the New Testament

The same approach is often needed with New Testament texts, since individual texts or pericopes have their own contexts and histories that may not directly discuss the gospel. They nonetheless can be understood to point to it or to serve as a portal from it. Thus, with these texts we also explore connections with the Easter event, however briefly, as a way to ground the gospel in the lives of the hearers. More on this will be said in the final chapters.

Mention of the cross and resurrection is not like some formula that magically transforms any discourse into a Christian sermon. However, preachers need to be able to use all of the faith resources and truths language makes available in order to nurture the faith of others with the widest array of banquet foods.

Linear and Polar Thought

Two ways of thinking strengthen theological expression in the pulpit. People tend to think that what they say is perfectly clear simply because it is usually clear in their own minds. However, people think in different ways—including linear thought, or progression and movement, and polar thought, or digression and association.

Linear thought moves in a line. It is deductive and convergent and focuses on principles or propositions. It is influenced by the left hemisphere of the brain, which is logical, informational, and sequential. Propositional preaching is associated with it, of the sort that dominated homiletics until the 1970s or beyond. Geared to logic and reason, it is often hierarchical in terms of authority and didactic.

Polar thought, by contrast, moves by digression and association to related subjects or situations. Modest forms of digression are essential to all preaching as a means of establishing relevance; without it listeners may ask, how does this connect with my life or the Bible? Dominant polar thinkers are gifted in making these connections, and they present their material with stories, images, and metaphors. Many sermons now are narrative or imagistic, geared to other ways of knowing beyond straight reason, like experience and emotion; they are conversational or dialogical in style.

Listeners, like preachers themselves, tend to be dominant in one form of thought or the other. Preachers need to know their own natural way of thinking and to work on the other so that both kinds of listeners are addressed. Each way of thought has its own signature forms of expression, thus preachers who are dominant linear thinkers need to strengthen polar thought and polar thinkers need to concentrate on developing linear thought or argument. Here are a few suggestions for each group. (I have developed these in greater detail elsewhere.)[25]

Exercises for Dominant Polar Thinkers

Polar thinkers are imagistic and metaphoric; to some people they may sound unfocused; thus, polar thinkers need to be more linear and build in logical signposts:

• Stick with the structures advocated here: develop a clear theme sentence. Let each Page deal with only one idea (a concern of the text or concern of the sermon). Ensure that each paragraph has a clear connection to the theme of each Page.

• Define terms: Any new theological term or doctrine needs to be defined. To define something say, "This is part of that"; in other words it belongs to a family of thought, so name the family and its particular traits. For instance, "The sovereignty of God concerns God's rule over everything. It is part of our understanding of God's nature who created all things out of nothing and who alone has the final say over all things."

- Determine a sequence of ideas in each part of the sermon. This might be on the basis of time or chronology, or it may start with the effect and then consider its causes or move from least important to most important. Point form is a way to give order to thought, provided it is not overused. Rhetoric teaches that one puts the second-best reason first, the weakest reason second, and the strongest reason last. Or, one can offer coordinate terms, for example, three characteristics of God's love.

- Avoid piling image on image and make chains of thought: one can test links by reviewing a composed sermon to identify link phrases between paragraphs (usually the first or last sentence) or larger sections or Pages. Alternatively, one can keep returning to a single image that becomes dominant.

Exercises for Dominant Linear Thinkers

Linear thinkers are logical and may seem too intense, too much in their heads. They need to be more polar and imagistic or poetic. Here are some things that linear preachers can try:

- Do not cover too many ideas: say a couple of things and say them well. Break down complex thought so that each paragraph moves only a small distance from the previous one. Listeners need not climb Mount Everest, just Calvary will do.

- Make significant comparisons or associations as a way of explaining: such analogies help slow down argument and make things clear for listeners. They also give a break from linear development, moving sideways, as it were, enabling listeners to catch up. Comparisons or associations can be made on the basis of similarities or differences.

- Allow for contradiction: this means, in part, to allow other viewpoints to be represented. It also means allowing paradox or seeming contradiction of the sort discussed earlier with key Christian tenets. When one depicts people in the sermon, contradictory behavioral elements often need to be included in the portrait to make the person seem more real.

- Build in digression: everything need not have an obvious link up front to what went before. That is, from time to time, just launch into a story about someone without explanation; by the end of the digression bring the story back to where you were.

- Make pictures with words. Use stories of people doing things. Ideas and abstractions are needed, but wherever possible, give a picture. Speak about real-life situations in the Bible or today.

Sermon Unity

To be persuasive, a sermon needs unity. Communication is best when it serves a unified purpose. In propositional preaching, unity is conceived in largely mechanical ways. H. Grady Davis wrote the following words, which are the earliest and best description we have of organic unity in preaching. He claimed that this is not a poem but an alternative to a traditional sermon outline. The first line is his "idea that grows." His words can be interpreted to be a preacher's version of the 1926 poem by Archibald Macleish, "Ars Poetica" (the epigraph of this book), in which he said, "a poem should not mean but be." Note also that Davis reworks Augustine's injunction that preaching should teach, delight, and persuade.

Design for a Sermon

A sermon should be like a tree.

It should be a living organism:
    With one sturdy thought like a single stem
    With natural limbs reaching up into the light.

It should have deep roots:
    As much unseen as above the surface
    Roots spreading as widely as its branches spread
    Roots deep underground
        In the soil of life's struggle
        In the subsoil of the eternal Word.

It should show nothing but its own unfolding parts:
    Branches that thrust out by the force of its inner life

Sentences like leaves native to this very spray
   True to the species
   Not taken from alien growths
Illustrations like blossoms opening from
   inside these very twigs
Not brightly colored kites
   Pulled from the wind of somebody else's thought
     Entangled in these branches.

It should bear flowers and fruit at the
   same time like the orange:
Having something for food
   For immediate nourishment
Having something for delight
   For present beauty and fragrance
   For the joy of hope
   For the harvest of a distant day.

To be all this it must grow in a warm climate:
   In loam enriched by death
   In love like the all-seeing and all-cherishing sun
   In trust like the sleep-sheltering night
   In pity like the rain.[26]

When one composes a sermon it is helpful to keep six things in mind that contribute to sermon unity:

One Text: Develop primarily one text in its historical setting. Refer to others only if they will be an obvious and quick help, not needing much commentary.

One Theme: Again, choose from your text a theme sentence or major concern of the text around which to focus the sermon. Everything should speak to it, even if one uses various points.

One Doctrine: Identify from your theme sentence on key teaching of the church that can help to inform the sermon.

One Need: Think of one person or group whose need or longing will be met by this sermon and, in your mind at least, address what you say to that need or longing.

One Image: From your text or perhaps your introductory story (if this is different) pick one image (visual or acoustic) to become dominant. It becomes dominant by being repeated. By the end of the sermon, that image ought to be linked in people's minds to the theme sentence. An image could be the Goliath in our life, or the fig tree, or the cup of blessing.

One Mission: What do you want people to do as a result of hearing this sermon? Offer one example of what faithful living might look like so that listeners start thinking about what they might do to practice the gospel this week.[27]

We will say more on doctrine and mission in upcoming chapters.

Sermon Drafts

Some of these features of unity are too much to attend to in the first draft of a sermon when you are trying to get your ideas down. They can be developed later, in a second draft. Anne Lamott speaks of two drafts in creative writing, the down draft and the up draft: "Start by getting something—anything—down on paper. A friend of mine says that the first draft is the down draft—you just get it down. The second draft is the up draft—you fix it up."[28] Many people resist second drafts. She says she knows many great writers: "Not one of them writes elegant first drafts. All right, one of them does, but we do not like her very much."[29] Ideally, preachers will allow as much sermon preparation time as possible spread over many days. Lamott says of many people, "They *kind* of want to write, but they *really* want to be published."[30] Maybe something like that is true for some preachers: they kind of want to compose properly but they really want to preach.

The Tiny Dog Now Is Mine: one text, one theme, one doctrine, one need, one image, one mission

Some of my own best friends resist starting to compose early in the week, and they start later in the week instead. Perhaps that works for them. Whenever I have done that on a regular basis I have hated the pressure; I now pressure myself even in the midst of a busy week to have the sermon well under way on Wednesday, finished by Friday, and then Saturday permits revision time. As Jana Childers humorously says, "The Holy Spirit needs an editor."[31] Saturday ought not to be the day on which the sermon goes from nothing to something but rather from something to something better.

In this section we have spoken about matters of style and substance. For convenience, these matters have been arbitrarily assigned to Friday, but they affect any of the last days of the week. The same is true for the assignment for Saturday—tending to the gospel—which is our final focus.

> Assignment 17: Revise your sermon with a view to oral issues. Try using the senses and making movies. Check to see if you use all three means of persuasion, logos, ethos and pathos. Will polar and linear thinkers both find themselves addressed? Check for unity using the acronym TTDNIM.

For Further Reflection and Study Concerning Friday

1. Concerning yourself, do you feel that oral communication is a matter of trying to be natural in the pulpit so that you speak the way you usually do, or is something more than this needed?

2. What reasons could you give in a sermon as to why someone might believe that Jesus did his miracles? Are you convinced by these reasons? Might a seeker be persuaded by them?

3. In preaching an Old Testament text it is suggested that one find God's message of salvation in the text at hand and then move to the resonance of that message with Jesus Christ. Do you feel this second step is necessary or helpful?

Section VI

Saturday: Gospel Matters

This section is assigned to Saturday, but it ought not to be left to Saturday, and in many ways, we have been tending to matters of the gospel all week: gospel matters. The things discussed here could be done on Thursday. However, if during the course of sermon composition the gospel is still not present by Saturday, that day presents itself as an excellent opportunity to attend to it in revision. We will tend first to the bed the gospel needs in the sermon by way of theological support and in the final chapter to practices that ensure the gospel is present.

CHAPTER TWELVE

STEPS TOWARD THE GOSPEL

How one does theology is an issue in the gospel being preached. What paths may preachers follow to prepare for the gospel to be heard? What foundation needs to be present in the sermon to facilitate the hearing of the gospel? What steps are needed to achieve the sermon's desired results? We will suggest two approaches that stand preachers in excellent stead. One comes from systematic/constructive theology. The other comes from homiletical theology.

Lessons from Systematic/Constructive Theology

Long before any of us actually set foot in seminary we were doing theology, that is, we reflected on our experience in light of our faith and the teachings of the church. What we began when we came to seminary was simply the formal and often systematic study of theology. One of the hardest tasks students face is how to do theology well. What can help? Four lessons recommend themselves for the pulpit, each having to do with method.

The first lesson from systematic or constructive theology is to *keep God near the center of one's discussions, instead of affording occasional glimpses of God at the periphery.* Too often, preachers are tempted to think that they are preaching a doctrine or a truth or a story or a text and forget the more basic truth: they are to preach God. Systematic theologians generally

229

agree that their appropriate focus is God, God's self-disclosure in the life, death, and resurrection of Jesus Christ in particular, and in human history in general. In addition, the focus is on human response to God, both actual and potential.

> An appropriate focus of theology is God, God's self-disclosure in the life, death, and resurrection of Jesus Christ in particular, and in human history in general; as well as on human response to God.

A second lesson from systematic theology can be to *imitate the theology of those who stand as models for the church*, including great preachers. Imitation awakens preachers to patterns of thought or expression that can be transformed into their own style, personality, and theology. Even by just copying an argument or paragraph into a notebook, they can learn a great deal about how someone thinks, and thus learn how to employ similar principles for themselves.

For centuries, art students learned by imitation in copying the works of great artists. Through the Middle Ages, theological method was primarily imitation and citation of the church fathers, their quoted words standing as automatic, semiautonomous, divine proofs. Still today, most of us formally learn theology initially by imitation in writing essays in which we quote others and by thinking through the received doctrines, propositions, and creedal affirmations of the church.

Few preachers receive direct formal instruction on basic theological method: discovering what there is to say about a subject (that is, the ancient rhetorical canon of invention), how to structure theological thought, how theological language works, what theological process is (not just content), the relationships between method and meaning and between form and meaning, and other issues.[1]

No standard theological method exists that is comparable, for instance, to the scientific method. We can listen at the open doorways of a few classrooms to overhear theologians. David Kelsey dismisses the possibility of a normative approach: "There is no special theological 'way' to argue or 'think,' if that is taken to imply a peculiarly theological structure to argument. Accordingly, analysis and criticism of theological 'systems' are not likely to be illuminating."[2] Richard Grigg says, "It is bad enough, a critic might say, that theologians cannot agree upon the specifics of the *how* of theological thinking. But there is no general agreement among theologians even about theology's *what*."[3] George Lindbeck notes that a universal norm is impossible because all cultural and linguistic expression is conditioned by the symbols of that culture.[4] Thomas Oden, in his deep suspicion of all that is modern, would have us return to classical theologians and the early church "because of its close adherence to apostolic faith and because a more complete ecumenical consensus was achieved in that period than any period since."[5] David Tracy would have us return to the classics for another reason, to discover new tools of interpretation with which we might make a new beginning.[6]

Method receives much attention in liberation theology, yet wide differences exist. James Cone insists on a new starting point for theology in the needs of the oppressed: "We must become black with God," he says, in an attempt to get away from pervasive racist assumptions that God is white.[7] Rebecca Chopp speaks as a feminist: "There is no one method or theory that can accomplish the needed transformation. There are, instead, insights and strategies that arise out of the margins that may allow for new possibilities and visions."[8] Among feminists and womanists, there are differences, and some see women's experience as the only norm, while others affirm that Christian tradition contributes to what is normative.[9]

Models in systematic theology are important. With so many competing theological positions in the postmodern world, to whom does one look? Effective preachers look to those theologians whose writing shows sensitivity to the realities of congregational life, needs, and experience. Students training for ordered ministry are training to speak, in the first instance, with and on behalf of the congregation and the wider church, not over and against the people or regarding them as the opposition. Servant ministry is the model Christ gives. Only out of this ability does the possibility of prophetic utterance of the preacher arise.

Common to all systematic theology is our third methodological principle: *test the logical consequences of any doctrinal position.* Ask, for instance, what is at stake for the church if this position is held? For instance, if one ceases to confess the full humanity of Jesus Christ, one calls into question whether God truly knows the human condition, and if one calls into question his full divinity, one calls into question whether he can help us.

Or to take another example, a student might have legitimate difficulty with the doctrine of the virgin birth, in spite of the fact that it is attested in Scripture and is part of classical creeds and teachings. By asking what is at stake in this doctrine, one discovers that its denial could be interpreted: (a) that Jesus is less than divine, (b) that Jesus was just another person, or (c) that Jesus was not born at all and only appeared to be human. Each of these positions has been taken in history and judged to be heretical. However, a theologian as orthodox as Emil Brunner believed that affirming the doctrine of the virgin birth could compromise Christ's true humanity and make his divinity dependent on the circumstances of his birth. So rich is the intellectual tradition of the church that most doctrines can be analyzed both by what they actually say and by what, if turned over, they avoid saying. In other words, in arguing with any doctrine, one needs to decide whether its flip side is a statement one wishes to defend.

> Lessons from Systematic Theology
> 1. Keep God at the center.
> 2. Imitate the theology of those who stand as models for the church.
> 3. Test the logical consequences of any doctrinal position you might take.
> 4. Identify your own (and your church board's) theological stance.

We come, then, to our fourth principle: *identify as clearly as possible your own theological method or approach.* Sometime early in your ministry to a congregation, sit down with your church board and have them do this as well. Most congregations have both defined and assumed theological limits and boundaries that the preacher should know. The excellent preacher keeps pushing at a congregation's limits and boundaries, calling people afresh to new claims of the gospel message; this can be done only within a relationship of mutual respect and trust. The preacher must never treat the congregation as the opposition or enemy and must never use the sermon as an opportunity to vent personal frustration or anger in ministry. Preachers should seek a personal counselor for such expression.

Four Theological Stances

Theologies vary widely on a variety of issues: sources of theology (Bible, tradition, experience, or some combination), interpretation and authority of Scripture, openness to other disciplines of knowledge, focus beyond the church (that is, the church's role in society and culture), and the like.[10] Here are the broad outlines of four theological stances. Most people would not find themselves totally in agreement with at least one of these, but they can serve as a tool to name one's own approach:[11]

Orthodox	Neoorthodox
starts with Christian tradition	starts with God's total otherness
responds to the modern	responds to cultural religion
historical and mystical	revelational and catastrophic
assumes conformity as normal	assumes experience is deceptive
truth is contained in established forms	truth is transcendent, not contained in human forms
theology "from established authority"	theology "from above, and beyond culture"
sin as corruption of the will and disobedience of God's will	sin as separation from God and rejection of human limitation
preacher relies on the authority of the institution or office	preacher claims the authority of revelation over experience
listeners accept the authority of the church to instruct	listeners affirm the totality of human sin
Liberal	Liberation/Feminist/Black
empirical starting points	starts with marginalized people
responds to the nonbeliever	responds to the oppressed
philosophical and metaphysical	sociological and political
assumes harmony and progress	assumes injustice as normal

searches for truth in premises and propositions	truth emerges out of theory and praxis using narrative
theology "from above"	theology "from below"
sin as egoism, lack of love, and failure of human potential	sin as injustice and covetousness in human systems
preacher draws on contemporary culture and Christian tradition	preacher is political and speaks for the oppressed
listeners test their own experience with tradition	listeners claim their own authority

Any method(s) one uses in theology will inform one's preaching, which is one reason preacher and congregation should be broadly compatible. It is too simple to say that the preacher's role is not to convert people to a particular theology, ideology, or political position, for one preaches from a particular theological perspective and seeks to foster actions and beliefs that conform to it. One is more accurate in saying that one preaches from particular perspectives and makes allowances for others.

Lessons from Homiletical Theology

Anne Lamott says, "Writing involves seeing people suffer and . . . finding some meaning therein."[12] She could have been speaking of preaching. Fred B. Craddock put the importance of theology into appropriate perspective: "Theology prompts preaching to treat subjects of importance and avoid trivia."[13] The ultimate subject of preaching is the gospel. It is supported by a number of theological practices that have been developed in preaching—certain things need to be in place in order for the gospel to be heard. Four recommendations leap out from the pages of preaching history: find a theological focus, concentrate on core doctrines, discuss mainly one doctrine per sermon, and develop theological movement in the sermon.[14] We will discuss each in turn.

Find a Theological Focus in the Text

A theological focus in a biblical text does not always seem apparent, yet the sermon needs to get to God. How to keep the focus on God will be our first focus here. How does one develop a theological theme when none seem evident?

We have already said in earlier chapters much of what needs to be said regarding the theme sentence. To review, a biblical text may not demonstrate sufficient theological focus in itself. Not all biblical texts mention God, and historical critics do not necessarily concern themselves with God or revelation. Many of the proverbs might seem to lack a theological theme and display a wisdom and common truth one scarcely needs to come to church to hear. Nonetheless, in one proverb one might legitimately discern a doctrine one could develop (for example, talk of money might imply stewardship); in yet another proverb one might find a structure or movement that matches the structure or movement of a doctrine (for example, "if . . . then" is the basic structure of covenant); in yet another, one might find theological focus in the function of proverbs as wisdom literature (for example, God is the source of all wisdom and gives it to us in order that we may respond appropriately to the world); in yet another, for instance a proverb about a widow, one might amplify the truth that is implied in the text (for example, God is acting when justice is done).

The book of Esther also does not mention God, and therefore, God may not be mentioned in a sermon on that book. One might only speak of Esther. However, it is a matter of what lenses are used to read the text. If the preacher uses the lens of faith and actually looks for God in the story, God's hand is seen throughout:

- Esther and her uncle are Jews acting on behalf of their people, and therefore, they are God's ambassadors in the story.

- Mordecai refuses to worship Hammon, the king's prime minister. Why? The text silently points to the first commandment.

- Mordecai tells Esther that if she does not act, she too will be killed as a Jew; if she does not act, "relief and deliverance for the Jews will rise from another quarter"—to what or whom does he refer if not to God?

- Esther herself has the Jews fast before she dares to enter the king's chamber—fasting is a form of prayer.

- When Esther goes in to the king, he does not kill her, though she expected he would. The Bible does not affirm chance; this is God at work, an answer to prayer.

- Who but God gave Esther her courage?

- At night, the king cannot sleep and is reading the court annals and discovers that Mordecai once exposed a plot against the king and was never rewarded. Suddenly he is in high regard. Is this coincidence or God's hand?

- The outcome of the story echoes the Exodus and anticipates the cross: God saves.

This practice of finding God is not reading something into the text that does not belong; it is finding what is already there and what can only be seen if one specifically looks for it when one claims the Bible as the church's book. The practice is identical to finding God in ordinary life: one looks for the signs and clues.

On other occasions with other texts, one faces a different problem: God may be implied or mentioned without significant emphasis. A second way to provide theological focus concerns magnifying one of the three persons of the Trinity. Magnification is the homiletic practice of enhancing God's action in or behind a biblical text or the present-day world in order that God may have significant focus in the sermon.[15] (Magnification is used, for instance, when someone taking a meal to a mourning family is claimed as Christ acting.)

> Magnification is the homiletic practice of enhancing God's action in or behind a biblical text or the present-day world in order that God may have significant focus in the sermon. It is used in both the biblical sense of praising God (for example, Psalm 34:3; Luke 1:46) and in the English sense of making larger or more evident the actions of God.

Here the term *magnification* is used in both the biblical sense of praising God (for example, Psalm 34:3; Luke 1:46) and in the English sense of making larger or more evident the actions of God. With every text we should at least be able to answer, what is God doing in or behind this text? even if we do not choose to use this approach to determine the theme sentence, as recommended here. For example, someone could conceivably preach Noah and never mention God since God is mentioned in only three verses of the entire three chapters of the Noah story.

In preaching on John the Baptist in the wilderness (Mark 1), it is important not to be enticed into proclaiming him. A similar point could be made concerning any of the disciples, apostles, prophets, or saints. Who is John the Baptist to us? We do not pray to him. He is not our source of hope. Still, God has chosen him and speaks through him, and that is the reason he is important to us. John points to someone else; it is to this One that we also point.

Concentrate on Core Doctrines

Many people today are questioning the role of preaching—in particular, the role of doctrine in preaching. The pressure on preachers can be acute where church membership is floundering or foundering, and they may be tempted to try anything that promises renewed interest. Doctrines are teachings. Since doctrines often divide congregations, should we not avoid them? Preaching and teaching are united; in a postmodern world of increasing fragmentation, doctrines hold our experience together. Their purpose is to help form ragtag groups of people into the body of Christ. Robert G. Hughes and Robert Kysar recommend, "We need to ask of every sermon, what is being taught here?"[16] To expand on this point: it is not a question of

> Concentrate on only a few core doctrines overall in the entire course of preaching, such as: Christ's death and resurrection, the inbreaking of the realm of God with power, as well as God's intervention in individual human lives and history.

whether we will teach doctrine in a sermon; it is a question of what that doctrine will look like. By seeking to avoid substantive ideas, we are implicitly teaching that God is weak or unconcerned with humanity or leaving it all up to us.

Many of the greatest preachers in history recommend that preachers concentrate on only a few core doctrines overall in the entire course of preaching. What are these central doctrines? They may be identified for us by our faith tradition. They are the doctrines the church identifies as core doctrines. For example, John Broadus in the 1800s identified the "great" doctrines as sin, providence, redemption, repentance, and atonement.[17] The great Scottish Presbyterian preacher of the 1900s, James S. Stewart, advocated Christ-centered preaching: Christ's death and resurrection, the inbreaking of the realm of God with power, God's intervention in individual human lives and history.[18] Stewart also contended that Christ-centered preaching is assisted by the Christian calendar (see the chart on pages 239-42).

Samuel D. Proctor reflects his own particular African American tradition when he identifies key doctrines, or what he calls "four themes that drive my preaching like strong, moving pistons":

1. God is present and active in human affairs and intervenes on our behalf [that is, immanence and transcendence].

2. Spiritual renewal and moral wholeness are available to us all [that is, conversion and transformation by the Holy Spirit].

3. Genuine community is a realizable goal for the human family [that is, church and the inbreaking of the realm of God].

4. Eternity moves through time, and immortality is an ever-present potential. We have already passed from death unto life when we love [that is, incarnation and eschatology].

Proctor adds to these a fascinating dynamic that is akin to what we have discussed with trouble-grace when determining the theme of Page One using the inverse of Page Three. He asks himself, "What is the opposite of this doctrine in the lives of my congregation?" Once found, he includes it in his sermon: "When I canvas the antitheses to these four main theses, I cannot find enough time or places to preach the sermons that are generated."[19]

Core doctrines themselves can be broad, thus it may be important to do what Hughes and Kysar suggest: identify the core of each doctrine in preaching. For instance, the core of the satisfaction theory of atonement is "the relationship between love and justice in God's actions." The preacher, in seeking to retain that core, will reflect on it using the congregation's own language and imagery and might tell a story "of one who has been offended by injustice but who corrects that injustice through self-sacrificial self-love."[20]

The church year was devised as a way to teach the Christian story through the year, and it names several key doctrines. Let us now turn to a chart to consider how the seasons of the church year guide preachers to predominant doctrines.

Doctrines of the Christian Year	
Advent	These four weeks prior to Christmas begin the Christian year. Preaching during Advent (= approach) anticipates God coming in three ways: Christ's birth in history (the doctrine of incarnation), Christ's birth in our own lives (the doctrine of faith), and Christ's second coming at the end of time (the doctrine of final things or eschatology). As nights (in the Northern Hemisphere) move to greatest length and human troubles threaten to overwhelm, the anticipation of God's saving action mounts. We may heighten the despair even as we accentuate the hope. We do not forget Easter in Advent: the One who comes is the Redeemer who died on the cross.
Christmas	December 25, the Western date, and the Sundays following it mark God becoming flesh in the Incarnation. God acts decisively on our behalf that through Christ we may know God and God's purpose for us. God's way is the way of weakness and vulnerability of a child, accepting the limitations of humanity. Christ is fully God and fully human. God has the final word on human affairs.

Epiphany	The Western date is January 6, followed by Sundays of the season and ending with Transfiguration Sunday. Epiphany literally means "appearance or manifestation of God." The preaching focus is on the appearance of God in Christ in his earthly ministry (the doctrine of Christology). Traditional readings during this season regularly include the following manifestations: the descent of the Spirit at Jesus' baptism; God's revelation to the Gentiles; and Jesus' first miracle at Cana.
Lent	Beginning with Ash Wednesday, these forty days, or six weeks (Sundays are not counted as they are days marking resurrection), traditionally made up a time of penitence in preparation for Christ's giving himself upon the cross on our behalf (the doctrines of repentance and atonement). Sundays reflect the season, yet they remain as celebrations of the resurrection even though they are somewhat muted celebrations. We preach the reality of sin and evil, and our own complicity in them, never underestimating their power or our capacity for deception. Against these we place Christ's refusal to give in to temptation; that is, his determination to accomplish our salvation for us. This is a traditional season of training for membership and is a good one in which to reexamine Christology, since the cross and resurrection are drawing near and are continually before us.
	The Season ends with Palm/Passion Sunday and Holy Week (including Good Friday). Preaching emphasis falls on human failure to recognize who Jesus was/is, our incomprehension of his mission, and our inability to reconcile ourselves with God (the doctrines of atonement, salvation, the full humanity of

	Christ). Our way is the way of the world. The way of the world is death, especially death of the innocent, even Jesus Christ.
Easter Sunday	The Easter date varies according to the first Sunday after the first full moon after the spring equinox. Since without Easter we would have nothing to preach, this can be interpreted to be the most important Sunday of the year, and resurrection is the key doctrine. Death has had its say, and God's power is greater. Christ overturns the powers of the world. A new age has dawned in which Christ rules in power and glory. Through most of this season, the gospel lessons feature resurrection appearances of Christ. (Preachers are advised to prepare a draft of the Easter sermon, the most celebrative of the year, well before becoming immersed in the penitential mood of Lent and the demanding pressures of Holy Week. Too many Easter sermons are, in fact, Good Friday sermons.)
	Every Sunday celebrates the resurrection, thus every Sunday of the Christian year reflects Easter joy. God has accomplished in Christ what we could not accomplish for ourselves. Forty days after Easter is Ascension Day, marking Christ's ascent into heaven to sit at the right hand of God. Without the ascension, Christ's promises would not be confirmed.
Pentecost	Fifty days (hence "pente") after Easter marks the descent of the Holy Spirit on the disciples, the birth of the church (doctrines of the Holy Spirit and the church). Next is the Season after Pentecost (Ordinary Time = Latin "counted time") that covers a range of doctrines even as the gospel lessons in the lectionary for this period concentrate on Christ's teachings. Included are Trinity Sunday (the

	first Sunday after Pentecost, the doctrine of the Trinity) and the Reign of Christ (the last Sunday before Advent). The preaching focus is the mission of the church and Christ's action through it. Though Christ has ascended, we are not left alone and powerless. Christ through the Holy Spirit is in the church and may be encountered in the world. The end of the story is known. Through the actions of Christ and the Holy Spirit, God empowers us to act in concert with the Creator's will.

The church year plainly has its weaknesses; where in the year is the sovereignty of God highlighted? or providence? or creation? Still, churches that follow the church year tend to follow the lectionary, and many texts still lead to these doctrines. To some degree, the church year imposes on the preacher the need to speak to the key doctrine(s) of the season. Does the church year impose doctrine on the biblical texts? To a degree: reading some of the Isaiah texts assigned to Advent and Holy Week means that they are heard in relationship to Christ, yet this connection with these texts already exists in the church. However, the lectionary texts were selected with the seasons in mind, such that their meanings are often enhanced by the season.

Discuss One Doctrine Per Sermon

A third way to prepare a foundation for the gospel in the sermon is this: in any one sermon try to speak concretely only to one doctrine or teaching of the church, one that arises naturally out of one's biblical text. (In the mnemonic device The Tiny Dog Now Is Mine, the letter D refers to one doctrine.) Without turning the sermon into a theological essay, allow the doctrine to inform and shape what is said.

Doctrines overlap; they arise out of biblical narratives that flow into one another; thus, clear separation is often neither possible nor desirable. Moreover, some overlap is essential: many sermons have a "from this to this" structure, for instance from sin to redemption, and to some degree one cannot talk about the one without the other. Still, the advice is to concentrate primarily on one doctrine and not to get lost in theological thickets.

Normally, the way to locate the doctrine of a sermon is with the theme sentence. Earlier we listed some text and some possible major concerns. Let us now return to that list and name one key doctrine that might be addressed.

Biblical Text	Possible Major Concerns	Possible Doctrine
Genesis 9—Noah and the rainbow	God initiates the covenant.	God's faithfulness
Exodus 20—Ten Commandments	God gives us the way to life.	God's love/ sovereignty
Ruth 4—Ruth and Boaz	God restores the outcast.	Ecclesiology/ new creation
Isaiah 6—Isaiah's call	God gives a new identity.	Salvation/ministry
Luke 11:33-36— Letting light shine	Christ lights our lives.	Fruits of the Spirit
John 4—The woman at the well	Christ bestows true identity.	Redemption
Acts 13—The Holy Spirit and Paul	The Spirit guides the church.	Ecclesiology
Philippians 2— Christ's self- emptying	God exalts the lowly.	Salvation
Revelation 21— God wipes away tears	God comforts the suffering.	Eschatology—the future present

Develop Theological Movement

A fourth guide from homiletical theology that helps provide a foundation for the gospel is this: *Find movement within theology to give direction to the sermon.* The doctrine one chooses normally arises out of the theme sentence. Most doctrines have an underlying plot or story line because they arise out of various biblical accounts. The doctrine of sin suggests the fall in the Garden of Eden or the wandering of Israel for forty years, the cruci-fixion, or countless other stories that move from sin to its consequences to being saved. The Incarnation moves from the dire need God perceived in humanity to the meeting of that need by God becoming flesh. Plot helps people listen. One of the ancient formulas for narrative plot that dates back all the way to Aristotle is complication/resolution. Thus, the doctrine of the sovereignty of God may be said to move from human resentment of God to the blessing that God is sovereign (not humans). Each of these movements is an expression of trouble to grace. In other words, though the doctrines one preaches vary, their deep structure bears the gospel.

Any sermon needs a theological deepening of thought as the preacher explores the issues. A beginning preacher is likely to just keep repeating and illustrating a theological truth—such as the people of Israel sin—and certainly repetition of key truths is essential for oral delivery. However, the preacher must help listeners know why people sin. It is generally best to try to find a reason on the horizontal plane; the vertical might just say it is wrong because the Bible or God says so. The horizontal tries to help people understand why they do what is wrong. For example, with exces-sive concern about material things, advertising often encourages people to believe that there is limited time and limited supply and people think supplies will run out; consequently, there will not be enough. Alternatively, people seek immediate gratification by turning to drugs when only God can truly satisfy. One can then discuss the remedy for sin in Christ.

When preaching on suffering, one might move from the reality of human suffering to typical human response (that is, the apparent absence of God in those situations) to God's actual response (that is, the manner in which God in Christ has already entered into that suffering and taken it upon himself).

Try Inversion

Finally, here is a suggestion that is designed to give a sermon more amps by heightening the flow of electricity through it. It is really a sup-plementary playful exercise to try with a text to ensure that the full range of ideas from the text is considered, or it is an exercise to try with a sermon draft that seems dull. Take your list of concerns of the text and make one column with two halves, trouble and grace. Now go through each column one at a time and invert it for the opposite column. Then check to see if the new idea can stand as a legitimate concern of the text.

Example using Luke 13:31-35:

START WITH	INVERSION TO
Trouble:	*Grace:*
Herod seeks to kill Jesus.	Jesus seeks to save Herod.
Jerusalem will kill Jesus.	Jesus will die for Jerusalem.
Jerusalem will not see Jesus until they know him.	Jesus will be present but unrecognized.
Grace:	*Trouble:*
Jesus casts out demons.	Demons would cast out Christ.
Jesus will finish his work.	Humans cannot finish what is required of them.
Jesus would be as a mother hen.	We do not choose nurture.
Jerusalem will name Jesus Blessed.	Without Christ we may feel cursed.

One could do the same exercise using concerns of the sermon:

START WITH	INVERSION TO
Trouble:	*Grace:*
We must trust God.	God gives us trust.
We must help others.	God works through us.
Do what God instructs.	God empowers us.

Doing this exercise, one can discover new angles that may be legitimate. If done on a regular basis, it produces theological facility and agility.

In this chapter we focused on ensuring a theological foundation in sermons that will facilitate the gospel, and we have latterly concentrated on four practical principles from preaching, namely:

1. Find a theological focus in the biblical text (a) when no theological theme is apparent or (b) when focus on God needs magnification.
2. Concentrate overall on core doctrines.
3. Select mainly one doctrine to inform each sermon.
4. Develop theological movement from within the doctrine.
5. Try inversion.

We now turn to where all of this has been leading, to the specific subject of preaching the gospel.

PREACHING THE GOSPEL

The principles discussed in the previous chapter help ensure a strong theological base in the sermon. It remains for us to propose more precisely in this concluding chapter what it might mean from a practical perspective to preach the gospel. Here we will explore what it means to employ a gospel hermeneutic, and later we will suggest that to proclaim the gospel need not be a mere synonym for preaching.

A Gospel Hermeneutic

A gospel hermeneutic connects preaching to the center of the faith. In using it, one reads a biblical text in light of the gospel, and one finds ways in the sermon to connect with the larger faith story. This book has dealt largely with the notion of a gospel hermeneutic, from the beginning, when the limitations of preach-the-text were first discussed. A central conceit here is that the gospel cannot be effectively communicated if it is simply added to the sermon at the last moment. The gospel cannot be incidental, something that might happen along the way; it needs to be intentional from the beginning. Thus, at the start, theological exegesis of biblical texts is needed with a view to revelation and matters of God and faith. Preachers employ exegesis ("to bring out" meaning) rather than eisegesis ("to bring in" meaning) in order that the text may be understood as much as possible in its original historical setting. Nonetheless, these texts were written and handed down by people of faith dealing with faith issues that historical criticism struggles to acknowledge. When one reads a biblical text, one reads it through history and also through one's tradition and faith—never merely on its own terms as a document of history, in isolation from Judeo-Christian heritage. Even as the Jewish community reads Scripture through the Mishnah (oral law) and the Gemara (rabbinic discussion of the Mishnah), taken together as the Talmud, likewise, Christians read Scripture through the cross and resurrection. If the gospel is to be proclaimed as Christ commissioned it to be, some link between the biblical text at hand and the larger gospel message needs to be part of the approach, otherwise how is it the gospel?

> Even when a sermon may speak about God in significant ways, the gospel may still not be proclaimed. Grace is not necessarily gospel, but it often is and it both leads to it and invites it.

This practice assumes what was said earlier: even when a sermon may speak about God in significant ways, the gospel may be missed, such as when judgment and law are the only focus. Even when grace may be the focus, the gospel may still not be proclaimed. This will be a radical idea to some. The gospel is not really the gospel if it is announced in the absence of trouble, if it does not connect to the real-life circumstances of the hearers, if salvation is not liberation from something. Gospel is truly gospel when resurrection occurs where there was death. Using the Four Pages of a sermon as a grammar, trouble on its own is not gospel, nor is grace on its own, but when harnessed in tension with each other, the gospel may be proclaimed. Even in such tension, grace is not necessarily gospel, but it often is and is certainly always close to it. One could say that grace leads and points to grace and invites its proclamation. Without grace, one cannot expound the gospel. The one opens a pathway to the other and authorizes it.

Two things may yet be missing when we have established grace in a sermon. First, the listeners need a means in the sermon to know the grace is for themselves (*pro me*). To say that God heals may be encouraging, but in what way can the listeners know that God intends that healing for them? Our means of claiming that grace as gospel is Jesus Christ who died for us. Only if Christ is risen from the dead is he able to be present through the power of the Holy Spirit to us. Through faith in him the promises of God to the people of Israel become promises to the listener. In accepting him as Lord and Savior, one locates oneself before the cross and the empty tomb as a witness to the resurrection. Second, the gospel is not the gospel until it meets us in the circumstances and particularities of our own lives. By allowing the text to lead to both trouble and grace in our situation, the possibility of an experience of gospel becomes possible because it is here and now, not once upon a time.

Several factors mitigate against preaching the gospel. The problem of no gospel can originate when a text is cut from surrounding texts in order to be preached. The present-day understanding of preach-the-text treats texts as isolated units or pericopes cut off from the larger story.[1] God is not necessarily sought. Other ages had different understandings of text, and they had flaws in their own approaches. For the first fifteen hundred years of the church and more, the church understood text to mean the Bible as a whole, and a particular verse or phrase was simply the entry point in the sermon to other places in the Bible that communicated similar topics, common places, or teachings, all of which led to the gospel. The problem of no gospel is compounded by an age that assumes that gospel is contained in its notion of a biblical text no matter what lenses are used to read it or that does not actively question what gospel means. However, the problem of no gospel is larger even than this, and it has to do with the offense of the cross at the center of the faith. Mary Donovan Turner speaks for some seminaries when she laments, "Who among our community talks openly about the resurrection?" It seems to be connected with "evangelistic zeal and fervor."[2] James F. Kay wonders if "without a saving cross, would the Christian message still be Christian?"[3]

Arguably, only in the last century or so has preaching the gospel been diminished as an objective of critical scholarly endeavor in biblical departments. The halls of the seminary are appropriately in conversation with disciplines in the university; this is a vital source of much ferment and growth in theological understanding. On the downside, these other disciplines are not rooted in faith; from our perspective they are anthropocentric. Continued borrowing from them has left some aspects of the theological enterprise anthropocentric as well, mute on matters of God and faith. Thus in preaching, too heavy a reliance on historical criticism fostered preach-the-text, which became the dominant twentieth-century emphasis. The New Homiletic christened it. Whereas the ongoing strengths of this movement are plainly evident in rendering a trustworthy text understood against the backdrop of its own times, its theological limitations only gradually became clear: the gospel was often missed. Or, rather, the gospel was hit-or-miss. Sermons in the New Homiletic might proclaim the gospel, but this, as a practice, was assumed and rarely tested or discussed; it was not named as the preaching goal, and no methodology was developed for obtaining or ensuring it.

Five Steps to Preaching the Gospel

Using the gospel as a lens to read texts is one of the least discussed practices in contemporary homiletics, yet it is one of the most important and vital steps for preachers to learn. The gospel hermeneutic that is developed here has five critical steps: (1) discern trouble and grace in the text; (2) seek the gospel in the text; (3) bring the text to the cross and resurrection; (4) bring the canon to the text; and (5) proclaim the gospel (where proclaim is not a mere synonym for preach). The first two of these steps are employed from the beginning of the sermon process.

1. Discern trouble and grace in the text. Little more needs to be said here. The gospel has a shape and movement—from trouble to grace, from the cross to the resurrection—and to preach the gospel requires that something of this form and movement be explored and experienced. This movement is also an excellent way of doing theology, of finding what texts have to say, by moving from the human perspective to the divine perspective, as it were. It is at the heart of Jesus' identity.

2. Seek the gospel in the text. Seeking the gospel in the text is what we did when we added theological exegesis to traditional historical-critical and literary exegesis in chapter 1. When we ask, what is God doing in or behind this text? we ask a question that will enable us to identify the gospel if it is in the text at hand. Some texts, as we understand that term, do contain the gospel. In the majority of instances, however, some action of saving grace will be the focus, an action that provides a solid foundation for the gospel to be proclaimed.

The remaining three steps to proclaiming the gospel can be used in the sermon once the biblical text has been largely developed in the sermon (that is, Pages One and Three, once the integrity of the text has been assured).

3. Bring the text to the cross and resurrection. In this third step of a gospel hermeneutic, one uses the particular biblical text as a lookout place from which to view the cross on the far horizon, thus each text and time affords a slightly different perspective. Bringing the text to the Easter event is a process of allowing the significance of what God has accomplished in Jesus Christ to modify, fulfill, or otherwise affect the final meaning of the text at hand. In other words, one says, how does the Easter message affect the message of this text? In being open to this, one also allows the light of the gospel to shine through the text to illuminate the listener's life in front of the text.

> Bringing the text to the cross allows the significance of what God has accomplished in Jesus Christ to modify, fulfill, or otherwise affect the final meaning of the text at hand. One allows the light of the gospel to shine through the text to illuminate the listener's life in front of the text.

There is little good news in the story of the rich young man who comes to Jesus in Mark 10:17-31, for Jesus commands him to do the one thing he cannot. Christians have always read the present times in light of both the beginning of time (creation) and the final times (the eschaton): the promise of the future helps determine our present steps. One uses the same practice in reading biblical texts; the ending of the book as well as the beginning affects the reading of every text in between. By reading this particular text in Mark in light of the ending of Mark's book, one realizes that all was not lost for the young man as the text seems to imply; in fact, we discover that Jesus goes to the cross for him and all who are like him and that Easter holds out that promise of new creation to each of us who, for our own reasons, cannot do what is required.[4] Only in light of the gospel can we ensure that we have allowed the text to correct and reform our own readings, attitudes, behaviors, and doctrinal convictions.

Too often in history, the cross and resurrection have been an "easy out" for the preacher, a quick exit from a tough text or a pious fire escape from a hellfire sermon, or from a sermon that is drawing to a close with still no hope on the horizon. In such instances, as the despairing sermon draws to a close, the desperate preacher adds, almost as an afterthought, "But the good news is that Jesus died for your sins, therefore go out into the world and sin no more." To switch metaphors, to do that and say no more is like standing on the deck of a ship shouting to someone washed overboard, "There is a life preserver on deck at the bow," and doing nothing else. Rather, the gospel needs to be fully expounded from within the text and administered to our time through the cross.

Let us take another example. In moving the parable of the rich man and Lazarus (Luke 16:19-31) to the cross and resurrection, it becomes a fuller expression of the Christian faith. The preacher follows the hints Jesus gives in the text. He says there are consequences for sin. He says that no man can cross the chasm. He says that even if a man was raised from the dead and sent to the rich man's five brothers, they would not believe. Yet even in using this language, Jesus himself points to the cross. He is no ordinary man in that he is both fully human and fully divine. He dies that people might believe in God's love. In other words, the text whispers, "Preach the resurrection." Thus, over and against the message of the text at one level (that is, "It is too late"), Jesus' words point to another theological truth (that is, "In Christ, it is not too late"). In other words, in Christ we have one who has come to us from the dead, and it is not too late to hear or to act upon the life that is offered.

Similarly, we saw that in the call of Isaiah, the angel comes to him and says, "Now that this [coal] has touched your lips, your guilt has departed and your sin is blotted out" (Isaiah 6:7). When we take this text to the cross and resurrection, we recognize that we have heard these words before. They were spoken to us by Jesus on the cross. Without this reading, the text primarily resonates with today's listener on a somewhat romantic level, "Here am I; send me!"—as listeners, we identify with Isaiah and imagine our own volunteer service to be so blessed, even though the specific details of Isaiah's call have little to do with us. Just because God calls Isaiah does not in itself mean that God calls us. However, when our call is located where it truly is, in the Easter event, when we hear Jesus say to us, "your guilt has departed and your sin is blotted out," Isaiah's call becomes our own and we rejoice in the same God and a similar call, a call to witness.

4. Bring the canon to the text. Here one carries the larger gospel story to the text to find echoes of the gospel. This movement essentially looks for images or words from anywhere in the Bible that connect with the heart of the gospel or its practice in the church. Having said what one can about the text at hand, one now asks, what echoes of God's sovereignty, providence, the Incarnation, redemption, ascension, the inbreaking of the realm of God with power, or the end times may be found in the text, and how is this linked to the cross? What echoes may be found of baptism, the meal at the Table, or ministry in the shape of the cross?

David Bartlett refers to this kind of reading as canonical criticism, treating the context of the text as the entire Bible. He discusses echoes and allusions that are in Scripture as well as those that one finds in intertextual readings and typologies. Preaching makes connections between the Bible and peoples' lives and social movements, "but sometimes the connections are between the text and other texts. This is made all the easier by the fact that often Scripture has begun to do that for us.... It is not cheating for Christians to see the verse in Psalm 2 where God calls the king his son, as foreshadowing Jesus

> Bringing the canon to the text one asks, what echoes of God's sovereignty, providence, the Incarnation, redemption, ascension, the inbreaking of the realm of God with power, or the end times may be found in the text, and how is this linked to the cross? What echoes may be found of baptism, the meal at the Table, or ministry in the shape of the cross?

as God's son. Canonically, Matthew, Mark, and Luke all make that con-nection, and so may we."[5]

Consider, for instance, Naaman in 2 Kings 5:1-14. Elisha says he is to wash seven times in the Jordan and he will be made clean; in doing this he discovers that the God of Israel is indeed sovereign. But what are we to make of this? What connection has it to us? When one listens for echoes of the gospel, one discovers resonance with the washing that we receive in our baptism through faith. In baptism we die to our old selves and rise with Christ to our new: we are made clean. Thus the cleansing that Naaman received is our own in Christ and his story becomes ours.

Similarly, in the parable of the wedding banquet (Matthew 22:2-14) preachers may affirm the stark consequences of not being prepared for the banquet. Still, that is not the fullness of the Christian message one pro-claims. One may set this against what our faith also affirms, namely, that in our baptism, Christ put on us a garment of high cost; through faith, he puts on us that which makes us fit to enter into God's presence (Revelation 3:4).

Of course, some biblical scholars may charge that this is promoting an uncritical allegorical method, but that is not the case. An important dif-ference exists between allegorizing a text and typology. The former twists a text to say what one wants. Typology, by contrast, uses the imagery and theology of the church to find connections and echoes between texts: the integrity of the original text is not put in question. The Bible frequently uses typology.

> Examples of New Testament typology include: John 6:49-59 (Jesus is "the living bread . . . from heaven" in contrast to the limited sustenance Israel received, manna in the wilderness); Romans 5:14 ("Adam, who is a type of the one who was to come"); Romans 10:6-10 (Moses' words in Deut. 30:12-14 are a type of justification by faith); 1 Corinthians 10:1-2 (the Red Sea is a type of baptism, and Israel is a type of the Corinthians); 2 Corinthians 3:7-17 (Moses' transfiguration is a type of Christ's); Galatians 3:16 (Abraham is a type of Christ); Ephesians 5:14 (citing Jon. 1:6, Jonah is a type of the awakening sleepers upon whom Christ's light will shine); Hebrews 9:24 (the sanctuary is a type of Christ's heavenly one); Revelation 5:12 (Christ is the Passover lamb); and Revelation 19:13-15 (vengeance on Edom in Isaiah 63:1-6 is a type of Christ's judgment). [6]

Both the Bible and the faith authorize such links. We make similar ones in the practice of the church when we read one text alongside another and make some connection between them on the basis of a resonant image.

To return to John the Baptist in Mark 1, the significance of that text lies in John pointing to Jesus and God's action through John. If we listen for the gospel in this story (if we bring it to the the cross and resurrection), it may seem hard to find. His message is Isaiah's message: "Prepare the way of the Lord, make straight his paths." The same message had been proclaimed for hundreds of years. If it had been possible for Israel to achieve on their own, they would have accomplished it. This is exactly the point. Try though one might, we are unable of our own resources to make straight our crooked ways, and that is why God comes in Jesus. Thus, this story is the beginning of God making straight our ways. In bringing the canon to the text and connecting it to the larger story, we interpret that Jesus comes in order to straighten out our relationships with God, and he does this ultimately on the cross. John announces what Jesus does. It is God who acts in John; it is God who acts in our preparations; it is God who enables us to do what John commands on behalf of God, and we do it through faith in Christ.

Take as another example the great commandment, love God and your neighbor as yourself. As a commandment, it leaves people finally cast upon their own resources to do the required loving. As such it kills us. However, when one brings the canon to bear on the text, one finds echoes of another great statement concerning love, the one made on the cross. The commandments say, "You do it; it's up to you"; Christ says in relation to the commandments, "You cannot do it; I do it for you." Theologically we may affirm that we are only able to love in the manner of the great commandment because we have first been loved by Christ. In fact, Jesus is the only person who was able to love God and neighbor as oneself. Through the resurrection and the gift of the Spirit, he has given us his power to love. Because Christ loved God and neighbor as he loved himself, it becomes possible for us to do the same because he has given us his Spirit. When we fulfill the great commandment, God acts in and through us.

Paul's description of love in 1 Corinthians 13 is typically read at weddings where it appropriately stands as an ideal for which to strive. The text actually stands as a condemnation of each of us because we all fall short of its requirements. However, when one brings the larger canon to this text, one can affirm that Paul's description of wonderful love is only fulfilled in Christ; in other words, the text describes God's love, and this love is available to us through faith.

In using these sorts of theological interpretation or gospel hermeneutic, the best reasons for believing are made evident. Many biblical texts that have been interpreted only to convict can now also serve as instruments to proclaim the gospel and to nurture God's community of love.[7] By a reverse strategy, texts that seem to imply only grace can be interpreted to convict as well, as we just saw with 1 Corinthians 13; preachers thereby enhance the text's ability to proclaim the gospel.

One uses a gospel hermeneutic with some caution. For example, one does not read the Old Testament only or primarily in typological fashion, as though the texts are mere types of the Christian story and exist only to serve it. Authentic good news arises first from the biblical text at hand. There is one God in both Testaments. Moreover, if good news is not seen to arise first from this text, and God's action in or through it, it is likely to seem in the sermon like something that is pasted on.

> To proclaim the gospel is to speak on behalf of God to the gathered community of faith with words that are at the heart of the gospel. It is first-person to second-person intimate speech, countless ways of God saying "I love you."

The gospel is then turned into a mere bandage; it is superficial, unconvincing, disconnected, and shallow—quite the opposite of God's Word.

5. Proclaim the gospel. It is important to provide a structure of trouble-grace to bear the gospel in the sermon, to look for the gospel in the text, to take the text to the cross, and to bring the canon to the text. It is yet another thing to proclaim the gospel, to dare to speak on behalf of God loving gospel words to the gathered community of faith; such words are one to one.

Arguably the highest expression of the gospel comes through proclamation used in this sense. The term is often used only as a mere synonym for preaching in general, yet in the history of preaching, it frequently has a more specific use. To proclaim is to speak on behalf of God to the community of faith with words that are at the heart of the gospel. It is first-person to second-person gospel speech that cannot happen without a proper foundation in teaching about the gospel from the Bible text at hand. Once established, grace in the text can be amplified into gospel and brought home to the listener through proclamation.

Proclamation takes the shape of a host of phrases, and one would look initially to one's own biblical text for words that are most appropriate. Proclamation is a free pronouncement of the gospel; it is an unconditional declaration of love from the cross. The message may sound something like any one of these statements (though said in this kind of list may make them sound foolish—they need to arise out of Scripture and theology in preaching): "I love you. I died for you. I will not let you go. I forgive you. Come to me, all of you that are weary and heavy laden, and I will give you rest. Take heart! Do not be afraid! Your faith has made you well. I am your Shepherd. Let not your hearts be troubled, neither let them be afraid. Well done my good and faithful servant. I am with you to the end of the age. This is my body, broken for you. This is my blood, poured out for you." These words are intimate words, supportive words, words that can only be spoken when the sermon has made clear the gospel identity of the risen One who speaks them. They are cruciform words that come bearing the gospel. Their variety is limited only by the number of ways God has to say "I love you."

Gerhard O. Forde speaks of proclamation as a "doing of what the text authorizes" to the listener and he offers this example:[8]

> Where the text on the healing of the paralytic ends, for instance, with words to the effect that the people were "afraid and glorified God who had given such authority to men" the text virtually insists on what the next move has to be. The proclaimer must exercise the authority so granted. The proclaimer must so announce the forgiveness to those gathered here and now as to amaze them with the audacity of it all. Perhaps they will even glorify God once again. The proclaimer must, on the authority of Jesus, have the guts to do again in the living present, what was done once upon a time. The proclaimer must dare to believe that the very moment of proclamation is the moment planned and

counted on by the electing God himself. The proclaimer is there to do the deed authorized, not merely to explain the deeds of the past.[9]

> Proclamation performs or actualizes the text, brings it to its intended completion as a liberating, loving word of forgiveness and empowerment from God.

It is a wonderful understanding that we do what the text authorizes. Understood this way, proclamation performs or actualizes the text, brings it to its intended completion as a liberating, loving word of forgiveness and empowerment from God. It is an eschatological occurrence in the now that puts an end to the old and makes a new beginning in the present. For Forde, proclamation is "the necessary and indispensable final move in the argument."[10] As such, it can be the place to which the sermon leads.

> Five Steps to Preach the Gospel: (1) Discern trouble and grace in the text; (2) find the gospel in the text; (3) bring the text to the cross and resurrection to see if its meaning is altered; (4) bring the larger gospel story to the text to find echoes; (5) proclaim the Gospel

Some preachers may not feel comfortable speaking on behalf of God—it might presume too much authority. One could respond that every time a preacher preaches, people listen with the expectation that God is speaking in and through the sermon. Some preachers might find the words too personal, too intimate, but that is the gospel. Some preachers might find proclamation too individualistic. It is spoken to the individual, but it is also spoken to the entire community. In fact, one could argue that these words form the community; these are the words that Christ speaks directly, the words that make the church a church, that invite profession of faith, that evoke confession and service of Jesus Christ as Lord and Savior. These words of proclamation are the same words that the Sacrament of the Eucharist enacts and seals. In short, proclamation takes information about God and turns it into a word spoken by God. It offers certainty and confidence in Christ. It slays death. It brings in a new era. It gives people life, identity, and mission.

Faithful Proclamation

Five steps are recommended, then, to assist preaching the gospel: trouble and grace, the gospel in the text, the text to the cross, the canon to the text, and proclaiming the gospel. Are preachers justified in using gospel interpretation in this way with a biblical text? Perhaps the question should be put another way: can preachers be fully faithful proclaimers of the gospel if they do not interpret in this way? The question may be put in yet another way: was it the intent of the New Testament communities, or has it been the purpose of the church, to isolate biblical passages from the larger Christian story in what is too often the contemporary manner? Do preachers preach the truth of one pericope on its own, or do they preach it within the saving message of Jesus Christ? Or to ask our starting question, are preachers to preach the text or preach the gospel?

Preaching the gospel means preaching the text, yet it means something more. Far from distorting biblical texts, could preachers be truer to their historical-critical settings and faith contexts? Is the cross and resurrection not a legitimate concern of every biblical text for Christians? Asked another way, can preachers ever do more than pretend to read a biblical text as though the incarnation, cross, resurrection, ascension, and descent and empowerment of the Spirit are not key lenses? All of this is to urge preachers to use gospel interpretation intentionally, with the utmost care and sensitivity, in order that they not distort God's Word but faithfully deliver and proclaim it.

Nothing may be more important for preaching in our time than recovery of the gospel: the church is seemingly in decline; its preaching often falls short of the gospel; many in the academy are distracted with other matters, yet the gospel is all that we have to offer to this world that God loves so much. Nothing is more urgent, for only with the gospel is it possible for us to exercise our ministries of outreach and justice in Christ's name and power.

Conclusion

Perhaps this is the right place to end our tour of the homiletical highlands, with our focus on proclaiming the gospel. This, after all, is a main goal of preaching: to send brothers and sisters everywhere, proclaiming the good news of Jesus Christ in both word and deed, and ministering to others in the power of the Holy Spirit.

The field of Homiletics has seen some remarkable and exciting changes in the last fifty years. The New Homiletic shifted the emphasis from propositions communicating information to greater emphasis on stories, images, and metaphors that communicate experience. In addition, sermons once moved primarily along lines of logic and argument; they now may honor plot and organic development and growth as well. Sermons now try to honor differences: different ways of knowing, different ways of learning, different backgrounds of listeners, different perspectives on issues, different ways of reading the Bible.

The crucial test of the New Homiletic can be posed as inquiring whether sermons have become better. Almost without pausing, one can say, "Yes, they are more listener orientated, more in tune with their cultural settings, better able to teach the Bible in ways that people can receive." Sermons typically are more biblically based, and they communicate what the text says; they have more variety in terms of form. Still, there is pause. One is not quite so ready to say yes when one shifts the question slightly and asks, have sermons become more faithful? Are they better at proclaiming the gospel?

Here, one is rightly hesitant. Most sermons in most pulpits continue to focus on human action and leave out God. Even when God is a significant focus, God's grace may not be. And even when God's grace may be developed, how that grace is "for me" is omitted. If Jesus Christ's life, death, and resurrection have made any difference to life today, it is not apparent. If he is alive today, listeners may not meet him. Thus, even when sermons are biblically based, the gospel may not be proclaimed. People may not experience God's love or be persuaded that its precious costly nature applies to them.

The gospel is not always the dedication of scholars in disciplines that serve preaching. This need not imply lack of faith, but lack of explicit focus on the gospel may imply a naive assumption that most biblical texts contain it. Many teachers who follow the preach-the-text approach have actually found intuitive or other ways to get to the gospel in preaching, but not necessarily with consistency or in ways students can follow, because these teachers are largely silent about how this is accomplished. Most of us who teach and uphold the value of preaching the gospel have assumed in the past that somehow by preaching the text it just happened.

Preachers must preach the text, but they must do more than this. The New Homiletic was preoccupied with other important matters that often had to do with the surface of preaching, such as moving from old conceptual ways of thinking and devising forms that fit the texts. The benefits of the New Homiletic are plain, yet the hermeneutical models of the New Homiletic (and the old) may be said never to have accomplished their task: they could not account for how the Word of God then is the Word of God now.[11] There is always the danger that preaching the text as text makes text an idol. In any case, it is time to take the learnings of the New Homiletic and move beyond it.

Preach-the-gospel moves to deep issues in promoting better preaching. Surface models afford variety but they provide no solution to the absence of gospel. What is needed is an entire hermeneutic from the beginning of the sermon process to the end that has gospel as the goal and focus. Thus the text is treated as a possible source of the gospel and as a lens or portal through which one looks to the cross and to the larger gospel story; the text is also understood to be a lens or window through which God shines the light of the gospel on a needy world. To the historical critical and literary models of exegesis in chapter 1 were added an essential third step of theological exegesis that approaches the Bible as Scripture, as revelation, as the church's book, which communicates something about God and creation; God in and behind the text becomes the key focus early in the exegetical process; trouble and grace bring the shape of the gospel into the sermon at a deep level and thereby prepare a foundation for the gospel to be explored and experienced, named and proclaimed; and a gospel hermeneutic and ways of proclaiming the gospel bring the sermon to completion.

Preaching is no better than the instruments one uses to guide its formation. If preachers do not look for God in texts, they may not find God. If they do not find God, how can they know they have found God's

Word? Without a focus on God one can have no grace. Without a focus on grace one can have no gospel. Without a focus on gospel one cannot live up to the commission Christ gave to preach it. If preachers do not intentionally seek the gospel, it may not be discerned.

The gospel has a shape, and it molds and transforms people in that shape, the shape of the cross, lives lived in service to others putting to death the old powers and giving testimony to Christ. The gospel is life and it implies movement in the sermon from doubt to faith, from the cross to the resurrection, from Good Friday to Easter, from the Exodus to the promised land, from expulsion from Eden to the New Jerusalem.

The gospel is more than this, however. It is encounter with the living God, meeting one's Savior, an inbreaking of God's eternal realm. The task of preachers is to facilitate this meeting such that Jesus Christ is heard to speak words of life to each person present. This is true proclamation; it necessarily arises from and is distinct from generic preaching. Said another way, proclamation ceases to be a synonym for preaching when gospel becomes the focus of it. These words of proclamation may be trusted precisely because they come from the other side of death with the power of the Holy Spirit.

The first disciples were told, "He has been raised from the dead, and indeed he is going ahead of you to Galilee; there you will see him" (Matthew 28:7). People today may go into the world as both Easter people and Pentecost people, in the knowledge that Christ goes with them and they are given his power. The closing words of the Gospel of John can be a constant inspiration for the preacher, for John was pointing to countless resurrection appearances even in his own day: "But there are also many other things that Jesus did; if every one of them were written down, I suppose that the world itself could not contain the books that would be written" (21:25).

The challenge is determining whether preaching in general can take the principles of the New Homiletic and move beyond them to recover proclamation of the gospel. Putting God at the center of the Bible and preaching is a big step, and perhaps the barriers are too great; or possibly the number of people teaching preaching is too few; or perhaps tradition is too strong; or maybe the academy is too resistant. Yet if God wills it, it will happen, and the church will have the only future it can have in faith—the one God intends.

Appendix

A Note to Teachers Using This Book

Teachers wishing to use this book for their introductory homiletics class might appreciate some idea of how this book is used elsewhere. It is designed to take students through the sermon-writing process from beginning to end one step at a time and one week at a time in relation to the course and one day at a time in relation to the preacher's week. Our school term consists of twelve weeks of two-hour classes. The term is split into two. The material of this book is covered in the first six weeks of the term, one section or "day of the week" for each week of class. (The course is front-end loaded, with the heaviest work coming in the first half, in contrast to many other courses.)

The first half of the term deals with class theory in the first hour and practice with a biblical text in the second, applying that theory. In addition, throughout the first half of the term, the students work in small groups outside of class; they work on class assignments using either an Old Testament or epistle text of their choice (that is, they have free choice and are not all working on the same text). The "Further Reflection and Study" questions found at the end of each section may be assigned to the small groups or used in class. Before midterm, students preach their first sermon to their small group, make changes, and submit their written sermon for grading. Students often elect to continue their small groups through the second half of term.

In the second half of the term, the students pick a gospel text and preach a second sermon to the entire class on their assigned day, this time using the lectionary for the upcoming Sunday. The reverse order is followed: the first hour is now practice in which the students preach their second sermon, and the second hour is devoted to class theory in which the class responds to one sermon at a time, dividing the time equally. Students are instructed to make no comparisons between or among preachers; each competes simply to be the best preacher he or she can be. Feedback is offered first by stating things that the listeners liked and later with possible suggestions. (An alternative, of course, is to divide the two hours by the number of students preaching and do sermon-response-sermon-response, and so on, a process that can increase the anxiety of the last preacher.) Students are allowed to take minimal notes during the sermon, trying as much as possible to maintain eye contact with the preacher, and fuller notes may be made in a time of silence after each sermon. Full written evaluations are to be submitted to the preachers the following week and submitted as a unit to the instructor at the end of term. Class sermons are videotaped, and students are to view and evaluate their own performance.

The student assignments include those listed below (for the first sermon only—an exegetical assignment is assumed for the second sermon), written evaluations of each of the class sermons in the second half of the term using course theory, and a book report on another book in homiletics.

The student assignments in this book are listed here in order that instructors may more easily decide which ones they want to assign for marking or for the small groups. They are listed according to each section, along with their exact location.

Student Assignments

Week 1

1. Do an exegesis of the text for your first sermon for the class following the model above. Chapter 1, page 25.
2. Using the exegesis exercise that you have done, list a few potential major concerns of the text. Now select one as your theme sentence. Chapter 3, page 52.

Week 2

3. Using your exegesis assignment, make a list of the concerns of the text. Chapter 4, page 63.

4. Indicate on your own list of concerns which texts are trouble and which are grace. Chapter 4, page 67.

5. Write your own poem/prayer based on your biblical text. Conclude with some powerful dimension of grace in the manner of McDonnell. Chapter 4, page 70.

6. Transpose your list of concerns of the text into concerns of the sermon. Transpose trouble into trouble and grace into grace. Chapter 5, page 78.

7. Choose from among your list of concerns of the text and concerns of the sermon two pairs, one to serve as trouble and one to serve as grace. Consider these as a possible outline of your sermon. Chapter 5, page 81.

Week 3

8. Do an exegesis of your congregation or of the class to which you will preach using the above questions and/or your own. Chapter 6, page 91.

9. Identify roughly a dozen probing questions and do an exegesis of yourself in relationship to your congregation or class. Chapter 6, page 95.

10. Using one of the above strategies, do an exegesis of a social situation or issue relevant to preaching. Chapter 6, page 104.

11. Identify in a sentence what is the moral sense of your text and write a paragraph that will help you employ it in your sermon. Chapter 6, page 105.

12. Using some of the above principles, write a portion of your sermon. For instance, write about the biblical text using a concern of the text or the major concern of the text to guide the paragraphs or page you compose. You may also start to connect with some experiences using a concern of the sermon to guide your writing. This is a rough draft so expect to refine it later, but it is good to get something down now on the page. Chapter 7, page 128.

Week 4

13. Make your own list of five situations that represent vertical trouble and convert them to horizontal. Find a paragraph in the sermon you are working on (or some other sermon, perhaps from a book) that deals with our world using vertical trouble. Rewrite the paragraph using horizontal trouble. Chapter 9, page 173.

14. Choose a sermon form from either this or the preceding chapter and complete a first draft of your sermon. Try using trouble and grace as the deep structure whatever exterior form you choose. Chapter 9, page 183.

Week 5

15. Make a list of as many metaphors and names for God as you might typically draw upon for a sermon. After doing this, go to a source like *The New Interpreter's Dictionary of the Bible* (Nashville: Abingdon Press, 2006—check under "God, names of," "God, metaphors for," and "Jesus, metaphors for") and make a list of all the metaphors and names for God that the Bible uses. Compare your two lists and identify ways of speaking of God that you might want to employ more in preaching and prayer. One might pay particular attention to lifting up feminine images of God. Chapter 10, page 193.
16. Using at least two of the above examples of concrete oral speech for the word of God, write two examples of your own. Chapter 10, page 197.
17. Revise your sermon with a view to oral issues. Try using the senses and making movies. Check to see if you use all three means of persuasion, logos, ethos and pathos. Will polar and linear thinkers both find themselves addressed? Check for unity using the acronym TTDNIM. Chapter 11, page 226.

Week 6

No student assignment for this week is given in this book but in a class this would be the week students would preach to their small group, make any desired changes, and hand it in. The class itself would focus on the material in section VI: Gospel Matters.

Weeks 7–12

Class sermons.

When dealing with the Four Pages of the sermon, it may be helpful to show one video example, such as *Great Preachers, Barbara Brown Taylor*, series 1, The Odyssey Channel Collection [video recording and published sermon] (Worcester, Pa.: Vision Video, 1997). I recommend distribution of the full, written manuscript inside the jacket since the editors cut out, not least, much of Page One from the videotape.

A Sermon

T his sermon was preached at the Calvin Symposium on Worship, Calvin Theological Seminary, Grand Rapids, Michigan, January 24-27, 2007. The theme sentence is God's glory abounds in ministry.

2 Corinthians 3:7-18

Now if the ministry of death, chiseled in letters on stone tablets, came in glory so that the people of Israel could not gaze at Moses' face because of the glory of his face, a glory now set aside, how much more will the ministry of the Spirit come in glory? For if there was glory in the ministry of condemnation, much more does the ministry of justification abound in glory! Indeed, what once had glory has lost its glory because of the greater glory; for if what was set aside came through glory, much more has the permanent come in glory!

Since, then, we have such a hope, we act with great boldness, not like Moses, who put a veil over his face to keep the people of Israel from gazing at the end of the glory that was being set aside. But their minds were hardened. Indeed, to this very day, when they hear the reading of the old covenant, that same veil is still there, since only in Christ is it set aside. Indeed, to this very day whenever Moses is read, a veil lies over their minds; but when one turns to the Lord, the veil is removed. Now the Lord is the Spirit, and where the Spirit of the Lord is, there is freedom. And all of us, with unveiled faces, seeing the glory of the Lord as though reflected in a mirror, are being transformed into the same image from one degree of glory to another; for this comes from the Lord, the Spirit.

Degrees of Glory

If you were not thrilled by Paul's words from 2 Corinthians 3, you may not be alone. One has the sense that Paul is excited about something, and if his excitement leaps off the page, his meaning often does not. He is like a schoolkid fresh off the playground reporting an event, and his words run ahead of his meaning. The last time I preached on 2 Corinthians, a goodly man in the church said, "I just don't understand Paul." This was after my sermon. I could have consoled him if he had said it before I preached. You know you have a tough text when after the sermon people are no clearer about it than before—either that or you are a poor preacher. The day my grade four class studied grammar, syntax, and punctuation with Mrs. Turner, Saint Paul skipped class. He looked mature for his young years, even back then. When one looks at his sentences in Greek they are all run-ons. At the end of the school year we were given a test. He left blank the question, "What is a circular definition?" which in hindsight strikes me as odd given that he comes close to giving one here in this passage on the subject of glory. He surely loves the word *glory*. He uses it here eleven times. In verse 10 alone glory appears five times: "Indeed, what once had glory has lost its glory because of the greater glory; for if what was set aside came through glory, much more has the permanent come in glory!" That is a whole lot of glory. In my years of ministry, I've never once heard anyone pick this Bible verse as their favorite. What does it mean? I might not have chosen to preach on this passage if my host had not assigned it to me, such is his passion for glory. Too bad, because if you get down to Paul's meaning, it is so rich. He says that ministry of the Spirit comes in glory. Glory is part of the package. Glory is God's nature. Glory is God's presence. If you are a disciple of Christ, God's glory is job benefit number one. God's glory abounds in ministry. But who today is going to have patience to stay with Paul long enough to get his meaning and get to the glory? Many folks prefer reading something they can easily understand, like the *Da Vinci Code* or the *Gospel of Judas*, never mind what it may do to the soul.

Paul is dense—we are not the first to say it—2 Peter 3:16 says there are some things in Paul's letters that are "hard to understand." No kidding. Who knew? Who today will have enough patience with Paul's prose to get to the glory? Paul says there are two ways to read Scripture: one way is his former way when the law was written in stone, and the other is his present way, when the law is written by the Spirit on his heart in the new covenant. Like any good preacher, Paul expounds his meaning using a biblical text: Moses' face shone with glory when he descended from Mount Sinai with the Ten Commandments; his face was so bright with the glory of God that the people of Israel could not look directly on it, and Moses had to cover his face with a veil. That is how it was before Paul met Jesus Christ. Now, having met Christ Jesus, he finds God fully revealed in him, and the veil that prevented him from looking on the brilliant glory of God has been removed. Paul speaks from experience: his Road to Damascus experience involved blinding glory. All the former glory was set aside. Now he ministers in the Spirit and by comparison, "how much more will the ministry of the Spirit come in glory."

Paul might be easier to understand if his own ministry was not in such trouble. His claim that God's glory abounds in ministry may seem odd. Things have not gone swimmingly in Corinth. His authority was challenged on his last "painful visit" (2 Corinthians 2:1). He then wrote them a letter of "tears" (2 Corinthians 2:4). He writes now instead of visiting them as he promised, fearing his actual presence would cause pain. Glory does not come to mind when one hears that in Asia recently he has been "so utterly, unbearably crushed that we despaired of life itself" (2 Corinthians 1:8). Sometimes it sounds more like the ministry of death as he later recalls that five times he has been flogged forty lashes minus one; three times beaten with rods; once he received a stoning (or as my youth group likes to say, once he was stoned); often he has been left near death; frequently he has been betrayed; and many times he has been without food, shelter, and clothing (see 2 Corinthians 11:23-27).

You may have to know suffering to understand Paul. Perhaps you are suffering today. You may minister in a church where the previous pastor served faithfully for thirty years, attended all the meetings, visited every home, never missed the sick, studied constantly, published two sermons each Sunday, never had a holiday, and certainly never took continuing education at Calvin Seminary. By comparison with this predecessor, who still worships in the church, you have somehow always fallen short. The church parking lot is nearly empty after church when the chairperson of the board comes into your office and says, "You are not preaching the gospel the way it needs to be preached, otherwise we would not be having these problems." If you know suffering you might connect with Paul. Truth be told, at the Second Coming, when Jesus comes to that church, he may even be found wanting.

We must go where the Spirit sends us. We must do the ministry the Spirit sets before us. It is not our choice. Why is it that ministry of the Spirit so often looks and feels like death not glory? I ask God why my own children seem not to have faith. What glory is there for you, O God, when we cannot communicate our faith to the next generation? So many people ask the glory question: What glory is there for you, O God, when a baby dies of SIDS? What glory is there for you when people live in despair and poverty, or when young people come home from war in body bags? Some of you may be able to fill in the sentence for yourselves because of experiences in your own lives: What glory is there for you, O God, in this ...? This question may have even crossed Jesus' lips at Gethsemane: What glory is there for you in not taking away this cup from my mouth?

You have to be really patient to get Paul's meaning that God's glory abounds in ministry. You almost have to be a saint, someone who finds God where others see nothing. It is as though for Paul there is a direct connection between suffering and glory. That is not quite right. Paul sees no merit in meaningless suffering: he is not into S&M; he does not poke himself with his sewing needle or go around dropping boulders on his sandals because he seeks to suffer. He does not. However, for Paul there is a direct connection between his suffering in ministry for Christ and Christ's suffering on the cross; and there is a direct connection between the glory Paul experiences in ministry and Christ's glory in the resurrection. As a follower of Jesus, when suffering comes, so eventually does God's glory. God's glory abounds in ministry. Out of death comes new life. How many times did Paul experience it, either God saving him when he could have died or God giving him what he needed to endure his thorn in the flesh (2 Corinthians 12:7)—"my grace is sufficient for you" (12:9)—or in God turning his suffering into something that works for a larger good, as his letters serve us today? The Spirit gives Paul the hope, healing, sustenance, and faith he needs. When by the world's standards Paul should feel most alone, despised, utterly rejected in Christ's name, he still claims God's glory. Even in this letter, Paul proclaims the gospel as best he can from a painful distance, not always with the simplicity and clarity we would like. Glory be to God, the Word that he preaches in this letter bears fruit; the church in Corinth apparently unites behind him, and they preserve his letter as a testimony to the Spirit for the posterity of the church.

You have to be almost a saint to understand Paul, and you may feel you are not good enough, but Paul thinks otherwise, and apparently so does God. God has appeared in glory to you. The God whose glory was seen in Moses and the prophets, whose glory was heralded by angels at the birth of Jesus, whose glory was made manifest in Christ at his baptism, whose glory dazzled the disciples in the transfiguration, whose glory was evident in Jesus' words and miracles, whose glory appeared to Mary on Easter morning, whose glory blinded Paul on the Road to Damascus, whose glory called forth saints in every age, this same God has appeared in glory to you. In ministry our lives take the shape of the cross. We willingly take on the suffering of others. We experience suffering ourselves. And God takes even our suffering and turns it into glory; it is like what Paul says in Romans 8:28, "All things work together for good for those who love God." We have one foot in the old creation of death and one foot in the new creation of Christ, and glory is all around.

God takes even our suffering and turns it into glory. Someone is experiencing an illness, and God uses the occasion to bring the family more closely together than it has ever been, such that some of them even pray together. That is glory. Someone here is experiencing the pain of a broken relationship. God in Christ has already walked over to you, held you, called you by name, taken that pain and is molding it into hope for tomorrow, perhaps even into the ability to minister to someone in the future who is in similar circumstance.

I remember in my first ministry placement going to visit a frail woman in long-term care. She had greeting cards all around, yet it was not Christmas, and her own hands were too gnarled to write. She used to be so active in the community. "Do your find the passing of time hard?" "Oh I did at first. But not now. I keep myself busy praying for everyone who writes and asks me for prayers." What looked like death is overtaken by glory. Isn't that what happened on the cross? God accepted our suffering and turned it into something else. Some call it salvation or sanctification and others just call it glory.

You may have been wounded in ministry, yet I am here to declare to you that God's glory abounds in your ministry; in faith you are a bright, shining, and treasured beacon of God's love. God takes even your suffering and turns it into glory. Paul says in our passage, "And all of us, with unveiled faces, seeing the glory of the Lord as though reflected in a mirror, are being transformed into the same image from one degree of glory to another; for this comes from the Lord, the Spirit." Charles Wesley said we are "changed from glory into glory, / till in heaven we take our place." If you want to see God's nature, if you want some affirmation of God's presence in your life, just look in the mirror; no, not in a vain way, not in the old creation mirror in the old creation way, "Why didn't you tell me my hair was all blown out of place?" No, look into the new creation mirror in a new creation way, in a testimonial way, "Oh, I am looking glorious today—I am the image of Christ and I am getting more glorious every day." Look back over your life; you may be able to see that you are becoming more and more like Christ. The Spirit is sanctifying you, making you holy. God's glory is seen in you. Christ's glory is seen in your neighbor. God's glory abounds. Turn to your neighbors on both sides and say, "You are looking glorious today." Go ahead, do it, as a testimony to faith, because I want to tell you, "You are looking glorious today."

NOTES

Preface to the Original Edition

1. David James Randolph, *The Renewal of Preaching* (Philadelphia: Fortress Press, 1969), 22–23.

1. Biblical Exegesis

1. In Lionel Crocker, ed., *Harry Emerson Fosdick's Art of Preaching: An Anthology* (Springfield, Ill.: Charles C. Thomas, 1971), 30.

2. Preachers only very rarely preach against texts—and even then they do so on the basis of other scriptural texts—so one might ask why not just preach the other text? See Clark M. Williamson and Ronald J. Allen, *A Credible and Timely Word* (St Louis: Chalice Press, 1991), 91–129, esp. 120–25; and Phyllis Trible, *Texts of Terror: Literary-Feminist Readings of Biblical Narratives* (Philadelphia: Fortress Press, 1984).

3. Thomas H. Troeger, *Imagining a Sermon* (Nashville: Abingdon Press, 1990), 15.

4. Michael J. Quicke, *360 Degree Preaching: Hearing, Speaking and Living the Word* Grand Rapids, Mich.: Baker Academic; Carlisle, Cumbria, UK: Paternoser Publishing,), 144.

5. Linda L. Clader, "Homily for the Feast of the Visitation," in Jana Childers, ed., *Birthing the Sermon: Women Preachers on the Creative Process* (St. Louis: Chalice Press, 2001), 54.

6. Ibid., 57.

7. Casey Barton, personal e-mail, 6/27/06.

8. See: Anthony C. Thiselton, *The Two Horizons: New Testament Hermeneutics and Philosophical Description* (Grand Rapids, Mich.: Eerdmans, 1980), 5; he cites Heinz Kimmerle.

9. Paul Ricoeur understands explanation in an interdisciplinary manner, having to do with scientific method, for instance using Freudian psychoanalysis as it applies to interpretation. Each of these human sciences discloses new texts. As he says, "It is indeed *another text* that psychoanalysis deciphers, *beneath the text of consciousness.*" Cited in Anthony C. Thiselton, *New Horizons in Hermeneutics* (Grand Rapids, Mich.: Zondervan, 1992), 344–50.

10. Understanding a text, says Ricoeur, is to follow its movement "from what it says to what it talks about." See Paul Ricoeur, "The Model of the Text: Meaningful Action Considered as a Text," in Paul Ricoeur, *Hermeneutics and the Social Sciences* (New York: Cambridge University Press, 1981), 210–13.

11. Otto Kaiser and Werner G. Kummel, *Exegetical Method: a Student's Handbook* (trans. E. V. N. Goetchius; New York: Seabury Press, 1967), 36; originally published in Munich: Chr. Kaiser Verlag, 1963. What follows is loosely drawn from the Seabury source, 37–70.

12. Eugene L. Lowry, *Living with the Lectionary: Preaching Through the Revised Common Lectionary* (Nashville: Abingdon Press, 1992), 20.

13. Augustine, *On Christian Doctrine* (trans. D. W. Robinson Jr.; Indianapolis: Bobbs-Merrill, 1958), III, 15.

14. See my *God Sense: Reading the Bible for Preaching* (Nashville: Abingdon Press, 2001), 57–68.

15. Cleophus J. LaRue, *The Heart of Black Preaching* (Louisville: Westminster John Knox Press, 2000), 69–71. See his chapter on hermeneutics, 68–113.

16. Warren H. Stewart Sr., *Interpreting God's Word in Black Preaching* (Valley Forge, Pa.: Judson Press, 1984), 14.

17. Quicke, *360 Degree Preaching*, 146.

18. David L. Bartlett, *Between the Bible and the Church: New Methods for Biblical Preaching* (Nashville: Abingdon Press, 1999), 102–28.

19. These questions are taken from my *God Sense*, 69–71. Robert G. Hughes and Robert Kysar offer five theological questions in *Preaching Doctrine: For the Twenty-First Century* (Fortress Resources for Preaching; Minneapolis: Fortress Press, 1997), 44–45.

2. Purposes of Preaching

1. Cleophus J. LaRue, ed., *Power in the Pulpit: How America's Most Effective Black Preachers Prepare Their Sermons* (Louisville: Westminster John Knox Press, 2002), 9.

2. O. C. Edwards has a much narrower definition of preaching as something that occurs in a liturgical setting. See his, *A History of Preaching* (Nashville: Abingdon Press, 2004), 3–4.

3. Alan of Lille, *Art of Preaching*, in Richard Lischer, *Theories of Preaching: Selected Readings in the Homiletical Tradition* (Durham, N.C.: Labyrinth Press, 1987), 9–13.

4. It generally does so in ways that are careful to safeguard the meaning of the original text and avoid the past excesses of bad allegory. For a more thorough treatment of this topic see my *God Sense: Reading the Bible for Preaching* (Nashville: Abingdon Press, 2001), esp. 112–36.

5. Ibid., 67.

6. See Edmund A. Steimle, Morris J. Niedenthal, and Charles L. Rice, *Preaching the Story* (Philadelphia: Fortress Press, 1980); and Robert P. Waznak, *Sunday After Sunday: Preaching the Homily as Story* (Mahwah, N.J.: Paulist Press, 1983).

7. Charles L. Bartow, *God's Human Speech: A Practical Theology of Proclamation* (Grand Rapids, Mich.: Eerdmans, 1997), 26.

8. Karl Barth, *The Word of God and the Word of Man* (trans. Douglas Horton; Boston: Pilgrim Press, 1928; repr., New York: Harper & Bros., 1957), 107–9.

9. Jana Childers, "Seeing Jesus: Preaching as an Incarnational Act," in Jana Childers, ed., *Purposes of Preaching* (St. Louis: Chalice Press, 2004), 39-47, esp. 40, 43.

10. Phillips Brooks, *Lectures on Preaching* (Manchester, UK: James Robinson, 1899), 126.

11. Thomas G. Long speaks of the listener creating the sermon in, *The Witness of Preaching* (Louisville: Westminster/John Knox Press, 1989), 131.

12. It gave rise to German existential theology, particularly the idea that Jesus' living word is an event today through the preaching of the church (thus the movement known as the New Hermeneutic sought to avoid the use of the term *kerygma* or proclamation of Jesus' victory because it separated the Jesus of history from the act of preaching). See James M. Robinson, "Hermeneutic Since Barth," in James M. Robinson and John B. Cobb Jr., eds., *The New Hermeneutic* (Vol. 2 of *New Frontiers in Theology*; New York: Harper & Row, 1964), 49–72.

13. Paul Scherer, *The Word God Sent* (Grand Rapids, Mich.: Baker Books, 1965), 24.

14. David James Randolph, *The Renewal of Preaching* (Philadelphia: Fortress Press, 1969), 19 (from Question 54 of the Methodist *Discipline* of 1784).

15. See also John Claypool, *The Event of Preaching* (Waco, Tex.: Word, 1980).

16. Eugene L. Lowry, "The Revolution of Sermonic Shape," in Gail R. O'Day and Thomas G. Long, *Listening to the Word: Studies in Honor of Fred B. Craddock* (Nashville: Abingdon Press, 1993), 110.

17. Sallie McFague, *Speaking in Parables* (Philadelphia: Fortress Press, 1975), 79.

18. Fred B. Craddock, *Overhearing the Gospel* (Nashville: Abingdon Press, 1978), 83; and *Preaching* (Nashville: Abingdon Press, 1985), 47.

19. Don M. Wardlaw, "Preaching as the Interface of Two Social Worlds: The Congregation as Corporate Agent in the Act of Preaching," in Arthur Van Seters, ed., *Preaching as a Social Act: Theology and Practice* (Nashville: Abingdon Press, 1988), 78.

20. Eduard R. Riegert, *Imaginative Shock: Preaching and Metaphor* (Burlington, Ontario: Trinity Press, 1990), 122.

21. David J. Schlafer, *Surviving the Sermon: A Guide to Preaching for Those Who Have to Listen* (Cambridge, Mass.: Cowley Publications, 1992), 31.

22. Justin Martyr, in Hugh T. Kerr, ed., *Readings in Christian Thought* (2nd ed.; Nashville: Abingdon Press, 1990), 20.

23. Long, *Witness of Preaching*, 23.

24. See James D. Smart, *The Divided Mind of Modern Theology* (Philadelphia: Westminster Press, 1967), 209.

25. James F. Kay, "The Word of the Cross at the Turn of the Ages," *Interpretation* 53, no. 1 (January 1999): 44–56.

26. Ibid., 50

27. David Buttrick, *Preaching the New and the Now* (Louisville: Westminster John Knox Press, 1998), 13, 18.

28. Ibid., 141.

29. Richard Lischer, *A Theology of Preaching: the Dynamics of the Gospel* (rev. ed.; Eugene, Ore.: Wipf and Stock Publishers, 2001), 26.

30. Joseph R. Jeter Jr. and Ronald J. Allen, *One Gospel, Many Ears: Preaching for Different Listeners in the Congregation* (St. Louis: Chalice Press, 2002).

31. Christine M. Smith, *Weaving the Sermon: Preaching in a Feminist Perspective* (Louisville: Westminster/John Knox Press, 1989).

3. The Gospel and the Theme Sentence

1. Fred B. Craddock, *As One Without Authority* (3rd ed.; Nashville: Abingdon Press, 1979).

2. David Buttrick, *Homiletic: Moves and Structures* (Philadelphia: Fortress Press, 1987), 29.

3. Ibid., 301, 294.

4. Richard L. Eslinger, *Narrative and Imagination: Preaching the Worlds that Shape Us* (Minneapolis: Fortress Press, 1995), 28–29.

5. Lucy Atkinson Rose, *Sharing the Word: Preaching in the Roundtable Church* (Louisville: Westminster John Knox Press, 1997), esp. 105, 177.

6. I have written extensively on the theme sentence in homiletics in my *Preaching and Homiletical Theory* (St. Louis: Chalice Press, 2004), 9–24. Most of those who oppose the theme sentence do not acknowledge that it now has a double-barreled character that makes it different from propositional models.

7. James S. Stewart, *Heralds of God* (New York: Charles Scribner's Sons, 1946), 31.

8. Edward Farley, "Preaching the Bible and Gospel," *Theology Today* 51:1 (April 1994): 90–104.; and "Toward a New Paradigm for Preaching" in Thomas G. Long and Edward Farley, eds., *Preaching as a Theological Task: World, Gospel, Scripture* (Louisville: Westminster John Knox Press, 1996), 165–75.

9. See: James F. Kay, "The Word of the Cross at the Turn of the Ages," *Interpretation* 53, no. 1 (January 1999): 44–56; and David Buttrick, *A Captive Voice: The Liberation of Preaching* (Louisville: Westminster John Knox Press, 1994), esp. his first two chapters, "Preaching and Bible" and "Preaching and Church." I would also include in this category Charles L. Bartow's *God's Human Speech: A Practical Theology of Proclamation* (Grand Rapids, Mich.: Eerdmans, 1997).

10. Paul E. Scherer, "The Perils of the Christian Life," in *Great Preaching Today: A Collection of 25 Sermons Delivered at the Chicago Sunday Evening Club* (ed. Alton M. Motter; New York: Harper & Bros., 1955), 190–92.

11. See my *Preaching and Homiletical Theory* (St. Louis: Chalice Press, 2004), esp. 15. Haddon Robinson uses, "What am I talking about?" and "What am I saying about it?" These are perhaps the closest thing today to the traditional propositional theme-sentence approach. Haddon W. Robinson, *Biblical Preaching: The Development and Delivery of Expository Messages* (2nd ed.; Grand Rapids, Mich.: Baker Academic, 2001), 41; see 33–50.

12. Fred B. Craddock, *Preaching* (Nashville: Abingdon Press, 1985), 123 (my italics).

13. See for instance, Thomas G. Long, *The Witness of Preaching* (2nd. ed.; Louisville: Westminster John Knox Press, 2005), 106–16, esp. 107. What the text is saying and doing is an updated version of "understanding" a text (*verstehen*) and "explaining" a text (*erklaren*), mentioned earlier.

14. Michael J. Quicke is critical of the bridge as an overall image or model of the sermon (a 180-degree model) because it misleads preachers "into thinking that they bear all the responsibility to connect the two poles." He wants a bigger, trinitarian picture. Michael J. Quicke, *360 Degree Preaching: Hearing, Speaking and Living the Word* (Grand Rapids, Mich.: Baker Academic; Carlisle, Cumbria, UK: Paternoser Publishing, 2003), 48. Nancy Lamers Gross is also critical of the bridge metaphor, for a different reason: it

implies a rigid progression from the text to the sermons when the pattern is more like swinging back and forth. See *If You Cannot Preach Like Paul . . .* (Grand Rapids, Mich.: Eerdmans, 2002), 74–76, 83, 114–15. Charles L. Campbell may well be arguing against the notion of bridges when he calls for the meaning of texts to be found within the logic and language of the texts themselves, never straying too far from the world of the text. His important argument centers on Jesus Christ. Charles L. Campbell, *Preaching Jesus: New Directions for Homiletics in Hans Frei's Postliberal Theology* (Grand Rapids, Mich.: Eerdmans, 1997).

15. Long, *Witness of Preaching*, 108.

16. Ibid., 97.

17. Here I think for instance of Long, ibid., esp. 99–116, and Ronald J. Allen, *Interpreting the Gospel: An Introduction to Preaching* (St. Louis: Chalice Press, 1998), esp. 120–50.

18. Jana Childers, "A Shameless Path," in Jana Childers, ed., *Birthing the Sermon: Women Preachers on the Creative Process* (St. Louis: Chalice Press, 2001), 42–43.

19. Robinson, *Biblical Preaching*, 94.

20. Gardner C. Taylor, "The Sweet Torture of Sunday Morning," *Leadership* 3, no. 3 (Summer 1991): 20.

21. Several places in Luther could be cited here, but the best discussion of this with notes may be found in Gerhard O. Forde, *Theology Is for Proclamation* (Minneapolis: Fortress Press, 1990).

22. James Forbes speaks of the "attitudes which urge silence or privacy regarding the role of the Spirit in our preaching" as being the same attitudes that "rob us of the full empowerment crucial for all who preach the Word." James Forbes, *The Holy Spirit and Preaching* (Nashville: Abingdon Press, 1989), 26.

23. Cleophus J. LaRue, *The Heart of Black Preaching* (Louisville: Westminster John Knox Press, 2000), 71.

24. Ronald J. Allen, *Preaching the Topical Sermon* (Louisville: Westminster/John Knox Press, 1992), 64.

25. Henry H. Mitchell, *Celebration and Experience in Preaching* (Nashville: Abingdon Press, 1990), 39.

Section II: Tuesday

1. See Paul Ricoeur, "The Model of the Text: Meaningful Action Considered as a Text," in Paul Ricoeur, *Hermeneutics and the Social Sciences* (New York: Cambridge University Press, 1981), 210–13.

4. Bridging from the Text

1. Gerald T. Sheppard, "Isaiah 1–39," in James L. Mays, ed., *Harper's Bible Commentary* (San Francisco: Harper & Row, 1988), 547.

2. Thomas G. Oden, *After Modernity . . . What?* (Grand Rapids, Mich.: Zondervan, 1977), 106.

3. Ibid., 106–8.

4. Ibid., 108.

5. Martin Luther, *Sermons* (vol. 52 of *Luther's Works*; ed. Hans J. Hillerbrand and Helmut T. Lehmann; Philadelphia: Fortress Press, 1974), 8–9.

6. Warren H. Stewart Sr., *Interpreting God's Word in Black Preaching* (Valley Forge, Pa.: Judson Press, 1984), 15.

7. Cleophus J. LaRue, *The Heart of Black Preaching* (Louisville: Westminster John Knox Press, 2000), 69.

8. Hans Georg Gadamer, *Truth and Method* (London: Sheed and Ward, 1975), 273.

9. Gardner C. Taylor, "God as a Troublemaker," in *Fifty Years of Timeless Treasures* (vol. 6 of *The Words of Gardner C. Taylor*; comp. Edward L. Taylor; Valley Forge, Pa.: Judson Press, 2002), 78–83.

10. The exception to this is grace in creation, where still, in the first verses of Genesis, either nothingness or chaos is implied.

11. Kilian McDonnell, "Joseph, I'm Pregnant by the Holy Ghost," in *Yahweh's Other Shoe* (Collegeville, Minn.: Saint John's University Press, 2006), 18–19.

12. Kilian McDonnell, *Swift, Lord, You Are Not* (Collegeville, Minn.: Saint John's University Press, 2003).

13. McDonnell, *Yahweh's Other Shoe*, 113.

14. Debra Farrington, "Healed, Not Cured," in *The Christian Century* (February 7, 2006): 16.

15. Roberta C. Bondi, "Learning to Pray: An Interview with Roberta C. Bondi" [cited April 19, 2007]. Online: http://www.religion-online.org/showarticle.asp?title=302.

5. Bridging to Today

1. David Buttrick, *Homiletic: Moves and Structures* (Philadelphia: Fortress Press, 1987), 258–60, 293.

2. See Paul Scott Wilson, *Imagination of the Heart: New Understandings in Preaching* (Nashville: Abingdon Press, 1988), 86–88 and 115–21.

3. Paul Tillich, "The Experience of the Holy," in *The Shaking of the Foundations* (New York: Charles Scribner's Sons, 1948), 87–92. This is an example of what is known as an exegetical sermon; it develops the text line by line.

4. Davie Napier, "The Burning in the Temple," and Allen M. Parrent, "The Humanity of the Call of God," both in James W. Cox, ed., *The Twentieth Century Pulpit* (vol. 2; Nashville: Abingdon Press, 1981), 141–50, 151–56.

5. Buttrick, *Homiletic*, 23–69. See also 309–12.

6. Nancy Lamers Gross, *If You Cannot Preach Like Paul . . .* (Grand Rapids, Mich.: Eerdmans, 2002), 114–15.

7. Stephen Farris, *Preaching That Matters: The Bible and Our Lives* (Louisville: Westminster John Knox Press, 1998), 80.

8. Ibid., 92.

Section III: Wednesday

1. Michael J. Quicke has a comprehensive vision of the entire preaching process that has some similarities to this in that it is a repeating cycle or circle. One value of his model is his attempt to present preaching as fully involving the Trinity. He also has something

that he calls the "preaching swim" that covers many of the activities in the preacher's hermeneutical circle: immerse, interpret, design, deliver, experience. See his *360 Degree Preaching: Hearing, Speaking and Living the Word* (Grand Rapids, Mich.: Baker Academic; Carlisle, Cumbria, UK: Paternoster Publishing, 2003), esp. 132.

2. Rudolf Bultmann, "Is Exegesis Without Presuppositions Possible?" in Kurt Mueller-Vollmer, ed., *The Hermeneutics Reader* (New York: Continuum, 1989), 242. Paul Ricoeur said that preunderstanding allows the reader to "guess" at a text's meaning. Paul Ricoeur, *Interpretation Theory: Discourse and the Surplus of Meaning* (Fort Worth: Texas Christian University Press, 1976), 75–79.

3. Bultmann, "Is Exegesis Without Presuppositions Possible?" 247. He says that continuity in understanding is nonetheless possible through historical-critical research and what he called the "guidance" that might pass from generation to generation.

4. See Elisabeth Schüssler Fiorenza, "Toward a Feminist Biblical Hermeneutic," in Donald K. McKim, ed., *A Guide to Contemporary Hermeneutics: Major Trends in Biblical Interpretation* (Grand Rapids, Mich.: Eerdmans, 1986), esp. 364–68.

5. José Miguez Bonino, "Hermeneutics, Truth and Praxis," in Donald K. McKim, ed., *A Guide to Contemporary Hermeneutics: Major Trends in Biblical Interpretation* (Grand Rapids, Mich.: Eerdmans, 1986), 348.

6. Schüssler Fiorenza, "Toward a Feminist Biblical Hermeneutic," 381.

7. Don S. Browning, building on the work of Gerhard Ebeling, David Tracy, and others, claims that, "the pastoral theologian is interested in the full contextual meaning" and proposes "descriptive research" (*A Fundamental Practical Theology: Descriptive and Strategic Proposals* [Minneapolis: Fortress Press, 1991], 48). David Polk speaks of using a "hermeneutic of situations," involving "thick description" (a diverse research combining narrative with identification of appropriate questions, categories and methods, verbatim reports, identification of cultural biases, and so on) as a means of adequately reflecting "the complexity of lived experience" ("Practical Theology," in Donald W. Musser and Joseph L. Price, eds., *A New Handbook of Christian Theology* [Nashville: Abingdon Press, 1992], 376.) Theology that does this is what Browning calls "descriptive theology" (Browning, *Fundamental Practical Theology*, 110).

8. Paul Scott Wilson, *Preaching and Homiletical Theory* (St. Louis: Chalice Press, 2004), 33.

9. Jana Childers, "A Shameless Path," in Jana Childers, ed., *Birthing the Sermon: Women Preachers on the Creative Process* (St. Louis: Chalice Press, 2001), 37.

10. Barbara Brown Taylor, "Bothering God," in Jana Childers, ed., *Birthing the Sermon: Women Preachers on the Creative Process* (St. Louis: Chalice Press, 2001), 163.

11. Wilson, *Preaching and Homiletical Theory*, 36.

12. O. Wesley Allen Jr. broadens the matrix further by identifying personal, sociohistorical, theological, and congregational conversation partners. See his *Homiletic of All Believers: A Conversational Approach* (Louisville: Westminster John Knox Press, 2005), esp. 48–49.

6. Exegesis of Today's World

1. Leonora Tubbs Tisdale, *Preaching as Local Theology and Folk Art* (Fortress Resources for Preaching; Minneapolis: Fortress Press, 1997), 42.

2. See also Stephen Farris, *Preaching That Matters: The Bible and Our Lives* (Louisville:

Westminster John Knox Press, 1998), who gives a helpful template for exegeting our situation, 30–33. Taking a different slant, Joseph R. Jeter Jr. and Ronald J. Allen offer important guidance on how to preach to varieties of listeners, including different: generations, modes of mental process, gender, multicultural settings, economic conditions, and theological perspective. See their *One Gospel, Many Ears: Preaching for Different Listeners in the Congregation* (St. Louis: Chalice Press, 2002).

3. James R. Nieman and Thomas G. Rogers, *Preaching to Every Pew: Cross-Cultural Strategies* (Minneapolis: Fortress Press, 2002), 147.

4. Ibid., 150.

5. Ibid., 151.

6. Tisdale, *Preaching as Local Theology*, 64–77.

7. Ibid., 77–90.

8. Ibid., 124.

9. Harry Emerson Fosdick, *The Living of These Days* (New York: Harper and Bros., 1956), 99.

10. Lucy Atkinson Rose, *Sharing the Word: Preaching in the Roundtable Church* (Louisville: Westminster John Knox Press, 1997).

11. John McClure, *The Roundtable Pulpit: Where Preaching and Leadership Meet* (Nashville: Abingdon Press, 1996).

12. Nieman and Rogers, *Preaching to Every Pew*, 147.

13. Donald Miller, *Blue Like Jazz: Nonreligious Thoughts on Christian Spirituality* (Nashville: Thomas Nelson, 2003), 47.

14. Farris, *Preaching That Matters*, 33–38.

15. Teresa L. Fry Brown, "A Love Letter Written in Blood," in Jana Childers, ed., *Birthing the Sermon: Women Preachers on the Creative Process* (St. Louis: Chalice Press, 2001), 22. See also the prayer prior to the pulpit in Cleophus J. LaRue, *The Heart of Black Preaching* (Louisville: Westminster John Knox Press, 2000), 17.

16. Phillips Brooks, *Lectures on Preaching: Delivered Before the Divinity School of Yale College in January and February, 1877* (Manchester, England: James Robinson, 1989), 8. The preacher's self-understanding is so important that James Henry Harris recently devoted an entire chapter to it in his *Word Made Plain: The Power and Promise of Preaching* (Minneapolis: Fortress Press, 2004), 1–29. On related matters, see Joseph R. Jeter Jr., *Crisis Preaching: Personal and Public* (Nashville: Abingdon Press, 1998).

17. Karl Barth, *Church Dogmatics* (vol. I.1; New York: Charles Scribner's Sons, 1969), 165–66.

18. An excellent treatment of ethos may be found in Gerard A. Hauser, *Introduction to Rhetorical Theory* (Prospect Heights, Ill.: Waveland Press, 1986), esp. 91ff. His discussion has informed the one offered here.

19. Craig A. Loscalzo, *Preaching Sermons That Connect: Effective Communication Through Identification* (Downer's Grove, Ill.: InterVarsity Press, 1992), 59–60.

20. Lucy Lind Hogan and Robert Reid, *Connecting with the Congregation: Rhetoric and the Art of Preaching* (Nashville: Abingdon Press, 1999), 61.

21. André Resner, *Preacher and Cross: Person and Message in Theology and Rhetoric* (Grand Rapids, Mich.: Eerdmans, 1999), 4.

22. Craig A. Loscalzo concentrates on this important question of identification (*Preaching Sermons That Connect*). His chapter on the preacher's integrity (59–80) is perhaps the best on this topic in recent memory.

23. David Buttrick, *Homiletic: Moves and Structures* (Philadelphia: Fortress Press, 1987), 45, 47.

24. Barbara Brown Taylor, *The Preaching Life* (Cambridge and Boston: Cowley Publications, 1993), 14.

25. G. Lee Ramsey Jr., *Care-full Preaching: From Sermon to Caring Community* (St. Louis: Chalice Press, 2000), 147–202.

26. "Individuals have been treated [in the past] as if they could be separated from their corporate reality. With this separation the world becomes merely a backdrop to God's personal encounter with individuals as though the entire world is profane, no longer part of God's creation." Arthur Van Seters, ed., *Preaching as a Social Act: Theology and Practice* (Nashville: Abingdon Press, 1988), 19.

27. Browning, *Fundamental Practical Theology*, 48–49.

28. Christine M. Smith, *Preaching as Weeping, Confession and Resistance: Radical Responses to Radical Evil* (Louisville: Westminster/John Knox Press, 1992), 6. See also the fine anthology she has published: Christine M. Smith, ed., *Preaching Justice: Ethnic and Cultural Perspectives* (Cleveland: United Church Press, 1998).

29. Charles L. Campbell, *The Word Before the Powers: An Ethic of Preaching* (Louisville: Westminster John Knox Press, 2002), 93–94.

30. Ibid., 141–53.

31. Smith, *Preaching as Weeping*, 41.

32. William K. McElvaney, *Preaching from Camelot to Covenant: Announcing God's Action in the World* (Nashville: Abingdon Press, 1989), 76.

33. Walter J. Burghardt, *Preaching the Just Word* (New Haven, Conn.: Yale University Press, 1996), x.

34. Ibid., 54.

35. Ibid., 55.

36. Ibid., 56.

37. Ibid., 57.

38. Arthur Van Seters, *Preaching and Ethics* (St. Louis: Chalice Press, 2004), esp. 12–17. Individual chapters are devoted to each of the five.

39. Kathy Black, *A Healing Homiletic: Preaching and Disability* (Nashville: Abingdon Press, 1996), 183–86. See also her "A Perspective of the Disabled: Transforming Images of God, Interdependence, and Healing," in Smith, *Preaching Justice*, 6–26.

40. Ronald J. Allen, *Preaching the Topical Sermon* (Louisville: Westminster/John Knox Press, 1992), 38–71.

41. Paul Scott Wilson, *God Sense: Reading the Bible for Preaching* (Nashville: Abingdon Press, 2001), 104–5. See also 91–111, devoted to the moral sense of Scripture.

42. James S. Stewart, *The Wind of the Spirit* (Eastbourne, UK: Victory Press, 1975), 179.

7. The Use of Stories, Images, and Experiences

1. David Buttrick, *Homiletic: Moves and Structures* (Philadelphia: Fortress Press, 1987), 59–61.

2. Julian N. Hartt, *Theological Method and Imagination* (New York: Seabury Press, 1977), 237.

3. Elizabeth Achtemeier, *Preaching as Theology and Art* (Nashville: Abingdon Press, 1984), 51.

4. Victor Jones, *Creative Writing* (London: English Universities Press, 1974), 46.

5. Anne Lamott, *Bird by Bird: Some Instructions on Writing and Life* (New York: Anchor Books, 1995), 55.

6. Aristotle said, for instance, "The life and soul, so to speak, of tragedy is the plot; and … the characters come second," in "Poetics," *The Complete Works of Aristotle* (vol. 2; Princeton: Princeton University Press, 1984), 2321.

7. William Foster-Harris, *The Basic Formulas of Fiction* (Norman: University of Oklahoma Press, 1963), 60.

8. Ibid., 9–10.

9. Ibid., 32.

10. Ibid., 77–92.

11. Lamott, *Bird by Bird*, 62. Lamott credits Alice Adams for the formula.

12. Barbara K. Lundblad, "After Emmaus," in Jana Childers, ed., *Birthing the Sermon: Women Preachers on the Creative Process* (St. Louis: Chalice Press, 2001), 126.

13. Professor David Newman was a much loved and respected worship and homiletics professor at Emmanuel College, University of Toronto, who died too young.

14. Long was drawing on August Wilson's play, *Ma Rainey's Black Bottom*. Thomas G. Long, "Praying for the Wrath of God," in Cornish R. Rogers and Joseph R. Jeter Jr., eds., *Preaching Through the Apocalypse: Sermons from Revelation* (St. Louis: Chalice Press, 1992), 137.

15. This plot is that of the movie *Rain Man*, directed by Barry Levinson (Los Angeles: United Artists, 1988).

16. Barbara Brown Taylor, "Bothering God," in Jana Childers, ed., *Birthing the Sermon: Women Preachers on the Creative Process* (St. Louis: Chalice Press, 2001), 156.

17. Ibid., 157.

18. L. Susan May, "Starting a Fire," in Ronald J. Allen, *Preaching the Topical Sermon* (Louisville: Westminster/John Knox Press, 1992), 122.

19. Peter Vaught, "Within Reach of the Dragon," in Cornish R. Rogers and Joseph R. Jeter Jr., eds., *Preaching Through the Apocalypse: Sermons from Revelation* (St. Louis: Chalice Press, 1992), 122–23.

20. Ibid., 124.

21. Charles L. Rice includes a helpful section on use of the arts in sermons in *The Embodied Word: Preaching as Art and Liturgy* (Minneapolis: Fortress Press, 1991), 93–124.

22. From Truman Capote and Eleanor Perry, "A Christmas Memory," in Truman Capote, Eleanor Perry, Frank Perry, *Trilogy: An Experiment in Multimedia* (New York: Collier Books, 1969), 248–52; as cited by Robert P. Waznak, "Christmas Is for Seeing," in his *Like Fresh Bread: Sunday Homilies in the Parish* (Mahwah, N.J.: Paulist Press, 1993), 39.

23. Mary Donovan Turner, "Not Silent," in Jana Childers, ed., *Birthing the Sermon: Women Preachers on the Creative Process* (St. Louis: Chalice Press, 2001), 181; see also, 175–76.

24. Charles L. Rice, "Ordinary People," in Don M. Wardlaw, ed., *Preaching Biblically: Creating Sermons in the Shape of Scripture* (Philadelphia: Westminster Press, 1983), 113–14.

25. The Reverend George Mayers made this observation in a graduate class.

26. William K. McElvaney, *Preaching from Camelot to Covenant: Announcing God's Action in the World* (Nashville: Abingdon Press, 1989), 26. This is an excellent book on globalization and preaching. See also Arthur Van Seters, ed., *Preaching as a Social Act: Theology and Practice* (Nashville: Abingdon Press, 1988).

27. *CBS Evening News* [television broadcast], October 16, 1996.

28. See my "Beyond Narrative: Imagination in the Sermon," in Gail R. O'Day and Thomas G. Long, eds., *Listening to the Word: Studies in Honor of Fred B. Craddock* (Nashville: Abingdon Press, 1993), 141–43.

8. Sermon Form I: Surface Structures

1. The term *New Homiletic* now seems to be the term of consensus for the homiletical revolution. The term derives from the New Hermeneutic in the 1960s and, in particular, to David James Randolph's *Renewal of Preaching* (Philadelphia: Fortress Press, 1969), in which he set forth a new vision of preaching that turned out to be somewhat prophetic. However, Randolph was not the first to anticipate later homiletical developments, and H. Grady Davis moved the discipline enormously with his *Design for Preaching* (Philadelphia: Fortress Press, 1958). To use the term *New Homiletic* to include Davis, as one must, involves something of an unavoidable anachronism.

2. Michael J. Quicke, *360 Degree Preaching: Hearing, Speaking and Living the Word* (Grand Rapids, Mich.: Baker Academic; Carlisle, Cumbria, UK: Paternoser Publishing, 2003), 154.

3. Samuel D. Proctor, *The Certain Sound of the Trumpet* (Valley Forge, Pa.: Judson Press, 1994), 93. See 93–104. Michael J. Quicke calls them "SW? and YBH?": So what? and Yes but how? (*360 Degree Preaching*, 154).

4. David Mains of Mainstream Ministries, Carol Stream, Ill. Cited by Quicke, *360 Degree Preaching*, 154.

5. Proctor, *Certain Sound of the Trumpet*, 93.

6. Thomas G. Long, *The Witness of Preaching* (2nd ed.; Louisville: Westminster John Knox Press, 2005), 172–87.

7. David Buttrick, *Homiletic: Moves and Structures* (Philadelphia: Fortress Press, 1987), 83–109.

8. Ibid., 86–87.

9. Ibid., 92–93.

10. David Schlafer takes the last three of our suggestions as an approach to the entire sermon in "'Where Does the Preacher Stand?' Image, Narrative, and Argument as Basic Strategies for Shaping Sermons," in *Homiletic* xix:1 (Summer 1994): 1–5.

11. Barbara K. Lundblad, "After Emmaus," in Jana Childers, ed., *Birthing the Sermon: Women Preachers on the Creative Process* (St. Louis: Chalice Press, 2001), 128.

12. Buttrick, *Homiletic*, esp. 103–8.

13. James S. Stewart, *Heralds of God* (New York: Charles Scribner's Sons, 1946), 140.

14. Mitchell adds, "For this we had a number of our own terms, such as 'coming on up at the end,' 'the gravy,' 'the rousements,' 'the whoop,' or just the generic 'climax.'" Henry H. Mitchell, *Celebration and Experience in Preaching* (Nashville: Abingdon Press, 1990), 12.

15. Cleophus J. LaRue, *Power in the Pulpit: How America's Most Effective Black Preachers Prepare Their Sermons* (Louisville: Westminster John Knox Press, 2002), 8.

16. Robert of Basevorn, *The Form of Preaching*, trans. Leopold Krul, in James J. Murphy, ed., *Three Medieval Rhetorical Arts* (Berkeley: University of California Press, 1971), 138.

17. See Craig A. Loscalzo, *Preaching Sermons That Connect: Effective Communication Through Identification* (Downer's Grove, Ill.: InterVarsity Press, 1992), esp. 25–28. He draws on the work of Kenneth Burke in exploring the importance of identification in the sermon.

18. Charles L. Rice, *Interpretation and Imagination* (Philadelphia: Fortress Press, 1970), 58.

19. Stephen Crites, "The Narrative Quality of Experience," *Journal of the American Academy of Religion* 39 (1971): 291–311. Reprinted in Stanley Hauerwas and L. Gregory Jones, *Why Narrative? Readings in Narrative Theology* (Grand Rapids, Mich.: Eerdmans, 1989), 65–88.

20. W. E. Sangster, *The Craft of Sermon Construction* (1949); republished as the *Craft of the Sermon: A Source Book for Ministers* (Philadelphia: Westminster Press, 1951), 84–87.

21. Davis, *Design for Preaching*, 177–80.

22. Fred B. Craddock, *As One Without Authority* (Nashville: Abingdon Press, 1971).

23. Buttrick, *Homiletic*, 321–90.

24. This example is in Gwyn Walters, *Towards Healthy Preaching: A Manual for Students, Pastors, and Laypersons*, published by Gwyn Walters (n.p., 1987), 81.

25. Michael Williams, ed., *The Storyteller's Companion to the Bible* (Nashville: Abingdon Press, 1991), is devoted to helping its readers primarily with this form, although it does much more than this.

26. Davis, *Design for Preaching*, 177–80.

27. This format was first advocated by Charles L. Rice, *Interpretation and Imagination*, esp. 110–55.

28. Eugene L. Lowry speaks of three hybrid forms (although he uses story as a synonym for biblical text): (1) delaying the story—the story entry delayed, possibly until midway; (2) suspending the story—start with story and later return to it; (3) alternating the story—there is a movement into and away from the biblical text. See Eugene L. Lowry, *How to Preach a Parable: Designs for Narrative Sermons* (Nashville: Abingdon Press, 1989). John Holbert identifies a fourth option, (4) a "frame narrative"—the narrative is "framed" with commentary or by a nonbiblical story to help listeners discern the narrator's intent. John Holbert, *Preaching Old Testament: Proclamation and Narrative in the Hebrew Bible* (Nashville: Abingdon Press, 1991), 42–49.

29. Eugene L. Lowry, *The Homiletical Plot: The Sermon as Narrative Art Form* (Atlanta: John Knox Press, 1980). See also his revision of this in his *The Sermon: Dancing the Edge of Mystery* (Nashville: Abingdon Press, 1997), 78, where his five "sequencing strategies" become four in one loop: conflict, complication, sudden shift, and unfolding. "Experiencing the gospel" may happen anywhere from the second to fourth strategy, but he suggests, "about three-fourths into the sermon. Perhaps five-sixths is better. On rare occasions it may happen on the last line."

30. Ella P. Mitchell, "For Such a Time," in Henry H. Mitchell, *Celebration and Experience in Preaching* (Nashville: Abingdon Press, 1990), 96–100.

31. Thomas H. Troeger, *Imagining a Sermon* (Nashville: Abingdon Press, 1990), 44–47.

32. Fred B. Craddock, "Praying Through Clenched Teeth," in James W. Cox, ed., *The Twentieth Century Pulpit* (vol. 2; Nashville: Abingdon Press, 1981), 47–52.

33. Eugene L. Lowry, *Doing Time in the Pulpit: The Relationship Between Narrative and Preaching* (Nashville: Abingdon Press, 1985), 15, 8.

34. Lundblad, "After Emmaus," 126.

35. See for instance John C. Holbert, *Preaching Job* (St. Louis: Chalice Press, 1999); also his *Preaching Old Testament: Proclamation and Narrative in the Hebrew Bible* (Nashville: Abingdon Press, 1991).

36. For a countering perspective see J. Kent Edwards, *Effective First-Person Biblical*

Preaching: The Steps from Text to Narrative Sermon (Grand Rapids, Mich.: Zondervan, 2005).

37. Lowry, *How to Preach a Parable*.

38. Christine M. Smith, *Weaving the Sermon: Preaching in a Feminist Perspective* (Louisville: Westminster/John Knox Press, 1989); Carol M. Norén, *The Woman in the Pulpit* (Nashville: Abingdon Press, 1991).

39. Aimee Semple McPherson, "A Certain Man Went Down," in *Aimee Semple McPherson, This Is That: Personal Experiences, Sermons, and Writings* (Los Angeles: Bridal Call Publishing House, 1923). Reprinted in O. C. Edwards Jr., *A History of Preaching* (vol. 2; Nashville: Abingdon Press, 2004), 458–70, esp., 461–63.

40. Edward Oren Grimenstein, "Teaching the Presence of Christ in Preaching," a draft of a proposed chapter for a doctoral dissertation in homiletics for the University of Toronto, June 2006.

41. The sermon by Tim Bauer was for a DMin class in preaching at Luther Seminary, June 23, 2006. The painting is anonymous Netherlandish, *The Healing of the Paralytic* (ca. 1560/1590), National Gallery of Art, Washington, D.C., Chester Dale Collection, 1943.7.7. It may be viewed online at www.nga.gov/cgi-bin/pinfo?Object=12210+0+none (use the "detail images" feature once you have arrived at the site), or one may get to it through the website for Text This Week using the Mark text reference (www.textweek.com/art/healing.htm).

42. Barbara Brown Taylor, "Bothering God," in Jana Childers, ed., *Birthing the Sermon: Women Preachers on the Creative Process* (St. Louis: Chalice Press, 2001), 156–57.

43. Proctor, *Certain Sound of the Trumpet*, 1–129.

44. Catherine Gunsalus González, *Difficult Texts: A Preaching Commentary* (Nashville: Abingdon Press, 2005), esp. 13.

45. Thomas G. Long, *Preaching and the Literary Forms of the Bible* (Philadelphia: Fortress Press, 1989), 24–34. See also Mike Graves, *The Sermon as Symphony: Preaching the Literary Forms of the New Testament* (Valley Forge, Pa.: Judson Press, 1997).

46. Long, *Preaching and the Literary Forms*, 47.

47. Ibid,. 122–26.

48. Graves, *Sermon as Symphony*, 6–8.

49. See the final chapter of Robert G. Hughes and Robert Kysar, *Preaching Doctrine: For the Twenty-First Century* (Fortress Resources for Preaching; Minneapolis: Fortress Press, 1997).

50. Evans E. Crawford with Thomas H. Troeger, *The Hum: Call and Response in African American Preaching* (Nashville: Abingdon Press, 1995), 13.

51. Cleophus J. LaRue, *The Heart of Black Preaching* (Louisville: Westminster John Knox Press, 2000), 11.

52. Ronald J. Allen, *Preaching the Topical Sermon* (Louisville: Westminster/John Knox Press, 1992), 75–78. See also his *Interpreting the Gospel: an Introduction to Preaching* (St. Louis: Chalice Press, 1998), 177–205.

53. Buttrick, *Homiletic*, 23.

54. For a practical demonstration of this, see David Buttrick, "Abraham and Isaac," in Richard L. Eslinger, *A New Hearing: Living Options in Homiletic Method* (Nashville: Abingdon Press, 1987), 166–69.

55. See my *Four Pages of the Sermon: A Guide to Biblical Preaching* (Nashville: Abingdon Press, 1999).

56. *Great Preachers, Barbara Brown Taylor*, series 1, The Odyssey Channel Collection [video recording and published sermon] (Worcester, Pa.: Vision Video, 1997).

9. Sermon Form II: The Deep Structure

1. For a fuller discussion of this, see my *Four Pages of the Sermon: A Guide to Biblical Preaching* (Nashville: Abingdon Press, 1999), 159–61.

2. Joseph R. Jeter Jr. and Ronald J. Allen, *One Gospel, Many Ears: Preaching for Different Listeners in the Congregation* (St. Louis: Chalice Press, 2002), 10.

3. Linda L. Clader, *Voicing the Vision: Imagination and Prophetic Preaching* (Harrisburg, Pa.: Morehouse Publishing, 2003), 12.

4. John Wesley in an open letter to "My dear friend," originally published in Wesley's own *The Arminian Magazine* in 1779; reprinted in Albert C. Outler, ed., *John Wesley* (New York: Oxford University Press, 1964), 232–37, esp. 237. Wesley was better than Luther in avoiding a dangerous identification of law with Old Testament and gospel with New Testament, when in fact, each is a dimension of God's Word, wherever it is found. See my "Wesley's Homiletic: Law and Gospel for Preaching," *Toronto Journal of Theology* 10:2 (Fall 1994): 215–25.

5. Charles Haddon Spurgeon, *Lectures to My Students* (Grand Rapids, Mich.: Zondervan Publishing House, 1954), 70.

6. Gerhard O. Forde, *Theology Is for Proclamation* (Minneapolis: Fortress Press, 1990), 15.

7. Milton Crum Jr., *Manual on Preaching: A New Process of Sermon Development* (Valley Forge, Pa.: Judson Press, 1977), 76.

8. For an in-depth discussion of Luther, Walthers, and the entire topic of law and gospel in preaching, see my *Preaching and Homiletical Theory* (St. Louis: Chalice Press, 2004), 73–115.

9. John Wesley, "Letter on Preaching Christ, December 20, 1751," in Richard Lischer, ed., *The Company of Preachers: Wisdom on Preaching, Augustine to the Present* (Grand Rapids, Mich.: Eerdmans, 2002), 131.

10. Karl Barth, *Prayer and Preaching* (trans. B. E. Hooke; London: SCM Press, 1964), 95. Barth is sometimes incorrectly cited as advocating a sermon movement of gospel to law to gospel, but in fact he was talking about the Third Reich and the need for gospel to influence the shaping of civil law. See my *Preaching and Homiletical Theory*, 79.

11. Richard Lischer, *A Theology of the Gospel: The Dynamics of the Gospel* (Abingdon Preacher's Library, ed. William D. Thompson; Nashville: Abingdon Press, 1981), 50.

12. Lowry's initial stages were: upsetting the equilibrium to analyzing the discrepancy to disclosing the key to resolution to experiencing the gospel and finally to anticipating the consequences. Eugene L. Lowry, *The Homiletical Plot: The Sermon as Narrative Art Form* (Atlanta: John Knox Press, 1980). He recently revised his to: conflict, complication, sudden shift, and unfolding. Experiencing the gospel may happen anywhere from the second to fourth stages, but he recommends, "about three-fourths into the sermon. Perhaps five-sixths is better. On rare occasions it may happen on the last line." Eugene L. Lowry. *The Sermon: Dancing the Edge of Mystery* (Nashville: Abingdon Press, 1997), 78.

13. Henry H. Mitchell, *Celebration and Experience in Preaching* (Nashville: Abingdon Press, 1990). See also Henry H. Mitchell, *Black Preaching: The Recovery of a Powerful Art* (Nashville: Abingdon Press, 1990), 110–12, 119–21.

14. James H. Harris, *Preaching Liberation* (Minneapolis: Fortress Press, 1995), 8–36.

15. See my *Preaching and Homiletical Theory*, 73–119.

16. David Buttrick, *Homiletic: Moves and Structures* (Philadelphia: Fortress Press, 1987), 25–27.

17. Stephen Farris, *Preaching That Matters: The Bible and Our Lives* (Louisville: Westminster John Knox Press, 1998), 98.

18. Calvin conceived of the third use of the law in this manner and was echoed by Wesley in his understanding of how the law works as we approach sanctification. John Wesley spoke about the life of the Christian as moving from "preventing grace" (the first "tendency toward life, some degree of salvation"); to "convincing grace" or repentance; to salvation by grace through faith, first by justification ("we are saved from the guilt of sin, and restored to the favour of God") and second by sanctification ("we are saved from the power and root of sin, and restored to the image of God"). This salvation, he says, is "both instantaneous and gradual." "On Working Out Our Own Salvation" (vol. 3 of *The Works of John Wesley*, ed. Albert C. Outler; Nashville: Abingdon Press, 1986), 203–4. To those "pressing on to the mark" of sanctification and glorification, the burden of the faith is "not only a command but a privilege also … a branch of the glorious liberty of the [children] of God." "On Preaching Christ," *John Wesley* (ed. Albert C. Outler; New York: Oxford University Press, 1964), 233.

19. Anne Lamott, *Bird by Bird: Some Instructions on Writing and Life* (New York: Anchor Books, 1995), 30

20. Herman G. Stuempfle called this "law as Hammer of Judgment," *Preaching Law and Gospel* (Philadelphia: Fortress Press, 1978), 21–27. In my discussion here I am indebted to his delineation of two kinds of law and two kinds of gospel.

21. Reinhold Niebuhr, *Beyond Tragedy: Essays on the Christian Interpretation of Tragedy* (New York: Charles Scribner's Sons, 1937), esp. chapter 8, "Christianity and Tragedy."

22. See my *Four Pages of the Sermon*.

23. See my *Four Pages of the Sermon*, 243–60; I give demonstration of numerous variations in *Broken Words: Reflections on the Craft of Preaching* (Nashville: Abingdon Press, 2004).

24. Farris, *Preaching That Matters*, 94.

25. Mike Graves, *The Sermon as Symphony: Preaching the Literary Forms of the New Testament* (Valley Forge, Pa.: Judson Press, 1997), 23–24.

26. Thomas G. Long says, "In short, the gospel is too rich, complex, and varied to be proclaimed through a single sermon form.… No one form is adequate to display the full-ness of the gospel. Many forms are used, each selected in turn to express some aspect of the gospel on a particular occasion." Thomas G. Long, *The Witness of Preaching* (2nd ed.; Louisville: Westminster John Knox Press, 2005), 131, 135.

10. Speaking for the Ear

1. Linda L. Clader, "Homily for the Feast of the Visitation," in Jana Childers, ed., *Birthing the Sermon: Women Preachers on the Creative Process* (St. Louis: Chalice Press, 2001), 61.

2. Charles L. Rice, *The Embodied Word: Preaching as Art and Liturgy* (Minneapolis: Fortress Press, 1991).

3. Kathy Black has argued the inadequacy of this understanding for the deaf and the

need for a new theology of "presence," in "Beyond the Spoken Word: Preaching as Presence," in *Papers of the Annual Meeting of the Academy of Homiletics*, 28th meeting, 1993, 79–88.

4. Quoted in Fred W. Meuser and Stanley D. Schneider, eds., *Interpreting Luther's Legacy* (Minneapolis: Augsburg Press, 1969), 19, 30.

5. T. S. Eliot, *Selected Essays*, 37. Cited in Peter Dixon, *Rhetoric* (London: Methuen & Co., 1971), 5.

6. Quoted by Yngve Brilioth, *A Brief History of Preaching* (trans. Karl E. Mattson; Philadelphia: Fortress Press, 1965), 113.

7. Karl Barth, *Prayer and Preaching* (trans. B. E. Hooke; London: SCM Press, 1964), 96. The same passage may be found in an awkward translation, in Karl Barth, *Homiletics* (trans. Geoffrey W. Bromily and Donald E. Daniels; Louisville: Westminster/John Knox Press, 1991), 83.

8. Walter J. Ong calls their thinking, "residually oral." See Walter J. Ong, *Orality and Literacy: The Technologizing of the Word* (London and New York: Methuen, 1982); see also Jack Goody, *The Domestication of the Savage Mind* (Cambridge: Cambridge University Press, 1977).

9. In addition to Ong, see Paul Saenger, "Silent Reading: Its Impact on Late Medieval Script and Society," in *Viator* 13 (1983): 367–414.

10. Thomas J. Farrell, "Early Christian Creeds and Controversies in the Light of the Orality-Literacy Hypothesis," in *Oral Tradition* 2/1 (1987), 133.

11. Eduard R. Riegert, *Imaginative Shock: Preaching and Metaphor* (Burlington, Ontario: Trinity Press, 1990), 120-21.

12. Aleksandr Romanovich Luria, *Cognitive Development: Its Cultural and Social Foundations* (ed. Michael Cole, trans. Martin Lopez-Morillas and Lynn Solotaroff; Cambridge, Mass.: Harvard University Press, 1976). Some of the following examples from Luria are also to be found in Ong's discussion of Luria in *Orality and Literacy*, 24.

13. Luria, *Cognitive Development*, 55.

14. Ibid., 102–4.

15. Ibid., 144.

16. All language is abstract in the sense that many words are abstracted from experience. Sallie McFague distinguishes between imagistic primary language rooted in experience and conceptual secondary language that arises out of experience. Sallie McFague, *Metaphorical Theology* (Philadelphia: Fortress Press, 1982).

17. Owen C. Thomas, *Introduction to Theology* (Cambridge, Mass.: Greeno, Hadden & Company, 1973), 18.

18. G. Robert Jacks, *Just Say the Word: Writing for the Ear* (Grand Rapids, Mich.: Eerdmans, 1996), 31. See also his *Getting the Word Across: Speech Communication for Pastors and Lay Leaders* (Grand Rapids, Mich.: Eerdmans, 1995).

19. Some of these are loosely inspired by Walter J. Ong, *Orality and Literacy*. For an understanding of orality that takes issue with Ong, see Viv Edwards and Thomas J. Sienkewicz, *Oral Cultures Past and Present: Rappin' and Homer* (Cambridge, Mass.: Blackwell, 1990).

20. Laura Sinclair, "Can Your Bones Live?" in *Those Preachin' Women* (ed. Ella Pearson Mitchell; Valley Forge, Pa.: Judson Press, 1985), 23–24.

21. Fred Craddock, "When the Roll is Called Down Here," *Preaching Today*, tape 50, side 2, 1987.

22. Ronald J. Allen, "The Social Function of Language in Preaching," in Arthur Van Seters, ed., *Preaching as a Social Act: Theology and Practice* (Nashville: Abingdon Press, 1988), 191.

23. Ola Irene Harrison, "This Bittersweet Season," in Cornish R. Rogers and Joseph R. Jeter Jr., eds., *Preaching Through the Apocalypse: Sermons from Revelation* (St. Louis: Chalice Press, 1992), 111.

24. Henry H. Mitchell, *Celebration and Experience in Preaching* (Nashville: Abingdon Press, 1990), esp. chapter 2.

25. Clader, "Homily for the Feast of the Visitation," 61. See also Pamela Moeller's *Kinesthetic Homiletic* (Minneapolis: Fortress Press, 1993), which was designed to help preachers involve their bodies in sermon preparation and delivery.

26. Charles L. Bartow, *God's Human Speech: a Practical Theology of Proclamation* (Grand Rapids, Mich.: Eerdmans, 1997), 21, 96.

27. Charles L. Bartow, *The Preaching Moment: A Guide to Sermon Delivery* (Nashville: Abingdon Press, 1980); Jana Childers, *Performing the Word: Preaching as Theatre* (Nashville: Abingdon Press, 1998); Richard Ward, *Speaking of the Holy: The Art of Communication in Preaching* (St. Louis: Chalice Press, 2001); and *Speaking from the Heart: Preaching and Passion* (Nashville: Abingdon Press, 1992). On related matters, see Mary Donovan Turner and Mary Lin Hudson, *Saved from Silence: Finding Women's Voice in Preaching* (St. Louis: Chalice Press, 1999); Joseph M. Webb, *Preaching Without Notes* (Nashville: Abingdon Press, 2001).

28. James Forbes, *The Holy Spirit and Preaching* (Nashville: Abingdon Press, 1989), 70.

29. Ward, *Speaking from the Heart*, 39.

30. John Mason Stapleton, *Preaching in Demonstration of the Spirit and Power* (Philadelphia: Fortress Press, 1988), 45. See also 41–57.

31. Robin R. Meyers, *With Ears to Hear: Preaching as Self-Persuasion* (Cleveland: Pilgrim Press, 1993), 117–18.

32. Augustine, *On Christian Doctrine* (trans. D. W. Robinson Jr.; Indianapolis: Bobbs-Merrill, 1958), IV:17. See also Cicero, *Orator*, § 69.

33. Jini Robinson, "What's Your Story?" in J. Alfred Smith, *Preach On!* (Nashville: Broadman Press, 1984), 101.

11. Composing to Persuade

1. Lucy Lind Hogan and Robert Reid, *Connecting with the Congregation: Rhetoric and the Art of Preaching* (Nashville: Abingdon Press, 1999).

2. Aristotle, "Rhetoric," in *The Complete Works of Aristotle* (ed. Jonathan Barnes, Bollingen Series LXXI-2, 2 vols.; Princeton: Princeton University Press, 1984), II:2155.

3. Lucy Lind Hogan, "Rethinking Persuasion: Developing an Incarnational Theology of Preaching" in *Homiletic* 24:2 (Winter 1999): 1–12; and Richard Lischer, "Why I Am Not Persuasive," in *Homiletic* 24:2 (Winter 1999): 13–16. Hogan and Robert Reid know that one of the reasons rhetorical argument is held with suspicion is that "what really matters in rhetoric is not truth, but whether arguments appear reasonable to the crowds." This is in contrast to dialectical argument that provides valid reasons. They make a strong case for rhetoric. Hogan and Reid, *Connecting with the Congregation*, 29, 12–13.

4. Hogan and Reid, *Connecting with the Congregation*. See also Ronald E. Sleeth, *Persuasive Preaching* (Berrien Springs, Mich.: Andrews University Press, 1981); Craig A.

Loscalzo, *Preaching Sermons that Connect: Effective Communication through Identification* (Downers Grove, Ill.: InterVarsity Press, 1992); John S. McClure, *The Four Codes of Preaching: Rhetorical Strategies* (Minneapolis: Fortress Press, 1991); Robin R. Meyers, *With Ears to Hear: Preaching as Self-Persuasion* (Cleveland: Pilgrim Press, 1993).

5. Henry H. Mitchell, *Celebration and Experience in Preaching* (Nashville: Abingdon Press, 1990), esp. 23–35. See also his *Recovery of Preaching* (San Francisco: Harper & Row, 1977), 54–73.

6. Meyers, *With Ears to Hear*, 14.

7. Ibid., 118.

8. Dorothee Sölle sees the debate between God-as-beyond-us and God-as-relationship to be "one of the most important arguments between male-patriarchal and feminist theology." Dorothee Sölle, *Thinking About God: An Introduction to Theology* (trans. John Bowden; London: SCM Press; Philadelphia: Trinity Press International, 1990), 181.

9. Gerard A. Hauser, *Introduction to Rhetorical Theory* (Prospect Heights, Ill.: Waveland Press, 1991), 71.

10. David S. Cunningham, a systematic theologian steeped in rhetoric, persuasively argues (he *is* a rhetorician!) that the very nature of speech prompts, in complex ways, readers or hearers to construct the character (that is, *ethos*) of the speaker and make their response to what is said partly on the basis of that character. Thus, he says, "Given our account of the relevance of character in assessing an argument, it seems that, not just for philosophical arguments, but for any act of persuasion whatsoever, we may justifiably claim that all arguments are *ad hominem*—directed toward the person." David S. Cunningham, *Faithful Persuasion: In Aid of a Rhetoric of Christian Theology* (Notre Dame: University of Notre Dame Press, 1992), 125.

11. Ibid., 5.

12. David J. Lose, *Confessing Jesus Christ: Preaching Jesus in a Postmodern World* (Grand Rapids, Mich.: Eerdmans, 2003), 62.

13. Ibid., 189.

14. Bruce E. Shields, *From the Housetops: Preaching in the Early Church and Today* (St. Louis: Chalice Press, 2000), 159–60.

15. Rebecca S. Chopp is one who would have us understand theological language as political activity and feminist theology in itself as rhetorical "proclamation" leading to "emancipatory transformation." Rebecca S. Chopp, *The Power to Speak: Feminism, Language, God* (New York: Crossroad, 1989), 3, 22; see Lucy Atkinson Rose, *Sharing the Word: Preaching in the Roundtable Church* (Louisville: Westminster John Knox Press, 1997); see also Cunningham, *Faithful Persuasion*, 41–42.

16. Cunningham, *Faithful Persuasion*, 41–42.

17. Classical rhetoric already recognized this kind of distinction. Aristotle saw that science, metaphysics, and logic primarily functioned using analytical method, particularly when the first principles or highest causes in a line of thought were not in dispute. However, subjects dealing with opinion, like ethics, politics, and poetics, used a dialectical method of inquiry involving question and answer or point and counterpoint when dealing with theory and involving rhetoric or persuasion when dealing with practical issues or applications. Analytic and dialectic methods were complementary, not hierarchical. See, Aristotle, "Metaphysics," in *The Complete Works of Aristotle* (ed. Jonathan Barnes, Bollingen Series LXXI-2, vol. 2; Princeton: Princeton University Press, 1984), IV:1 ff. See also Cunningham, *Faithful Persuasion*, 16.

18. O. Wesley Allen Jr., *Preaching Resurrection* (St. Louis: Chalice Press, 2000), 8.

19. Ibid., 120.

20. André Resner, *Preacher and Cross: Person and Message in Theology and Rhetoric* (Grand Rapids, Mich.: Eerdmans, 1999), 147.

21. This is what Robin R. Meyers calls self-persuasion in his *With Ears to Hear*.

22. Horace Bushnell, "Preliminary Dissertation on the Nature of Language as Related to Thought and Spirit" (1849), 55. This can also be found in *Horace Bushnell* (ed. H. Shelton Smith; New York: Oxford University Press, 1965), 93–94.

23. Gardner C. Taylor, "Two Words at the End," in his *How Shall They Preach* (Elgin, Ill.: Progressive Baptist Publishing House, 1977), 145.

24. Clark M. Williamson and Ronald J. Allen, *Interpreting Difficult Texts: Anti-Judaism and Christian Preaching* (London: SCM Press; Philadelphia: Trinity Press International, 1989). See also their *Preaching the Gospels without Blaming the Jews: a Lectionary Commentary* (Louisville: Westminster John Knox Press, 2004).

25. See my first edition of this book, chapters 11 and 12.

26. H. Grady Davis, *Design for Preaching* (Philadelphia: Fortress Press, 1958), 15–16. Davis's image may be fruitfully contrasted with dominant medieval understanding of the "ladder of spirituality" (Jacob's ladder with seven rungs) that had preaching at the top. See Alan of Lille, *The Art of Preaching* (Cistercian Fathers Series 23, trans. Gillian R. Evans; Kalamazoo, Mich.: Cistercian Publications, 1981), 15. An even earlier precedent is Augustine's five spiritual steps for interpretation of Scripture in *On Christian Doctrine* (11:7).

27. These were first developed in my *Four Pages of the Sermon: A Guide to Biblical Preaching* (Nashville: Abingdon Press, 1999), chapter 2.

28. Anne Lamott, *Bird by Bird: Some Instructions on Writing and Life* (New York: Anchor Books, 1995), 25.

29. Ibid., 21–22.

30. Ibid., 13.

31. Jana Childers, "A Shameless Path," in Jana Childers, ed., *Birthing the Sermon: Women Preachers on the Creative Process* (St. Louis: Chalice Press, 2001), 41.

12. Steps Toward the Gospel

1. Methodological suggestions in systematics have taken a different approach. See, for instance, Friedrich Schleiermacher, who gave guidelines for the division of theology into philosophical, historical, and practical in his *Brief Outline on the Study of Theology* (trans. Terrence N. Tice; Richmond: John Knox Press, 1966). Gerhard Ebeling stood in a long tradition from Schleiermacher in suggesting three possible methodologies for theology in our pluralistic age: apologetic (that is, developing a supporting foundation for theological inquiry that can withstand challenges put to it); encyclopedic; or foundational (examining the ground rules for the disciplines). See his *Study of Theology* (trans. Duane A. Priebe; Philadelphia: Fortress Press, 1978), 154–55.

2. Cited in Richard Grigg, *Theology as a Way of Thinking* (Atlanta: Scholars Press, 1990), 35.

3. Ibid., 103. Grigg offers four positions in relation to the plurality of theological positions available and suggests ways in which each might be held responsibly: (1) no theology can provide knowledge of the divine—the position of the skeptic; (2) one theology can provide knowledge of the divine—one chooses the most coherent; (3) many

theologies can provide knowledge of the divine—if one admits that everyone has some knowledge of God (that is, the position of Karl Rahner); and (4) although no theology can provide knowledge of the divine, the task of theology can be reformulated in which the concept of God as a symbol or ideal (that does not correspond to a theological reality) becomes the foundation for exploration.

4. George A. Lindbeck, *The Nature of Doctrine: Religion and Theology in a Postliberal Age* (Philadelphia: Westminster Press, 1984).

5. Thomas G. Oden, *After Modernity . . . What?* (Grand Rapids, Mich.: Zondervan, 1977), 160–61.

6. David Tracy, *The Analogical Imagination* (New York: Crossroad, 1981).

7. See Dorothee Sölle's discussion of black theology in her *Thinking About God: An Introduction to Theology* (trans. John Bowden; London: SCM Press; Philadelphia: Trinity Press International, 1990), 95–110.

8. Rebecca S. Chopp, *The Power to Speak: Feminism, Language, God* (New York: Crossroad, 1989), 127.

9. Pamela Dickey Young, *Feminist Theology/Christian Theology: In Search of a Method* (Minneapolis: Fortress Press, 1990), 17–21.

10. Students wishing to explore this subject in greater depth should consult Hans W. Frei, *Types of Christian Theology* (New Haven and London: Yale University Press, 1992).

11. This chart is devised from several sources, including Robert McAfee Brown as cited in Grigg, *Theology as a Way of Thinking*, 75–78; Werner G. Jeanrond, "Theological Method," in Donald W. Musser and Joseph L. Price, eds., *A New Handbook of Christian Theologians* (Nashville: Abingdon Press, 1992), 480–86; Gordon D. Kaufman, *An Essay on Theological Method* (Missoula, Mont.: Scholars Press, 1975); Dorothee Sölle, *Thinking About God*, esp. 65.

12. Anne Lamott, *Bird by Bird: Some Instructions on Writing and Life* (New York: Anchor Books, 1995), 97.

13. Fred B. Craddock, *Preaching* (Nashville: Abingdon Press, 1985), 49.

14. At a simple level, Luther had three very practical suggestions for preacher-theologians, guidelines that he said, "have made a fairly good theologian of me": (1) know that the Scriptures turn "all other books into foolishness"; (2) "meditate . . . not only in your heart, but also externally" by saying out loud the words of Scripture many times and comparing them with the written words; and (3) seek not just knowledge but also experience and love of the sweet truth of God's majestic Word. This experience and love he called "*tentatio, Anfechtung* . . . For as soon as God's Word takes root and grows in you, the devil will harry you, and will make a real doctor of you, and by his assaults will teach you to seek and love God's Word." Martin Luther, "Luther Concerning the Study of Theology," in Gerhard Ebeling, *The Study of Theology* (trans. Duane A. Priebe; Philadelphia: Fortress Press, 1978), 167–68.

15. For a fuller treatment of this see my *Broken Words: Reflections on the Craft of Preaching* (Nashville: Abingdon Press, 2004), 31–39, which contains a sermon demonstrating this subject.

16. Robert G. Hughes and Robert Kysar, *Preaching Doctrine: For the Twenty-First Century* (Fortress Resources for Preaching; Minneapolis: Fortress Press, 1997), 26. Another excellent book on preaching doctrine is Millard J. Erickson and James L. Heflin, *Old Wine in New Wineskins: Doctrinal Preaching in a Changing World* (Grand Rapids, Mich.: Baker Books, 1997). See also, Ronald J. Allen, *Preaching Is Believing: The Sermon as*

Theological Reflection (Louisville: Westminster John Knox Press, 2002); Burton Z. Cooper and John S. McClure, *Claiming Theology in the Pulpit* (Louisville: Westminster John Knox Press, 2003.)

17. John Broadus, *The Preparation and Delivery of Sermons* (10th ed.; New York: A. C. Armstrong & Son, 1887), 89–95.

18. James S. Stewart, *Heralds of God* (New York: Charles Scribner's Sons, 1946), 62–66, 89. Stewart's idea of focusing on Christ became the organizing principle of his Lyman Beecher Lectures on Preaching at Yale, and they give proof of the variety that Stewart advocates. James S. Stewart, *A Faith to Proclaim* (London: Hodder and Stoughton, 1953).

19. Samuel D. Proctor, *"How Shall They Hear?": Effective Preaching for Vital Faith* (Valley Forge, Pa.: Judson Press, 1992), 10.

20. Hughes and Kysar, *Preaching Doctrine*, 30.

13. Preaching the Gospel

1. See my *Preaching and Homiletical Theory* (St. Louis: Chalice Press, 2004), 53–54.

2. Mary Donovan Turner, "Not Silent," in Jana Childers, ed., *Birthing the Sermon: Women Preachers on the Creative Process* (St. Louis, Chalice, 2001), 173.

3. James F. Kay, "The Word of the Cross at the Turn of the Ages," *Interpretation* 53, no. 1 (January 1999): 45.

4. One of my sermons on this is in my *Broken Words: Reflections on the Craft of Preaching* (Nashville: Abingdon Press, 2004), 63–70

5. David Bartlett, *Between the Bible and the Church: New Methods for Biblical Preaching* (Nashville: Abingdon Press, 1999), 72; see also 64–72 and 17–24. For the most thorough recent treatment of typology see Sidney Greidanus, *Preaching Christ from the Old Testament: a Contemporary Hermeneutical Method* (Grand Rapids, Mich.: Eerdmans, 1999), esp., 90–97; 249–61.

6. Paul Scott Wilson, *God Sense: Reading the Bible for Preaching* (Nashville: Abingdon Press, 2001), 125. See also on this topic, 112–63.

7. See my discussion of what I then called a "resurrection hermeneutic" in *Imagination of the Heart: New Understandings in Preaching* (Nashville: Abingdon Press, 1988), 140–42.

8. Gerhard O. Forde, *Theology Is for Proclamation* (Minneapolis: Fortress Press, 1990), 155.

9. Ibid., 156–57.

10. Ibid., 5.

11. Richard Lischer, who teaches homiletics at Duke University, has said, "Perhaps . . . preachers will reclaim the center when homiletics reclaims the center, when homiletics grounds the rhetorical act of preaching in God's own speech act." Richard Lischer, "Preaching and the Rhetoric of Promise," *Word and World* 8 (Winter 1988): 70.

Index